The Digital Finance Era

Babak Naysary · Amine Tarazi

The Digital Finance Era

A Journey Through Fintech and Cryptocurrency

palgrave
macmillan

Babak Naysary
Birmingham City University
Birmingham, West Midlands
United Kingdom

Amine Tarazi
Economics Department
University of Limoges
Limoges, France

ISBN 978-981-97-3969-1 ISBN 978-981-97-3970-7 (eBook)
https://doi.org/10.1007/978-981-97-3970-7

Cover credit: Andriy Onufriyenko

This Palgrave Macmillan imprint is published by the registered company Springer Nature Singapore Pte Ltd.
The registered company address is: 152 Beach Road, #21-01/04 Gateway East, Singapore 189721, Singapore

Contents

List of Figures

CHAPTER 1

Introduction and Overview

Introduction

This chapter outlines a sketch and a brief overview of the topic, including the genesis of FinTech and its development in the past decade along with the subsequent challenges and opportunities that its various segments are posing to the incumbent banking and financial institutions; the main argument in this chapter will be the fact that disruption is a real phenomenon taking place in a fast pace in financial industry and that financial institutions, particularly banks which were immune to severe disruption, under the idea of "Too big to fail" (TBTF) until recently, are now hit with transformations in the form of disintermediation in financial services industry.

The Emergence of Digital Sharing Economy

Technology has been one of the major contributors to the economic growth in the past few decades across the globe. Expansion of internet access (Fig. 1.1) coupled with development of online platforms and applications has provided businesses with the abundance of information and an opportunity to produce and market products and services in ways which were not possible before. According to predictions by market research

B. Naysary and A. Tarazi, *The Digital Finance Era*,
https://doi.org/10.1007/978-981-97-3970-7_1

firm IDC,[1] by 2023, more than 65 percent of global GDP will be digitalized (driven by digitally transformed enterprises) which can be considered as a new tipping point for digital supremacy. This also, in part, plays into a generational culture shift for Millennials and Generation Z (born after 1981), who are tech-savvy and spend a sizeable portion of their waking hours online. These have given rise to new business models which are shaping an emerging phenomenon called sharing economy. Although sharing economy has been studied and referred to as an independent concept, it cannot be denied that it is one of the by-products of digital economy; and considering the fact that sharing has always existed in the economic transactions in various forms and is not a new event, the term digital sharing economy has been used by researchers and practitioners and appears to do more justice to the term in conveying its underlying meaning.

Digital sharing economy can be defined as the application of technology and innovation leveraging digital solutions (such as internet,

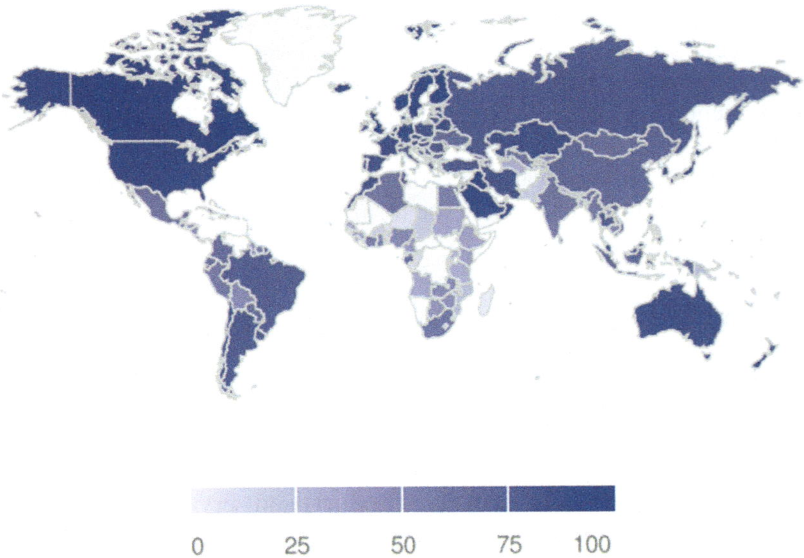

Fig. 1.1 Global internet penetration

[1] https://www.idc.com/research/viewtoc.jsp?containerId=US46880818.

mobile devices, and applications) to collaboratively engage communities in numerous transactions such as accommodation, transportation, multimedia exchange, finance, health, and education. It can be viewed as the emergence of software platforms performing the role of intermediaries between the private buyers and private sellers and facilitating the exchange of resources. The significance of digital sharing economy stems from the fact that the traditional forms of sharing and collaboration (which might not necessarily contribute to the economy) are transforming into organized, formal, and larger scale online processes whose direct benefits to the GDP can be observed and measured. The promising prospects of digital sharing economy for socioeconomic development have urged many firms to adopt new business models. Some examples of successful companies emerging from the digital sharing economy ecosystem include Airbnb and Couchsurfing (short-stay accommodation), Uber and BlaBlaCar (ride sharing and transportation), Lime (electric scooter rental), Lending Club and Kickstarter (peer-to-peer lending and crowdfunding), edX and Coursera (educational platforms), Freelancer (on demand professional services), American Well, Doctor On Demand, and Cohealo (healthcare service).

Among the reasons for rapid expansion of digital sharing economy over the past decade and emergence of a new breed of firms and startups are (i) widespread internet availability and access to smartphones, (ii) explosive innovation and technological advancements in online platforms and applications. This has led to emergence of another recent and significant phenomenon called big data analytics which is extensively used by firms and startups to match supply and demand and even set the optimum pricing using advance algorithms, (iii) ease of entry into the market which has increased democratization of entrepreneurship by reducing barriers for new firms and startups to enter into the marketplace through creating apps and online platforms, (iv) facilitated financial transactions between individuals through innovative payment solutions, (v) increased availability of data and subsequent enhancement of transparency regarding the information about buyers, sellers, and products and services offered. This has helped to alleviate some of the security risks issues associated with online services, and finally, (vi) economic turmoil in the past few two decades, which has led many people to relinquish their dependency on the traditional employment channels and seek new sources of income.

The digital sharing economy is an ecosystem where various players and parties interact at three levels. At the core are sharing economy digital platforms that connect suppliers and consumers at the individual level. The ecosystem is complex, involving organizations that interact with these platforms at the organizational level, leading to new business models. It also includes government agencies at the country level, acting as supervisors and regulators to ensure healthy operations and prevent fraud and market failures.

The idea of sharing idle capacity in digital sharing economy is central for considering it as one of the drivers of sustainability, following Frenken et al. (2015)'s definition of sharing economy as "consumers granting each other temporary access to under-utilized physical assets (idle capacity), possibly for money." One of the apparent benefits of this model, which has been the subject of much research and debate, is the environmental impacts. The fact that ownership of products has become secondary to usage, in light of the possibility to access them with a lower price through borrowing or renting, has theoretically contributed to the decline in the number of new goods produced (the pinnacle of which is car sharing). Apart from environmental impacts, digital sharing economy is believed to have created a platform for sharing peers to experience meaningful contacts and increase the social mixing of individuals with different socio-demographic background. From an economic standpoint, the digital sharing economy platforms are creating a new market that is expanding the volume of transactions and at the same time due to lower associated costs, it is injecting additional purchasing power to the economy and possibly leads to more consumer welfare.

However, critics argue that the advantages of sharing economy are exaggerated and more complex and there are still shortcomings which hinder its development such as lack of trust and security risks issues, unfair competition created by under-regulated marketplace which also facilitates tax avoidance and possible violation of workers' rights in terms of health insurance, pensions, and other benefits. Nevertheless, the digital sharing economy has proven to have disruptive impact on the business sectors. The lack of overhead (such as rental fees) and inventory enabled the share-based business models to operate more efficiently and deliver their value to customers, which calls for traditional firms adapting to this changing landscape. The next section describes the impact of disruptive technologies focusing on the financial services industry.

Disruption and Disintermediation in Financial Services Industry

The original foundation of our modern economic system was created through individuals exchanging goods and services directly to fulfill mutual benefits. The economic system has only become more organized and centralized after the emergence of more sophisticated firms followed by popularization of money and credit. However, the current transformations taking place in the digital world and technological advancements are creating a fertile ground for people to connect, communicate, and trade; this is giving rise to a shift back toward decentralized economic exchanges. The traditional role of market, shaped over the past hundreds of years, can be characterized with two distinct functions and features: first is the mechanism by which sellers can have access to buyers and therefore transactions are facilitated (necessitating the ubiquity of intermediaries) and second is the use of sovereign-issued fiat currencies under the supervision of central banks and market authorities. These roles are now being challenged by the rise of digital sharing economy in which the concept of peer-to-peer (P2P) sharing and also the expansion of cryptocurrencies is posing challenge before traditional trading mechanisms. In many industries, this challenge introduces itself as the risk of disintermediation which simply means discontinuation of providing intermediation services. The concept of intermediation itself can be considered as the process by which agents participate in a commercial relationship to facilitate supply of goods and services for a price. Although disintermediation may not take place as fast or as dramatic as projected by some experts and researchers, it can certainly be viewed as a decreasing role of middlemen and third parties in the supply chain of goods and services. This concept in the financial services industry should be particularly viewed in light of the global financial crisis of 2008/2009 which underlined the inefficiencies of the financial system structure at the heart of which lies banks and other financial institutions. After the financial crisis most of the focus has been targeted to the point whether the existence of intermediaries is necessary for the well-functioning of the markets. Subsequently, the emergence of distributed ledger technologies, such as blockchain which is considered as a decentralized ecosystem to perform transactions, has indeed contributed to the discussions and concerns surrounding disintermediation. One area which has been significantly affected by the disruptions is payment industry where cryptocurrencies are becoming more and more the preferable mode of transferring value across the globe. This has removed the necessity to use fiat currencies and refer to the banks and other financial institutions to make payments; instead, the payments can now be made directly from sender to receiver on a P2P basis executed electronically using a shared ledger structure where all transaction are settled and recorded.[2] Another prominent sector exposed to challenges posed by disintermediation process is the lending industry with P2P lending being introduced as an alternative to bank lending. P2P platforms provide an opportunity for lenders and borrowers to match without an intermediary bank. Contrary to banking institutions, P2P platforms do not invest in loans and do not issue debt and the loans come directly and fully from the investment of lenders. Overall, these transformations have led to diminishing the monopolistic role of the banks through development of FinTech and the shift in customer preferences.

Apart from banking industry, the technologically enabled financial services have the potential to improve the allocation of funds in the capital markets. As one of the major issues between investors and borrowers in the capital market has always been the information asymmetry which provided the intermediaries the chance to exploit investors, FinTech and more particularly in this case crowdfunding platforms offer firms and startups an alternative source of capital by channeling investors' (crowd) money to provide necessary financing. Although an Uber-like situation for capital market is not likely to happen in the near future, however, the impact of gradual transformation in the capital market and the foregoing disintermediation is posing the question of what value do banks capitalistic intermediaries create for their customers. Another highlight in the technological transformation in the financial services industry is the use of artificial intelligence (AI) which allows firms to reduce their risks, expense and enhance their productivity and efficiency. Robo-advisory is one of FinTech sectors which utilizes AI to provide financial services which were previously offered by financial planners and advisors. Although current services provided by robo-advisory platforms are more passive, the current shift taking place in the field of machine learning and particularly deep learning, there are promising prospects of more personalized wealth management services provided by autonomous robo agents.

[2] https://internationalbanker.com/finance/is-disintermediation-the-future-of-finance/.

It is worth mentioning that the foregoing disintermediation and fading role of the human component in the financial transactions have raised concerns over the regulatory perspectives. Whereas traditionally individuals such as bankers, investment managers, and advisors were the subject and focus of intense regulations, the rise of algorithmic processes in the financial industry calls for due diligence from the regulatory bodies to certify the algorithms and create trust and transparency among investors and borrowers in the market.

Decentralized Finance

Decentralized finance (DeFi) refers to a multitude of blockchain-enabled applications challenging current financial ecosystem. These applications normally include smart contracts, which are automated and enforceable contracts which could be accessed and evaluated by anyone with an internet connection with no centralized intermediaries to execute. Before considering the characteristics of DeFi, it is essential to overview the functions of traditional market-based finance. The intermediaries operating as financial institutions, such as banks and insurance companies, or market providers, such as securities exchanges, are the focal point of what is known as the financial system. These institutions centralize the provision of various financial services, whereby participants with extra financial resources who seek earnings are indirectly linked to participants in need of funds and are willing to pay the cost. Over the past century, these financial hubs have developed locally, regionally, and globally. The foundation of the traditional financial system is built upon the element of trust and confidence from the participants' side, which necessitated the establishment and evolution of laws and regulations imposed and monitored by respective states and international bodies. This implied intrinsic instability, which is to be supposedly addressed by regulation (full achievement of which has proven to be unsuccessful in various occasions, particularly during financial crises), is one of the main weaknesses of the traditional mode of finance. This underlies the significance of DeFi, the premise of which is challenging the centralization of finance and eliminates its foregoing inherent flaws (coupled with the shortcomings of state-imposed regulations) through technologically enabled infrastructure underpinning the decentralization of finance.

At the very root of DeFi lie a number of key technologies presented by the acronym "ABCD": A for Artificial intelligence, B for Big data,

C for Cloud, and D for Distributed ledger (including blockchain and smart contracts). These four technologies are the cornerstone of decentralization and are rapidly developing. This constant and exponential development has brought about convenience and efficiency in providing services together with a remarkable reduction in the cost of acquiring, processing, storing, and analyzing data which in turn has given rise to cooperation and financial exchange among a multitude of participants in a decentralized fashion. The positive attitude toward and wide acceptance of DeFi is magnified by the idea of democratization of finance and independence form monopoly and control in the traditional financial system. Increased financial inclusion brought about by use of digital technologies and provision of funds and services to individuals, businesses, and regions which were intentionally or unintentionally excluded from the financial system attests to this optimistic view.

Despite the wide adoption and excitement over the promising prospects of DeFi, it comes with a number of challenges. As the underlying concept of DeFi is ruling of "codes" as the ultimate law, it is posing a systemic threat to the regulatory bodies and government authorities who seek control over the market. On the other hand, due to its boundless nature, users across the globe can transact with each other, which makes the determination of jurisdictions in charge and relevant laws increasingly difficult. Generation and storage of data on clouds throughout multiple servers are also rendering the data protection controls inefficient and, in some cases, impossible. However, these challenges can be the ultimate opportunity for the regulatory bodies and RegTech to build a better functioning financial market by embracing these new technologies, which ironically implies that the full manifestation of decentralized financial system can only be achieved through centralized government cooperation.

Societal Implications of FinTech

In previous sections, we discussed how FinTech has influenced the traditional financial ecosystem. One of the major effects of FinTech is perpetuating new ways of collaboration among participants in the market, new business models and its customer centric approach. These impacts have reached far beyond the financial industry to influence the social norms and financial culture of individuals and businesses in society. This is particularly evident in mobile payment as the biggest FinTech segment.

Due to ever-increasing usage of mobile devices, the payment systems have evolved from cash or credit card transactions to various ways by which customers can process the payments for their transactions. This has, in turn, changed the business climate and consumer spending behavior. The modes of mobile payment have evolved to include near field communication (NFC) and quick response (QR) codes, which facilitate the payments made in person at the store or at any terminal by simply approaching the terminal. Among the various advantages of mobile payment are facilitating payments of bills, loans, lending and borrowing, and even international payments in a secure and convenient manner. Consequently, the access to financial system has been facilitated to a great extent, which contributed toward financial inclusion with the ultimate impact of increasing overall financial well-being of unserved and underserved individuals and businesses. By resolving some of the issues related to the traditional financial system such as information asymmetry, credit scoring mechanisms, risk assessment, and high cost of lending, FinTech has improved the chances of the poor accessing their required funds. Increasing evidence also indicates the implication FinTech on economic development which indirectly contributes to alleviate poverty.

It has been argued that FinTech can serve as a tool to reduce gender inequality. As reported in the Global Findex Database, in general the number of women with bank accounts is significantly lower than men. This is even more pronounced in the case of developing countries and rural areas. Among the barriers hindering women from having proper access to financial services are lack of identity cards, insufficient initial financial resources, limited means of mobility, and lower financial literacy. FinTech startups are providing low literates with user-friendly applications and reducing the complexity of performing financial transactions. The promotion of micro-entrepreneurship programs using FinTech across the world has also included women in the business ecosystem and helped service financially deprived women and generate employment opportunities in a more gender-neutral way.

Finally, the advent of FinTech has nurtured a more environmentally conscious attitude among consumers. Overall, the financial industry plays a big role in the battle against the climate change and environmental problems which are one of the biggest global issues now. Various attempts have been made by the financial sector to advance sustainability and develop strategies more in line with responsible investment decisions. The link between FinTech and sustainability has become more pronounced during the Covid-19 pandemic. Inclusion of "sustainable digital finance" as one of the key priorities of the G-20 work stream attests to the impact of FinTech on sustainability. This impact can be enforced though enhancing the usage and allocation of existing financial resources, and also provision of necessary funds for the establishment of environmentally sustainable firms in a faster, cheaper, and more affordable way. Additionally, artificial intelligence and big data facilitate processing information on the environment behavior of companies which helps investors to incorporate ESG considerations into their financial decisions. Overall, FinTech contributes to sustainability by making the financial services more resilient, efficient, and less energy intensive.

References

Alińska, A., & Czepirska, I. (2016). The development of payment services as an example of disintermediation in the financial system. *E-Finanse, 12*(2), 60–73.

Bennett, J. (2016). *An introduction to FinTech: Key sectors and trends* (pp. 1–19). S&P Global Market Intelligence.

Berlančić, T., & Miškulin, I. (2019). Future of sharing economy in medicine in Croatia. *Interdisciplinary management research* (Vol. XV, pp. 1758–1772).

Cheng, X., Mou, J., & Yan, X. (2021). Sharing economy enabled digital platforms for development. *Information Technology for Development, 27*(4), 635–644.

Dolgui, M. (2021). *Market structure and government policy implications of FinTech and the digital transformation of financial services* (Vol. 22, pp. 1–2).

Felländer, A., Ingram, C., & Teigland, R. (2015). *Sharing economy: Embracing change with caution* (Vol. 11, pp. 1–67).

Frenken, K., & Schor, J. (2019). Putting the sharing economy into perspective. *A research agenda for sustainable consumption governance* (pp. 121–135).

Frenken, K., Meelen, T., Arets M., et al. (2015). Smarter regulation for the sharing economy. *The Guardian*, May 20, Accessed February 18, 2022 at https://www.theguardian.com/science/politicalscience/2015/may/20/smarter-regulation-for-the-sharing-economy

Kaili, E., & Psarrakis, D. (2021). *Disintermediation economics: The impact of blockchain on markets and policies* (pp. 1–336).

Kaja, F., Martino, E. D., & Pacces, A. M. (2021). FinTech and the law and economics of disintermediation. *Routledge Handbook of Financial Technology and Law* (No. September, pp. 78–95).

de Luna, I. R., Liébana-Cabanillas, F., Sánchez-Fernández, J., & Muñoz-Leiva, F. (2019). Mobile payment is not all the same: The adoption of mobile payment systems depending on the technology applied. *Technological Forecasting and Social Change, 146*(August 2018), 931–944.

Lyaskovskaya, E., & Khudyakova, T. (2021). Sharing economy: For or against sustainable development. *Sustainability (Switzerland), 13*(19). https://doi.org/10.3390/su131911056

Pachenkov, O., & Yashina, A. (2017). When sharing economy meets digital one. *Association for Computing Machinery* (pp. 91–98).

Perini, F., Schwarten, G., & Comolli, L. (2013). The power of sharing: Exploring the digital sharing economy at the base of the Pyramid. *NESsT*, No. May.

Ponce, J. (2019). *Key aspects around financial technologies and regulation policy report* (pp. 1–68).

Wigand, R. (2020). Whatever happened to disintermediation. *Electronic Markets, 30*, 39–47.

Zamani, E. D., & Giaglis, G. M. (2018). With a little help from the miners: Distributed ledger technology and market disintermediation. *Industrial Management & Data Systems, 118*(3), 637–652.

Zetzsche, D. A., Arner, D. W., & Buckley, R. P. (2020). Decentralized finance. *Journal of Financial Regulation, 6*(2), 172–203.

CHAPTER 2

Fiat Money: History and Features

Introduction

A brief history of the emergence of fiat money will be brought forth in this chapter in an attempt to illustrate its significance as a large part of human life since several thousand years ago. The importance of this chapter stems from the fact that, in order to understand the concepts of new digital transaction systems, it is essential to familiarize the reader with the role of money as one of the most important achievements in the history of humankind.

To this end, evolution of currencies as a means for transactions, from barter, use of gold and other precious metals, to the current international system of government fiat monies managed by discretionary central banks is expounded. The ultimate aim of this chapter is to explain the status quo and at the same time explore the fundamental and controversial ideas that are revolutionizing the monetary systems and are caused by the increasing demand for the elasticity of money supply to cater to the need of current business environments.

Barter and Commodity Money

As human civilization progressed, a need was created for the exchange of goods and services among people. This need was due to the fact that the goods that one individual or family was producing were not necessarily

B. Naysary and A. Tarazi, *The Digital Finance Era*,
https://doi.org/10.1007/978-981-97-3970-7_2

the goods they needed for consumption. Additionally, people wanted to have a means for storing value for the times that they did not have any reserves and also to transfer this value from one generation to another. One of the oldest means of exchange among people was barter. The word barter has old French origins and means the act or practice of trading goods or services for other goods or services. At the beginning of bartering, the attitude and view of primitive man toward this exchange were not to take any economic advantage but rather simply acquire the commodities to the extent that satisfies the current demands and short-term necessities. One of the significant stages in human civilization that underscored the need for barter was the transformation of the early man lifestyle from hunter and food-gatherer to food-producers. Early settlement of individuals in small villages and expansion of tool-making industry from materials such as stone, bone, and wood brought about a necessity for some sort of exchange among producers of these materials and other community members. Another interesting progression of early man toward more advanced communities which marked a significant era of flourishing barter-exchanges was the development of pottery-making techniques. This was a turning point in the economic ecosystem particularly in the South Asia region and India[1] where a majority of people were engaged in the exchange of their animals and food supplies for pottery products.

But it was only in rare occasions that two people with the need for each other's exact goods had the chance to meet at the same time; more often than not, the situation presented itself as individual 'A' in need of commodities owned by individual 'B' and individual 'B' in turn in need of goods and services owned by individual 'C' and this goes on in an endless circle. On the other hand, the key underlying problem with barter was the negotiation over determining and calculating the value of each commodity as it was rarely the case that the value of 1 unit of a certain commodity was equal to the value of the other commodity in a barter exchange. For example, cloth was plentiful but corn was scarce and more sought-after. These issues were analyzed by Karl Menger[2] under the concept of saleability of commodities which means the ease with which

[1] See Thakur, U. (1972). A study in barter and exchange in ancient India. *Journal of the Economic and Social History of the Orient*, 297–315.

[2] See Menger, Karl (1892, June). On the Origin of Money. *The Economic Journal*, *2*(6), 239–255.

they can be disposed of at a market at any convenient time. The saleability of items was determined by the number of people in need of the item (demand), purchasing power of those people, and availability of the item in relation to the demand for it (supply).

Therefore, gradually, objects that had the element of scarcity in nature and whose circulation could be properly monitored started to be used as units of value to solve the aforementioned issues. For example, cowrie shells were widely used and circulated in most parts of the globe in about 1200 B.C. Some advantages of shell were the similarity in shapes and forms, easy to carry, and durability. The expansion of trade between coastal waters of Indian and Pacific Ocean (where cowrie shell was used) and Europe accelerated the acceptance of shells as currency. Some other forms of objects used as currency include wampum and beads, which were originally used in ceremonies and then became a unit of exchange, especially in North America. High demand commodities such as tobacco, rice, animal fur, and cattle are other popular examples. Cocoa was used as food and beverage in Mesoamerica and then became a form of money prior to and during the Spanish invasion. Tea as an important and widely consumed beverage was stored in brick-shaped forms and also later used as currency in many parts of the world. Another item which was initially worn in rituals and ceremonies in Fiji Islands and then became a currency was Whale's teeth. These items shared three fundamental characteristics of being a widely accepted medium of exchange, having a store of value and having a unit of account. Although using these items resolved a number of problems which were faced while bartering: some of them were not easy to carry and transport, some were perishable or difficult to store and with the development of trade among nations and advancements of transportation, some of these items did not meet the criteria of acceptability. It was also often the case that the owner of these items could not rely on their value, for example, if an item such as one unit of cotton was exchanged with one unit of corn, there was no certainty that it could be exchanged later having the same value. In other words, the price at which a person exchanged an item and commodity in a certain market at a given time was not necessarily equal to the price at which that person could dispose the item later on in another market. This made individuals very conscious of the saleability of their item and resulted in regular attempts to exchange their less saleable belongings not only for the items they needed but also for the items that were more saleable and might not have been necessarily useful for them. The idea was to be in possession of commodities whose value was less limited to space and time and was not only accepted by many but finally by all. This gradual discrimination of the different degrees of saleability in commodities has eventually led people to turn to more unified and widely used items such as precious metals including gold, silver, and copper, which later led to the creation of coins.

Precious Metals

Almost all civilizations throughout the history of humankind had and still have the desire to acquire and maintain precious metals, either as ornaments and decorations or as a store of value and medium of exchange. One of the main reasons why precious metals became a widely accepted means of exchange among various nations is their superior saleability as compared to other commodities and the fact that it was accepted by the people of the same nation in different times and different nations at the same time. Another quality of precious metals is that, despite their scarcity, they are finely distributed across various regions in the world and, compared to other metals, are relatively easy to extract. Although the ratio of available quantities of precious metals such as gold and silver to the amount of needs and demand in the society was always very small, their great divisibility has been an immense advantage for their continuous and dominant role as the most famous medium of exchange, in a way that even a small quantity of precious metals could satisfy the needs of a wide range of individuals. This was in addition to the significant ease in storing precious metals, convenience and low cost of transportation and almost unlimited durability, which is not comparable to any other commodity mentioned in the previous section. Therefore, precious metals could perfectly perform the role of money in any economy as the holders of these metals not only were able to convert them into any item at any time but also the price at which they could carry out this conversion was the optimum value without any loss and in many cases even carried added value. Then it became a norm among intellectuals and ordinary individuals that even the exchange of goods in return for other goods should also be laid out according to their corresponding value of precious metals; soon after, in any economic transaction a conversion of a value of the equivalent precious metals was inevitable even if either party to the transaction did not intend to use precious metals for the exchange. Among other reasons contributing to the popularity of precious metals as the most suitable medium of exchange was its far less fluctuation of value in economic exchanges and also their homogeneity. Given their durability, color, and specific density, the practice of stamping their quality and weight was very convenient, which in turn has significantly strengthened their widespread adoption and diffusion as money.

It is worth mentioning that states and governments did not have any role in the emergence of precious metals as accepted currencies, and this phenomenon was merely a consequence of a social trend. However, the rules and regulations imposed by authorities have contributed to betterment and adjustments of this role to meet the requirements of commerce and changing economic ecosystems. This was made possible through coinage of precious metals, which further enhanced their saleability. Fixing of coinage in a way that according to their weight, various grades, and qualities they could be supplied to the market was a contributing factor in maintaining public confidence and addressing some of the concerns over the genuineness of coins. This was eventually an answer to the manifold of difficulties associated with the trade of goods using different commodities as a medium of exchange; however, this process and also the initiative by states and authorities should not be considered as creating money out of precious metals but rather polishing and perfecting their function as money and currency.

Transition to Paper Money

Money is one of the greatest creations of human beings. It is important to note that it is not a natural product and, much like language, it is a man-made invention (the very meaning of coin refers to invention). There is no equivalent system among other species in nature and it is one of the main contributors to the development of human culture and modern societies. As for the origin of money, there are records of the use of gold and silver as a mode of payment in Mesopotamia in 2500 B.C. as inscribed on clay tablets in cuneiform. These uniform weights of gold and silver were called minas, shekel or talents. Although this system of payment was very effective for merchants trading large amount of goods, but due to scarcity and high value of these metals, they could not be easily incorporated in the day-to-day life of lower-class individuals seeking to buy or sell a basket of fruit or their home-brewed wine and beer. With the development of the exchange system and advancement of tools, small coins which were affordable by the average person had appeared and widely used. This revolutionary leap in the widespread use of coins by society members took place in West Asia in what is known today as Turkey and within a short period it permeated all around the world and constitute the foundation of the monetary system which we experience today.

The history of paper money is traced back to China when the well-known traveler Marco Polo wrote about and made it widely known in Europe. Although some writings associated the invention of paper money to Mongols who were reigning China at that time, creation and circulation of paper money in China dates way earlier than Mongols' dynasty in China to the beginning of the Tang dynasty (about A.D. 807) when copper became scarce to the point that there were even prohibitions on the usage of copper in dishes and utensils. Therefore, traders and rich families were encouraged to deposit their coins with the government and in return they received a type of security called "flying money" which further facilitated trade among them. The use and circulation of flying money during the Tang dynasty however lasted about three years, after which, they were no longer current. The next development in the issuance and circulation of paper money in China relates to Song dynasty (A.D. 960) who encouraged traders to deposit their coins and even merchandise with any government treasury in return for which they received a security named "convenient money" which was widely accepted and circulated everywhere.

Europeans began to use paper money during the seventeenth century. The first Europeans to use paper money were Swedes who started to develop and issue notes for reasons similar to Chinese. The first bank in Sweden, called Stockholm Banco, started to issue banknotes in Europe in 1661. These notes were issued as deposit certificates by founder of the bank Johan Palmstruch. These notes became rapidly popular and widespread due to the convenience of carrying them compared to silver and copper. By the end of the eighteenth century, paper currency was widely used by most European countries and their colonies. Paper money issued in Europe came in two forms: drafts which were given to depositors as receipt for the value held in their accounts and bills which were not linked with any deposit and were issued merely based on a promise to repay the holder with the equivalent amount of coin based on their value and weight. This system continued up until the middle of the twentieth century, whereby money didn't have any intrinsic value of its own and its value was dependent on what it could be exchanged for. Most of the paper money under this system was exchangeable at specified locations, mainly at treasury offices or at specific banks. Paper money has remained the foundation of modern economies for the last 150 years.

Emergence of Banks

The emergence of banking system can be traced back to around 1118 in the Jerusalem by a group of crusaders and religious Knights called Templars. Apart from their military activities, templars became businessmen and laid the foundation of what later became the banking system. They were mainly young men who dedicated their lives to service the church and led a very modest lifestyle, much like monks. Most of them were virgins and unmarried; however, married men could join, but should have abandoned their families and stay away from women. Throughout the years, they accumulated the proceeds from wars and also donations from their followers and heads of states in Europe, which were all deposited in their castles. Gradually, they started to provide services such as deposit taking and lending mortgages throughout Europe, for which they charged a transaction fee. These transactions were performed in various currencies. This continued to the point where their headquarters in Paris became one of the greatest treasure-houses in Europe, lending money to kings and high-profile individuals. At the highest point of their operations, there were 7000 individuals working in their organization and they owned around 870 castles across Europe and the Mediterranean. In 1291, templars lost their military dominance and a few years later their properties were seized by King Philip IV of France who later expelled and executed them. At this stage, there was a gap in the financial system in Europe as the church was not as active and powerful as before and the governments started to fully take control of financial transactions. In light of this gap, some of the wealthy families in northern Italy started to build a set of private family banks which although in the beginning were not performing in the same scale as the system created by templars, but they had the advantage of not being bonded by the religious restrictions. Therefore, they were able to transact with people across various religions and also play around the concept of usury, which was one of the main hurdles in the system run by templars. Another distinction between the banking system by Italian families and templars was that they were living among and dealing with ordinary people such as landlords and vendors and, hence, were able to extend their services to a wider demography of individuals. One of the distinguished aspects of their operations was that they set up large tables and benches in the marketplace to provide loans or payment services. The name bank, as we know today, comes from the word bench representing how they used to run their business and soon became a global expression. One of the main tools in the transactions carried out by these bankers was the bill of exchange, which was a document signed as a promise to make a payment to an individual at a certain time and location. People in need of money would refer to merchants for cash and, in return, they signed the bill of exchange to pay back the money, normally with a surcharge. This repayment could take place in various locations and different currencies. This boosted commerce in Europe to a great extent by facilitating the payments and eliminating the physical restrictions associated with coins. One of the interesting facts about the bill of exchange which was the foundation of banking system was that by channeling the idle wealth, the lender was earning some profit and still owned his wealth, the bank was recording that value in its accounts and the borrower was holding the money with which he/she could manage to run business and earn profit. Although Italian bankers were later on pushed away from the scene by their overinvolvement in government, particularly due to their heavy investment to finance Edward III in his war with France which he later on defaulted, but the system and innovations they created were very valuable for merchants and therefore their legacy survived and further flourished particularly in the city of Florence where at one point around 1422 seventy-two banks were operating. The accounting science and double entry system have also emerged in Italy in 1487 by Luca Pacioli which significantly contributed to the development of banking system and commerce.

However, the first organized institution with great resemblance to our today's banks was established in Venice where due to a shortage of funds by the government, caused by wars, a corporation named chamber of loans was established to receive contributions and pay an annual interest of four percent. During the course of its operations, the chamber engaged in the business of buying and selling bills of exchange, which, after some time, having the name of chamber imprinted on it, became a very popular and valuable instrument. Later on, the chamber discovered the advantage of discounting the bills and lending money upon mercantile papers. It was also found to be a safe place for keeping money by Venetian merchants, which later transformed into the business of deposit taking. The table of exchange in Barcelona and the chamber of chamber of St. George in Genoa replicated this idea and obtained the same level of respect and credit. As a response to depreciation of the value of coins due to wear and tear, the bank of Amsterdam created a system where subscribers could pay a certain amount of money and, in return, they received credit known as bank money. This created a uniform mode of payment for performing transactions in commerce by merchants whose value even rose above the coins at that time. Bank of Amsterdam created a system of receiving coins from depositors and issuing a receipt entitling bearer the withdrawal rights from the bank within six months from the date of receipt. It charged one quarter of a percent for coins and silver billions as commission. These commissions, together with bank money premiums, generated a considerable profit for the bank; however, one significant difference from modern banks was that it did not engage in the loan business. Similar institutions were later established in Hamburg and other major cities in Germany.

Established in 1694, the bank of England was one of the best examples of modern banks. One of the unique characteristics of bank of England was the introduction of bank notes which were given to depositors instead of coins, in return for purchase and sale of bills of exchange. These bank notes were made payable by the bank and were widely accepted by merchant. Although at the beginning the bank kept the same amount of coins as notes in circulation up until 1796, over the years notes were exchanged with a low possibility of being presented to the bank for withdrawals. Consequently, the bank issued more notes than coins in its vault and the amount of interest in the difference between them was a huge source of income. As a result, the entire business of bank was carried out using bank notes including major tasks of managing public debt, financing the government, circulating and exchanging the bills, and finally discounting the bills of exchange. Following the increase in the wealth of European countries and in England in particular at the time, and observing the amount of profit gained by government banks, private banks started to emerge imitating the function of government banks, including issuing their own notes. Despite the disinterest of government and enforcing limiting laws, private banks continued to evolve and grow.

In America, the first bank was established based on the premise of the bank of England and private banks in Britain. Bank of North America was established in Philadelphia in 1781. During this period, the revolutionary war was still going on and the government was facing difficulties in funding the war and paying for its expenses. The superintendent of finance, who was an officer corresponding to secretary of treasury in the present, proposed the idea of issuing bank notes similar to those in

England to facilitate the operations of the treasury and managing public debt, which was accepted by the congress. Soon, the bank of North America managed to gain the public trust and its notes were widely accepted and circulated. This success encouraged merchants in other cities to seek the same model, such as the Massachusetts Bank in Boston and the Bank of New York both starting their business in 1784. The first bank of the United States was incorporated in 1791 by Alexander Hamilton, which is considered as the precedent of the Federal Reserve. The main purpose of the bank was to help the government in dealing with its financial affairs. The powers of the bank bestowed by the congress included the ability to issue notes which were accepted for payments to the federal government and was the only bank which had the ability to open various branches across other states. Despite acceptance by various economic sectors in different regions of the country, the private ownership of the bank became a cause for unpopularity and disagreements which led the congress not to renew its charter. The second bank of the United States founded in 1816 had a similar fate where, on September 1833, President Andrew Jackson decided to discontinue its operation and remove all federal funds from the bank from this point up to 1861. There were conflicts and disagreements among various states on the whole concept of banking in the sense that while some states were trying to prevent the rise of any banking institutions, other states were trying to push for a possibility for any citizen to set up bank with the fewest regulation possible. The discontinuation of second bank encouraged other states to charter their own bank and facilitate establishment of private banks by citizens. This was a "free banking" movement postulating the right for citizens to set up banks instead of being forced to solely rely on state-owned banks. Consequently, the number of banks doubled between 1830 and 1836 from 330 to 713 and even reached the pre-civil war apex of 1601 banks in 1861. Naturally, there were varying quality of banking services offered across states depending on the governing legislation. There was an overflow of notes, most of which traded at a discount.

The changes in the political ecosystem created by the civil war, coupled with the increasing cost of banking crises, called for centralization in the banking system, which led to the establishment of the Federal Reserve in 1913. By the time, central banks were already in operation throughout Europe and Japan as a government measure to ensure the soundness and effectiveness of banking services. The initial role of central banking, which still holds to this day, was first to act as the fiscal agent for the government, second to control the currency by monopolizing the issuance of money, and third to manage the credit system on a wider scale. However, after 1914, especially post-World War I, central banks started to be concerned with the domestic economic stability and endeavored to align their operations in a manner which could contribute to the employment and stabilizing price levels. This, in turn, affected the political decisions of the countries regarding export–import, labor movement, and migration. Similarly, maintaining the financial stability became one of the crucial functions of central banks by playing the role of the lender-of-the-last-resort and bailing out the banks in trouble by issuing public funds. To further safeguard depositors' money, a financial safety net, including deposit insurance and a firewall between financial and commercial institutions, was put in place. Consequently, central banks have proven to be essential for a well-ordered banking system and a stable economy. However, in recent years, the advent of technologically enabled innovation has posed challenges ahead of the banking system and central banks, which will be discussed in the next chapters.

International Monetary Systems

International monetary system has always been the focus of world major powers and one of the main contributors in shaping the global economy and has undergone considerable transformations throughout the history. International monetary system encompasses a network of institutions through which international payment transactions are settled and the system by which the exchange rates among nations are determined. A well-functioning international monetary system can facilitate a smooth flow of investment and trade and a poorly operating system can lead to economic disruptions. One of the key factors which is the focal point of an international monetary system is the exchange rate mechanism. Throughout history, the exchange rate system has undergone three major pivotal transformations. First, fixed-exchange rate system, according to which governments determine a rate to be used in foreign transactions. Second, a free and flexible or floating exchange rate which is merely set based on the supply and demand without any manipulation by governments. And finally, a managed exchange rate, which is a mixture of previous systems, according to which governments, by exerting their monetary policy and interest rate adjustments, can influence the exchange rates.

From 1717 to 1933, the gold standard was used in the banking system across the globe, which dictated a fixed-exchange rate system. According to the gold standard, the value of each currency was determined by the amount of gold reserves held by each country. Therefore, it was the responsibility of the governments to manage the gold reserves and control the prices. It created a monetary discipline for many years since the money supply was closely adjusted to real money demand, resulting in a symmetric monetary adjustment. However, there were a number of disadvantages to this system, including the inability of governments to utilize monetary policies to fight economic turbulences such as unemployment and economic recession. Additionally, expansion of population and global trade called for an expansion of money supply to settle the transactions while the amount of gold was limited; therefore, the gold standard was hindering economic growth from various accounts. And finally, there was a global imbalance of gold production where countries with greater gold production had the ability to influence the global macroeconomic situation by market sales of their gold.

During the World War I, governments could not adhere to the restrictions and had no option other than printing money without considering gold resources to cover their expenditure and that was the beginning of gold standard collapse. Although from 1918 to 1939, which was the period between the two world wars, some countries oscillated between sticking to and abandoning the gold standard. With the outbreak of great depression, the apex of which was experienced in Germany, many countries renounced the gold standard obligations and resorted to the floating system in the foreign exchange market. World War II was another impactful incident shaping the global economy dynamic where global trade, currency exchange, and cross-border credit transfer were reduced to the lowest amount. By the conclusion of World War II and as an attempt to reconstruct the war-torn economies, in July 1944, delegates from 44 countries gathered in Bretton Woods which is a small city in New Hampshire, United States, to bring back order to the global monetary and financial system. The agreements signed in that conference gave birth to the two of the most significant and influential international financial organizations, namely the International Monetary Fund (IMF) and the World Bank Group (initially known as bank of reconstruction and development). Bretton Woods agreements intended to create a fixed (but adjustable) exchange rate system by salvaging the key elements of the gold standard. It was after this conference that the United States was recognized as a major player in the global economy and its dollar was regarded as international currency, incorporated in global transactions and other countries' reserves. This meant that United States Dollar (USD) was treated as good as gold and, while the value of other currencies was fixed to gold, they were not obligated to exchange them for gold. However, world's major currencies were evaluated based on the USD and that in turn created a so-called two-tier system in which the value of USD was pegged to gold, and the value of other currencies was pegged to USD. This exchange rate mechanism was adjustable within a one percent band range, either fluctuating upward or downward. This equilibrium was maintained by buying and selling the USD. It gave rise to the role of the IMF, which up until now acts as the global central bank and channels the funds to countries which have issues with their balance-of-payments. The lending to member countries, however, comes with conditions and monitoring powers of the IMF over the borrowing countries' policies. Under the established system by Bretton Woods, countries became reliant on the supply of the USD and issues with the coordination of national policies and the concerns over the sovereignty of governments contributed to the downfall of Bretton Woods. Suspension of USD convertibility to gold in 1971 marked the beginning of floating exchange rates against USD. Currently, foreign exchange market hosts a mixture of different regimes and exchange rate systems determined by individual countries. As a result, the current international monetary system is highly flexible which contributed to the expansion of global economy. USD has still remained as the dominant global currency, accounting for around half of the transactions in the foreign exchange market; although during the past decade rapid technological innovations have transformed the financial industry. Digital money and cryptocurrencies at the forefront of financial technology advancements have made payments easier, faster, cheaper, and more accessible particularly in case of cross-border transactions. While potential benefits of these advancements are notable, significant challenges are also to be dealt with, threatening the financial stability and efficiency of monetary systems. Following chapters attempt to provide a clear picture of the status quo of financial technology and its implications for the monetary policies.

References

Bordo, M. (2007). A brief history of central banks. In *Federal reserve bank of Cleveland* (pp. 9–42).

Champ, B., & Freeman, S. (2001a). A simple model of money: Building a model of money. In *Modeling monetary economics* (pp. 3–33).

Champ, B., & Freeman, S. (2001b). Barter and commodity money. In *Modeling monetary economics* (pp. 34–46).

Conant, C. (1896). *A history of modern banks of issue*. G. P. Putnam's Sons.

Cooper, R. N. (1982). The facts gold and standard: Future historical prospects. *Brookings Papers on Economic Activity, Harvard University, 1*, 1–56.

Davies, G. (2002). *A history of money from ancient times to the present day* (pp. 1–741).

Dorrucci, E., & McKay, J. (2011). *The international monetary system after the financial crisis* (pp. 1–64). European Central Bank.

Dunbar, C. (1891). *The theory and history of banking* (pp. 1–333). https://medium.com/@arifwicaksanaa/pengertian-use-case-a7e576e1b6bf

Dunbar, C. (1917). *The theory and history of banking*.

Espinoza, A. R. (2019). *Barter old fashioned or a modern alternative* (p. 624).

Gentle, P. F. (2021). Early forms of money, besides currency, which may include coins. *Financial Markets, Institutions and Risks*, *5*(4). https://doi.org/10.21272/fmir.5(4).62-65.2021

Goldberg, D. (2005). Famous myths of fiat money. *Journal of Money, Credit and Banking, 37*(5), 957–967.

Hildreth, R. (2001). The history of banks: To which is added, a demonstration of the advantages and necessity of free competition in the business of banking. *Batoche Books* (p. 78).

Hoppe, H.-H. (1994). How is fiat money possible? Or, the devolution of money and credit. *The Review of Austrian Economics, 7*(2), 49–74.

Menger, C. (2005). On the origin of money. *Readings in the Economics of the Division of Labor: The Classical Tradition, 2*(6), 251–269. https://doi.org/10.1142/9789812701275_0024

Pickering, J. (1844). The history of paper money in China. *Journal of the American Oriental Society, 1*(2), 136–142.

Robertson, J. (2007). *The history of money: From its origins to our time*. Autrement.

Stanley Jevons, W. (1989). Money and the mechanism of exchange. *General Equilibrium Models of Monetary Economies*, 55–65. https://doi.org/10.1016/b978-0-12-663970-4.50009-8

Thakur, U. (2014). A study in barter and exchange in Ancient India. *Journal of the Economic and Social History of the Orient, 15*(3), 297–315.

Tourpe, H., Liu, Y., He, D., Mancini-Griffoli, T., Sandoval, E., & Mathai, K. (2021). *The rise of digital money—A strategic plan to continue delivering on the IMF's mandate* (pp. 1–28). https://www.imf.org/en/Publications/Policy-Papers/Issues/2021/07/28/The-Rise-of-Public-and-Private-Digital-Money-462919?cid=em-COM-789-43478

Weatherford, J. (1997). *The history of money* (pp. 1–308). Crown Publishing.

CHAPTER 3

Financial Technology Sectors and Business Models

Introduction

This chapter sets out to provide an overview of the FinTech sectors and their business models. By contextualizing the origin of FinTech industry's growth and some of the biggest inroads made by FinTech startups in areas backdropped by financial institutions, this chapter highlights the opportunities this emerging industry has to offer and also the process of disintermediation brought about by the concept of sharing economy, rapidly expanding by the widespread access, and use of internet and smart phones.

The aim of this chapter is twofold: on the one hand, it attempts to layout a comprehensive picture of FinTech sectors including cryptocurrencies, payment systems such as e-wallets, asset management with robo-advisors and alternative finance such as crowdfunding and peer-to-peer (P2P) lending, their evolution and status quo in the market; on the other hand, it aims also to expound their innovative business models as a basis to explain advantages and disadvantages compared to incumbent financial institutions and identify the potential areas where they can compete or cooperate.

This chapter also acknowledges the fact that it is equally essential to have a balanced view of the benefits offered by FinTech as well as traditional financial institutions.

B. Naysary and A. Tarazi, *The Digital Finance Era*,
https://doi.org/10.1007/978-981-97-3970-7_3

FinTech, Definition and Background

From a general perspective, FinTech refers to an emerging financial services sector which is transforming banking and financial industry by utilizing technological infrastructure combined with innovative business models. Financial stability board defines FinTech as the "technologically enabled financial innovation in financial services that could result in new business models, applications, processes or products with an associated material effect on financial markets and institutions and provision of financial services.[1]" The term is normally associated with startups and Bigtech companies which provide innovative and pioneering financial services and products using technologically enabled platforms. The term FinTech was first coined by Abraham Leo Bettinger in 1972 as "an acronym which stands for financial technology, combining bank expertise with modern management science techniques and the computer" (in his work entitled "FinTech: A series of 40-time shared models used at manufacturers Hanover trust company"). However, the application of technology in financial transactions is not a recent phenomenon, and it has always been a big part of the financial sector. The practical commencement of FinTech dates back to 1866 with the successful implementation of transatlantic cable project which laid the necessary infrastructure for the rapid financial globalization throughout the next century and facilitated services such as Fedwire fund transfers with the help of telegraph and Morse code in 1918. This era up until 1967 is considered as the first stage of FinTech evolution (FinTech 1.0). However, most of the technology was still analogue. Transformation of technology from analogue to digital marks the second stage of FinTech revolution called FinTech 2.0 which brought us the first ATM by Barclays in 1967. This stage till 2008 was an eventful period for FinTech during which the first digital stock market (National Association of Securities Dealers or NASDAQ) began trading on 1971, and also Society for Worldwide Interbank Financial Telecommunications (SWIFT) started its operation on 1973. This era marks the invention of internet banking and integration of cloud computing in the financial sector.

In 2008, due to occurrence of global financial crisis and diminishing trust and confidence toward the traditional financial services industry, the general inclination of the public to use alternative services has increased,

[1] https://www.fsb.org.

which led to an accelerated increase in emergence of startups. During this era, which is also known as FinTech 3.0, Bitcoin was introduced which was later followed by a multitude of other cryptocurrencies. Widespread access to internet and ubiquity of smartphones were major contributing factors in massive development of FinTech at this stage.

The next and current stage, also known as FinTech 4.0, is signified by the expansion of FinTech from both the perspective of disruptive business models and startups and integration of technology in incumbent products and services. This era is marked by the entrance of Bigtech companies such as Meta, Google, Amazon, Tencent, Samsung, and Apple in the realm of financial services. This was a significant contribution, particularly due to the wide scale of these firms' operations and the considerable number of users to whom they have access.

The success of Bigtechs and the fact that most of them were foreign to the financial industry and mainly involved in social media, search engines, and telecommunication highlights the significance of data combined with sophisticated analytical tools such as AI which is evermore viewed as a valuable currency. The new business models are based on facilitating interaction among a massive group of users which result in a large amount of data collected, exploitation of network, and stimulating activity which is called DNA (data-network-activities) feedback loop and is a distinguishing characteristic of Bigtech operations. As Bigtechs attract more users on their platforms, they are able to provide complementary services such as payments to further enhance the interaction among users. These services are expanding onto other financial services such as credit and insurance by application of technology, which is far more effective and efficient than traditional forms of finance, since they have the proven capability to reach the unbanked and under-banked individuals and businesses. This evolutionary growth, which is transforming the banking and financial industry in general and how individuals handle their day-to-day financial affairs in particular, is very likely to be underestimated due to the current structure of disclosure frameworks; therefore, the following sections aim at shedding light on various FinTech segments and their business models.

Alternative Payments

The history of alternative payments is intertwined with the evolution of technology and changing consumer preferences. The emergence of the internet in the 1990s paved the way for early alternative payment methods. Companies like CyberCash and DigiCash introduced digital currencies and electronic payment systems, laying the groundwork for future developments. PayPal, founded in 1998, played a significant role in popularizing online payments. Initially serving as a payment solution for eBay, PayPal quickly gained traction as a digital wallet that allowed users to make online transactions securely. Contactless payment technology began to emerge in the early 2000s. Companies like MasterCard and Visa introduced contactless payment cards, enabling users to make payments by tapping their cards on compatible terminals. This technology laid the foundation for later innovations in mobile and wearable payments. The proliferation of smartphones in the late 2000s opened up new possibilities for alternative payments. Apple's introduction of the iPhone and the App Store in 2007 set the stage for mobile payment innovations. In 2009, the launch of Square's mobile card reader revolutionized mobile payments by enabling small businesses to accept card payments using their smartphones. The 2010s witnessed the rise of e-wallets, also known as digital wallets. Companies like Google, Apple, and Samsung introduced their own e-wallet solutions, allowing users to store their payment card information securely on their mobile devices and make contactless payments. P2P payment platforms gained popularity during this decade, offering users the ability to send money directly to friends and family. Services like Venmo, launched in 2009, and Cash App, launched in 2013, provided a convenient and social way to split bills, share expenses, and reimburse individuals. The launch of Bitcoin in 2009 marked the beginning of cryptocurrencies and blockchain technology. Cryptocurrencies offered an alternative form of digital currency, while blockchain technology provided secure and transparent transaction records. The subsequent growth of cryptocurrencies like Ethereum and the development of blockchain-based platforms expanded the possibilities for alternative payments. The 2010s also saw the rise of Buy Now, Pay Later (BNPL) services. Companies like Klarna, Afterpay, and Affirm provided consumers with the option to make purchases and pay for them in installments, often interest-free. BNPL services gained popularity, particularly in e-commerce, as they offered greater flexibility and convenience.

The history of alternative payments demonstrates the ongoing pursuit of convenience, security, and flexibility in the way we make transactions. Advancements in technology, changes in consumer behavior, and the need for more diverse payment options have driven the development of these alternative payment methods over time. In the followings, some of the major types of alternative payments are further explained.

E-wallets

E-wallets, also known as digital wallets or mobile wallets, are electronic accounts that allow users to store and manage their payment information securely. E-wallets enable users to store various forms of payment information, such as credit card details, bank account information, and even loyalty cards. Users can add funds to their e-wallets or link them directly to their existing bank accounts. E-wallets are typically accessed through mobile applications, which are available for smartphones and tablets. These apps provide a user-friendly interface for managing payments, transactions, and other related features. One of the primary functions of e-wallets is to facilitate contactless payments. Users can make purchases by simply tapping or scanning their mobile devices on contactless payment terminals, using technologies like Near Field Communication (NFC) or Quick Response (QR) codes. This allows for fast, convenient, and secure transactions. Users can also select the e-wallet as their preferred payment method during the checkout process on e-commerce websites or within mobile apps. The payment information stored in the e-wallet is used to complete the transaction. Some e-wallets offer cross-border payment capabilities, allowing users to make international transactions easily. This is often supported through partnerships with global payment networks or by leveraging blockchain technology for efficient and secure cross-border transfers. They offer additional features like transaction history, spending analysis, bill payments, ticket purchases, and integration with other financial services. Some e-wallets also provide financial management tools, budgeting features, or the ability to split expenses among multiple users.

E-wallet Business Model

The e-wallet business model involves offering digital wallet services to consumers and generating revenue through various channels. The providers focus on acquiring a large user base to establish a strong market presence. They employ various marketing strategies, partnerships with banks or merchants, and user incentives to attract users to their platforms. User acquisition may involve targeted advertising, referral programs, or integration with popular apps and platforms.

E-wallet providers enable users to create accounts by downloading their mobile apps and completing a registration process. This typically involves providing personal information, verifying identities, and linking payment instruments, such as credit cards or bank accounts. The providers prioritize user experience during the onboarding process to ensure ease of use and quick setup. They act as intermediaries between users and merchants, facilitating payment transactions. When users make purchases using their e-wallets, the providers process the payment, deduct the amount from the user's e-wallet balance or linked payment source, and transfer funds to the merchant. This involves integration with payment networks, acquiring banks, and payment processors to ensure smooth and secure transactions. E-wallet providers generate revenue through various fee structures and revenue-sharing models. Providers charge a small fee or a percentage of the transaction amount for facilitating payments. These fees may vary based on the transaction type, such as P2P transfers, online purchases, or merchant payments. They may earn a portion of the interchange fees charged by payment networks for processing transactions. These fees are typically a percentage of the transaction value. Some e-wallets offer additional services or features within their apps, such as premium features, faster withdrawals, or access to exclusive offers. Users may pay for these services, generating revenue for the e-wallet provider. E-wallet providers may establish partnerships with merchants, enabling them to offer special promotions, discounts, or advertising opportunities to users. These partnerships may involve revenue-sharing agreements or referral fees. Service providers can earn interest income by investing the funds held in users' e-wallet accounts. However, regulatory requirements and limitations may apply to how e-wallet providers manage and invest these funds.

To differentiate their offerings and enhance user engagement, e-wallet providers often provide value-added services. These may include loyalty programs, cashback rewards, integration with other financial services like insurance or investments, bill payment services, ticketing, or access to financial management tools. These services can generate additional revenue or strengthen user loyalty.

e-wallet Providers

Bank e-wallets are typically integrated with users' bank accounts. Users can link their existing bank accounts to the e-wallet, allowing them to access funds and make transactions directly from their bank balance.

This integration offers convenience and eliminates the need for separate transfers between accounts.

Card scheme e-wallets refer to digital wallet solutions provided by major card networks such as Visa, MasterCard, American Express, and Discover. These e-wallets leverage the existing card infrastructure and payment networks to offer digital payment services. Some examples include Visa Checkout and MasterPass.

E-wallets can be offered by FinTech companies. These e-wallets leverage technology and digital advancements to offer convenient and user-friendly payment experiences. In recent years, big tech companies such as Google, Apple, Amazon, and Samsung offer digital wallet solutions. These companies leverage their extensive user base, technological prowess, and ecosystem of services to provide seamless and integrated payment experiences. Bigtech e-wallets are often integrated with their respective ecosystem of products and services. For example, Apple Pay is integrated with Apple devices and the Apple ecosystem, allowing users to make payments using their iPhones, Apple Watches, or other compatible devices. This integration enhances convenience and promotes a unified user experience.

Big merchants are more and more involved in offering digital wallet solutions. These merchants leverage their existing customer base, extensive product offerings, and online platforms to provide convenient and streamlined payment experiences. E-wallets offered by big merchants are often integrated with their existing ecosystem of products and services. They are designed to facilitate seamless transactions within the merchant's platform, like Starbucks, which adds a lot of value and offers convenient payment options in their stores for adopters of their mobile e-wallets. These wallets do not expand into other stores currently, but are very popular, especially in the US and the UK.

P2P Payments

P2P payments refer to the transfer of funds between individuals without the need for intermediaries, like banks or traditional payment processors. P2P payment services typically operate through dedicated mobile apps or online platforms. Users create accounts, link their bank accounts or payment cards, and initiate transactions by providing the recipient's contact information or username associated with the P2P payment service.

Cryptocurrencies

Cryptocurrencies are digital or virtual currencies that utilize cryptographic techniques to secure transactions and control the creation of new units. Unlike traditional fiat currencies issued by central banks, cryptocurrencies operate independently of any central authority, relying on a decentralized network of computers known as the blockchain. Bitcoin, the first and most well-known cryptocurrency, paved the way for the proliferation of thousands of other cryptocurrencies. The underlying technology behind cryptocurrencies, blockchain, is a distributed ledger that records all transactions across multiple computers in a transparent and immutable manner. Each transaction, or block, is linked to the previous one, forming a chain of blocks. The decentralized nature of blockchain technology ensures that no single entity has control over the network, enhancing security, trust, and eliminating the need for intermediaries in financial transactions. Chapter 4 is dedicated to provide more in-depth information on cryptocurrencies.

CBDC

CBDCs are digital representations of fiat currencies, issued and controlled by central banks. Unlike cryptocurrencies, CBDCs retain the full faith and backing of the issuing central authority. They are designed to operate within a regulated framework, combining the benefits of digital currencies with the stability and trust associated with traditional fiat currencies. There are two main types of CBDCs: retail CBDCs and wholesale CBDCs. Retail CBDCs are accessible to the public and enable individuals and businesses to hold and transact in digital currency directly with the central bank. Wholesale CBDCs, on the other hand, are designed for interbank transactions, facilitating settlement between financial institutions and enhancing efficiency in the financial system. Chapter 5 is dedicated to provide more in-depth information on CBDCs.

Buy Now, Pay Later (BNPL)

BNPL is a consumer financing model that allows shoppers to make immediate purchases and delay payment over time. BNPL platforms partner with retailers to offer customers the option to split their purchase amount into instalment payments, typically interest-free or with low-interest charges. Users can enjoy the benefits of their purchase immediately while spreading the cost over a specified period. One of the primary advantages of BNPL is the convenience and flexibility it offers to consumers. It eliminates the need for upfront payment, enabling individuals to make purchases they might otherwise postpone due to financial constraints. BNPL platforms often have user-friendly interfaces, making the checkout process quick and seamless, enhancing the overall shopping experience.

Crowdfunding

Evolution and Growth of Crowdfunding

Crowdfunding, a revolutionary concept that harnesses the power of the crowd to fund projects, ideas, and ventures, has come a long way since its inception. In the early 2000s, crowdfunding emerged as a novel approach to financing projects. Platforms like ArtistShare and Kiva pioneered the concept, primarily focusing on donation-based crowdfunding. These platforms provided individuals with the opportunity to support creative endeavors and charitable causes. The advent of the internet played a pivotal role in facilitating crowdfunding, as it provided a scalable and accessible platform for connecting project creators and backers.

As crowdfunding gained traction, the need for a regulatory framework became apparent. In 2012, the United States passed the Jumpstart Our Business Startups (JOBS) Act, which eased regulations for startups and small businesses. This legislation played a significant role in legitimizing equity-based crowdfunding by allowing individuals to invest in early-stage companies in exchange for equity. Similar regulatory developments occurred in other countries, providing a secure environment for crowdfunding to expand beyond donations and rewards.

With the proliferation of crowdfunding platforms, the concept evolved to encompass various models. Platforms like Kickstarter and Indiegogo rose to prominence, pioneering reward-based crowdfunding. They allowed creators to offer exclusive rewards to backers who financially supported their projects. Equity-based crowdfunding platforms, such as Seedrs and Crowdcube, provided individuals with an opportunity to invest in startups and early-stage companies. Additionally, debt-based crowdfunding platforms, including LendingClub and Funding Circle, facilitated peer-to-peer lending.

The advent of social media platforms transformed the crowdfunding landscape. Platforms like Facebook and Twitter provided powerful tools for campaigns to reach a wider audience, generate momentum, and facilitate viral sharing. Moreover, advancements in technology, particularly the widespread adoption of mobile devices and secure online payment systems, made it easier for individuals to participate in crowdfunding campaigns anytime, anywhere.

The success of high-profile crowdfunding campaigns captured media attention and generated public interest. Projects like Oculus Rift,[2] Pebble Time,[3] and Exploding Kittens[4] showcased the transformative potential of crowdfunding in bringing innovative products and ideas to market. These success stories garnered widespread media coverage, fostering trust and awareness in crowdfunding as a viable funding option. As a result, more project creators and backers were attracted to the crowdfunding ecosystem.

Crowdfunding expanded beyond traditional creative projects, finding application in various sectors. Technology startups embraced equity crowdfunding as an alternative to traditional venture capital, enabling greater access to capital for early-stage ventures. Nonprofit organizations leveraged crowdfunding to support charitable initiatives, leveraging the power of the crowd to drive social change. Furthermore, real estate crowdfunding emerged as a disruptive force, providing opportunities for individuals to invest in real estate projects with lower barriers to entry.

Crowdfunding transcended geographical boundaries and experienced rapid global growth. They emerged in different countries, embracing diverse cultures and catering to local needs. The rise of collaborative consumption, shared economy, and community-driven initiatives contributed to the cultural shift that fueled the growth of crowdfunding worldwide.

[2] https://www.kickstarter.com/projects/1523379957/oculus-rift-step-into-the-game.

[3] https://www.kickstarter.com/projects/getpebble/pebble-time-awesome-smartwatch-no-compromises.

[4] https://www.kickstarter.com/projects/elanlee/exploding-kittens.

Types of Crowdfunding

Donation-Based Crowdfunding

Donation-based crowdfunding is a form of crowdfunding where individuals contribute voluntarily to support a project, cause, or personal need without the expectation of financial return. Backers are motivated by empathy, compassion, and a desire to make a positive impact. This type of crowdfunding fosters a sense of community and collective responsibility toward social and philanthropic initiatives.

The business model of donation-based crowdfunding revolves around providing a platform and support services to facilitate the fundraising process between project creators and backers. While donation-based crowdfunding platforms enable individuals and organizations to raise funds, they also sustain their operations by employing various revenue generation strategies. These platforms typically charge fees on the funds raised by project creators. These fees are usually a percentage of the total amount collected and cover the costs of operating the platform, including maintaining the infrastructure, payment processing, customer support, and platform enhancements. Fees can vary across platforms and may range from 3 to 10% or more.

Some crowdfunding platforms offer additional services to project creators for an extra fee. These services may include marketing and promotion assistance, campaign consulting, premium customer support, data analytics, and customized campaign features. By providing these value-added services, platforms generate additional revenue streams while supporting project creators in optimizing their campaigns. Donation-based crowdfunding platforms often form partnerships and secure sponsorships with organizations or brands that align with their mission or target audience. These partnerships can involve cross-promotion, shared marketing efforts, or providing exclusive benefits to users. By leveraging partnerships and sponsorships, platforms can generate revenue while expanding their reach and attracting more project creators and backers. Crowdfunding platforms have access to valuable data and user insights, which can be leveraged to generate revenue. They may offer aggregated data reports, market trends, and analytics tools to project creators, investors, or researchers for a fee. This data can help inform decision-making, campaign strategies, and market analysis, providing value to those seeking insights into crowdfunding trends.

Some crowdfunding platforms may engage in corporate social responsibility initiatives to support social causes and create a positive brand image. This can involve dedicating a portion of their revenue or facilitating corporate matching programs, where companies match the donations made on the platform. Such initiatives align with the ethos of donation-based crowdfunding and contribute to the platform's sustainability. Donation-based crowdfunding platforms may offer premium accounts or membership tiers with additional benefits and features for project creators or backers who are willing to pay a subscription fee. Premium accounts can provide access to advanced campaign management tools, personalized support, priority customer service, or exclusive networking opportunities within the crowdfunding community.

Reward-Based Crowdfunding

Reward-based crowdfunding is a funding model in which project creators offer rewards to backers in exchange for their financial support. Unlike donation-based crowdfunding, backers receive something of value in return for their contribution. These rewards can vary from simple acknowledgments and personalized messages to exclusive experiences, limited-edition merchandise, or early access to products.

The business model of reward-based crowdfunding revolves around creating a platform that connects project creators and backers, facilitating the exchange of financial support for tangible or intangible rewards. While supporting creative projects and entrepreneurs, reward-based crowdfunding platforms sustain their operations through various revenue streams.

Reward-based crowdfunding platforms typically charge fees on the funds raised by project creators. These fees are usually a percentage of the total amount collected and cover the costs of operating the platform, including maintaining the website, payment processing, customer support, and platform enhancements. The platform fee can range from 5 to 10% or more, depending on the platform. The primary source of revenue for reward-based crowdfunding platforms is the transaction fees generated from backer contributions. When backers make financial pledges to support a project, the platform charges a transaction fee for processing the payment. This fee is deducted from the total amount contributed by the backer. To provide additional value and generate additional revenue, crowdfunding platforms may offer premium services to project creators. These services can include enhanced campaign features, personalized support, marketing assistance, or analytics tools. By offering premium services, platforms cater to the needs of project creators, who are willing to pay extra for additional support and resources.

Crowdfunding platforms often engage in advertising and partnerships as a revenue generation strategy. They may collaborate with brands, organizations, or other stakeholders to promote campaigns, provide sponsored content, or offer exclusive perks to backers. These partnerships can involve cross-promotion, sponsored campaigns, or promotional activities that generate revenue through advertising or partnership agreements. Some crowdfunding platforms extend their business models by enabling project creators to sell their products directly through the platform. This can include pre-orders or early access to the products being developed. The platform may take a percentage of the sales revenue generated through these transactions, allowing project creators to reach a wider audience and generate additional income. Selling aggregated and anonymized data can serve as an additional revenue stream for the platform. Some crowdfunding platforms offer add-on services that project creators can opt for to enhance their campaigns. These services can include professional video production, campaign consultation, graphic design, or copywriting. By providing these supplementary services, platforms generate additional revenue while supporting project creators in maximizing the effectiveness of their campaigns.

While reward-based crowdfunding primarily focuses on offering rewards to backers, some platforms have adopted a hybrid model that combines reward-based crowdfunding with equity crowdfunding. In equity crowdfunding, backers receive shares or ownership stakes in the project or company they support. This model allows platforms to generate revenue by facilitating equity investments and taking a percentage of the funds raised as a fee.

Equity-Based Crowdfunding

Equity-based crowdfunding, also known as investment crowdfunding or crowd-investing, allows businesses to raise capital from a large number of investors, each contributing relatively small amounts. In return, investors receive equity shares or ownership stakes in the company. Unlike traditional venture capital or angel investments, equity crowdfunding allows startups and small businesses to access capital from a broader pool of backers, including retail investors.

The business model of equity-based crowdfunding revolves around facilitating the exchange of capital between entrepreneurs seeking funding for their ventures and investors looking for investment opportunities. Equity crowdfunding platforms provide the infrastructure and services necessary to connect these two parties, while sustaining their operations through various revenue streams. Here are the key components of the business model:

Equity-based crowdfunding platforms typically charge fees to both entrepreneurs and investors for utilizing their services. Entrepreneurs may be required to pay a listing fee to create an investment campaign on the platform. Investors, on the other hand, may be charged a percentage-based transaction fee or a management fee for investing in the listed companies. These platform fees contribute to the platform's revenue and cover the costs of operating and maintaining the crowdfunding infrastructure. To participate in equity crowdfunding, entrepreneurs set a fundraising target, which represents the amount of capital they aim to raise for their venture. The platform may require entrepreneurs to reach a minimum threshold of investor commitments or the full fundraising target before the funds are released to the entrepreneur. This ensures that there is sufficient interest and commitment from investors before the venture receives the funds.

Equity crowdfunding platforms have a responsibility to verify the eligibility of investors participating in campaigns. Depending on the regulatory framework in the jurisdiction, platforms may restrict participation to accredited investors or open it up to a wider pool of retail investors. Platforms may implement investor verification processes to ensure compliance with legal requirements and mitigate risks associated with fraudulent or unauthorized investments. Equity crowdfunding platforms conduct due diligence on the entrepreneurs and their ventures to assess their viability and mitigate risks for potential investors. This involves evaluating the business model, market potential, management team, financials, and legal compliance of the venture. The platform may also request additional documentation or perform background checks on the entrepreneurs to verify their credibility and ensure transparency.

Equity crowdfunding platforms facilitate communication and interaction between entrepreneurs and investors throughout the investment process. They provide tools and features for entrepreneurs to update investors on the progress of their ventures, share financial reports, and address any questions or concerns. This fosters transparency and allows investors to stay informed about the performance of their investments.

Some equity crowdfunding platforms offer secondary marketplaces, enabling investors to buy and sell their equity stakes in listed companies. This provides liquidity and exit opportunities for investors who wish to divest their holdings before the venture reaches a liquidity event, such as an acquisition or initial public offering. Platforms may charge transaction fees or commissions on secondary market transactions to generate additional revenue.

Equity crowdfunding platforms may form partnerships with venture capital firms, angel investors, or other investment entities. These partnerships allow for syndication, where multiple investors pool their capital to invest in a venture collectively. By collaborating with established investors, platforms enhance the credibility and attractiveness of the investment opportunities listed on their platform.

Equity crowdfunding platforms must adhere to legal and regulatory requirements specific to their operating jurisdiction. They need to comply with securities laws, investor protection regulations, and anti-money laundering guidelines. Compliance ensures transparency, protects investors from fraud or misconduct, and maintains the platform's reputation and integrity.

The Crowdfunding Process

Campaign Creation

The crowdfunding process begins with the project creator or entrepreneur conceptualizing and creating a compelling campaign. The campaign serves as a persuasive pitch that outlines the project's objectives, timeline, target funding amount, and the value proposition for potential backers. Project creators often leverage various media formats, including videos, images, and textual descriptions, to effectively communicate their vision and engage potential supporters.

Platform Selection

Once the campaign is ready, project creators must choose an appropriate crowdfunding platform that aligns with their project's nature and goals. There are numerous crowdfunding platforms available, each catering to specific niches such as creative arts, technology, social causes, or entrepreneurial ventures. Project creators must consider factors such as platform reputation, target audience, fees, and the level of support and resources offered by the platform.

Campaign Launch
With the campaign and platform selected, project creators launch their crowdfunding campaign. They share their campaign page across various channels, including social media, email marketing, personal networks, and relevant communities. The objective is to generate visibility and attract potential backers to the campaign page. Project creators often employ storytelling techniques, compelling visuals, and persuasive messaging to capture the attention and interest of potential backers.

Backer Engagement and Outreach
Throughout the crowdfunding campaign, project creators actively engage with potential backers, answering questions, providing updates, and fostering a sense of community. Backers appreciate transparent and timely communication, as it builds trust and strengthens their connection to the project. Project creators may also utilize stretch goals and exclusive rewards to incentivize backers and encourage them to spread the word about the campaign to their own networks.

Funding Goal and Timeline
Project creators set a funding goal, representing the amount of money they aim to raise through the crowdfunding campaign. This goal should be realistic and aligned with the project's financial needs. Crowdfunding campaigns typically have a predefined timeline, ranging from a few weeks to a couple of months. It is essential for project creators to establish a sense of urgency and momentum during the campaign period to drive backer participation.

Backer Contributions
Interested individuals who resonate with the project and its goals become backers by contributing and financial support. Backers typically have the option to choose from various predefined pledge levels or contribute a custom amount. The crowdfunding platform handles the collection of funds through secure payment processing systems. Depending on the platform, backers may be charged immediately upon making their contribution or at the end of the campaign if the funding goal is met.

Stretch Goals and Updates
During the campaign, project creators may introduce stretch goals, which represent additional funding targets beyond the initial goal. If the campaign surpasses the original funding goal, stretch goals offer incentives for backers to continue supporting the project by unlocking new features, rewards, or project enhancements. Regular campaign updates keep backers informed about the project's progress, achievements, and any adjustments made to the timeline or goals.

Campaign Conclusion
At the end of the campaign period, the project creator assesses the total funds raised. If the campaign successfully reaches or surpasses the funding goal, the project creator moves forward with executing the project, utilizing the funds for its intended purpose. If the funding goal is not met, project creators may explore alternative options, such as refining the project, relaunching the campaign, seeking other funding sources, or scaling down the scope of the project.

Challenges and Risks of Crowdfunding

Market Saturation and Competition
One of the primary challenges in crowdfunding is the increasing market saturation and competition. As crowdfunding gains popularity, numerous projects and ventures vie for the attention and support of potential backers. This makes it challenging for individual campaigns to stand out and attract sufficient funding. Project creators must develop unique value propositions, compelling narratives, and targeted marketing strategies to differentiate their campaigns from the crowd.

Funding Goal Achievement
Setting and achieving the funding goal is a critical aspect of crowdfunding success. However, many campaigns fail to reach their targets. Insufficient planning, unrealistic funding goals, inadequate campaign promotion, or lack of backer engagement can contribute to the failure to achieve the desired funding. Project creators must conduct thorough research, set realistic goals, develop comprehensive marketing plans, and actively engage with potential backers to maximize their chances of reaching their funding targets.

Trust and Credibility

Building trust and credibility is crucial in the crowdfunding space, as backers rely on the information provided by project creators to make investment decisions. However, trust can be undermined by fraudulent campaigns, exaggerated claims, or the inability of project creators to deliver on their promises. To mitigate this risk, crowdfunding platforms should implement verification processes, conduct due diligence on project creators, and provide transparent communication channels. Project creators, in turn, should be transparent, honest, and accountable throughout the campaign and post-campaign phases.

Intellectual Property and Idea Theft

Crowdfunding exposes project creators to the risk of intellectual property theft or idea replication. Sharing detailed project descriptions and concepts on public platforms can make ideas vulnerable to being copied by unscrupulous individuals or businesses. Project creators should consider protective measures, such as filing patents, trademarks, or copyrights, before launching their campaigns. Additionally, maintaining a competitive advantage through unique features, branding, or execution can deter potential idea theft.

Regulatory Compliance and Legal Risks

Crowdfunding operates within legal and regulatory frameworks that vary across jurisdictions. Non-compliance with these regulations can expose participants to legal risks and potential penalties. Crowdfunding platforms must ensure adherence to securities laws, consumer protection regulations, anti-money laundering requirements, and other relevant statutes. Project creators should also familiarize themselves with the applicable regulations to avoid legal complications and protect their interests.

Reputation Management

In the crowdfunding ecosystem, reputation plays a pivotal role. Negative experiences, such as project delays, miscommunication, or failure to deliver rewards, can tarnish the reputation of project creators and crowdfunding platforms. Negative reviews and feedback can deter potential backers and harm future fundraising efforts. Maintaining a strong reputation requires timely and transparent communication, delivering on promises, and addressing any issues or concerns raised by backers promptly and professionally.

Financial Risks

From the perspective of investors and backers, crowdfunding carries financial risks. Investments in startups or early-stage ventures inherently involve uncertainties and the potential for loss of capital. Project creators may encounter financial challenges during project execution, leading to delays, cost overruns, or project abandonment. Backers should carefully evaluate the risks associated with a project and diversify their investments to minimize the impact of potential failures.

Lack of Post-Funding Support

Once a crowdfunding campaign successfully raises funds, project creators must navigate the post-funding phase effectively. Managing funds, executing the project, and fulfilling promises made to backers require efficient project management and organizational skills. Inadequate planning, resource allocation, or unforeseen obstacles can contribute to the challenges faced during the post-funding phase. Project creators should establish clear project timelines, allocate resources effectively, and maintain open lines of communication with backers to provide regular updates on progress, potential setbacks, and any adjustments to the project plan.

Scalability and Growth

For successful projects, scaling and managing growth can present additional challenges. Meeting increased demand, expanding operations, and maintaining quality standards while managing cash flow can strain resources and create logistical complexities. Project creators should anticipate growth scenarios, develop scalable business models, and seek additional funding or strategic partnerships to support their expansion plans.

Cultural and Global Considerations

As crowdfunding transcends geographical boundaries, cultural and global considerations come into play. Language barriers, differences in consumer behaviors and expectations, and regulatory disparities can pose challenges for international campaigns. Project creators should undertake market research, adapt their messaging to target specific audiences, and ensure compliance with the local legal and regulatory frameworks when conducting cross-border crowdfunding campaigns.

Peer-to-Peer lending

Definition and Overview

The peer-to-peer (P2P) industry refers to a decentralized marketplace where individuals can directly interact and transact with each other without the need for intermediaries. It is built on the principle of sharing resources, services, or information between peers, facilitated by technology platforms that connect them. P2P platforms enable individuals to engage in various activities, such as lending and borrowing money, making payments, sharing assets, and conducting commerce. These platforms leverage technology to match supply with demand, creating efficient and transparent marketplaces that challenge traditional models of finance, commerce, and sharing.

The P2P industry has gained significant importance and witnessed exponential growth in recent years. It has emerged as a viable alternative to traditional systems, offering numerous benefits to participants. The growth of the P2P industry can be attributed to several factors, including advancements in technology, changing consumer behaviors, dissatisfaction with traditional intermediaries, and the desire for more personalized and efficient solutions. P2P platforms have disrupted industries such as finance, lending, payments, rental, and e-commerce by providing individuals with greater control, transparency, and access to resources.

Historical Development of P2P Industry

The roots of the P2P industry can be traced back to the early days of the internet when pioneers recognized the potential for direct peer-to-peer interactions. Concepts, such as file-sharing protocols, such as Napster and BitTorrent, allowed individuals to share digital files directly without relying on centralized servers. These early developments showcased the power of decentralized networks and laid the foundation for the P2P industry. The P2P industry gained momentum with the emergence of platforms that expanded the scope of peer-to-peer interactions beyond file sharing. In 2005, the launch of eBay's subsidiary, PayPal, revolutionized online payments by enabling individuals to transfer funds directly to one another. This marked a significant step in facilitating P2P financial transactions. Around the same time, platforms like Zopa, Prosper, and LendingClub pioneered the concept of peer-to-peer lending, connecting borrowers and lenders directly through online marketplaces. These platforms disrupted the traditional banking model by providing borrowers with access to loans and offering lenders the opportunity to earn interest in their investments.

As the P2P industry continued to evolve, new sectors emerged, such as peer-to-peer rental platforms like Airbnb and Uber, which revolutionized the hospitality and transportation industries. These platforms enabled individuals to monetize their underutilized assets, such as spare rooms or vehicles, by directly connecting with those in need of accommodation or transportation services. The proliferation of smartphones and the widespread adoption of mobile applications further fueled the growth of the P2P industry. Mobile payment platforms like Venmo and Alipay simplified P2P money transfers by allowing individuals to send and receive funds using their mobile devices. The historical development of the P2P industry highlights the continuous expansion of peer-to-peer interactions across various sectors, driven by technological advancements and changing consumer preferences. This evolution has reshaped traditional industries, disrupted established models, and empowered individuals to engage in direct and decentralized exchanges.

Key Sectors in the P2P Industry

One of the prominent sectors within the P2P industry is peer-to-peer lending. P2P lending platforms connect borrowers directly with lenders, bypassing traditional financial institutions. Borrowers can access loans for various purposes, such as personal loans, business loans, or student loans, while lenders have the opportunity to invest their capital and earn interest on their loans. However, there are other sectors in various industries which integrated the P2P concept into their business models.

The sharing economy has been revolutionized by peer-to-peer rental platforms. These platforms connect individuals who have assets or services to share with those in need. Examples include home-sharing platforms like Airbnb, car-sharing platforms like Getaround, and equipment-sharing platforms like Fat Llama. By leveraging the underutilized assets of individuals, these platforms create new opportunities for earning income and accessing resources more efficiently.

Additionally, P2P e-commerce platforms provide a direct channel for individuals to buy and sell goods and services without the need for traditional retail intermediaries. These platforms enable individuals to create online stores, list products, and reach a wider customer base. Popular examples include marketplace platforms like Etsy and Poshmark, where individuals can sell handmade or vintage items, and classifieds platforms like Craigslist and Facebook Marketplace, where individuals can buy and sell various goods locally.

Business Models in the P2P Industry

Marketplace Model

The marketplace model is a prevalent business model in the P2P industry. P2P marketplace platforms act as intermediaries, facilitating transactions between individuals. These platforms provide a user-friendly interface where participants can list their offerings, search for desired products or services, and engage in direct transactions. The platform typically earns revenue through transaction fees, subscription fees, or advertising.

Examples of marketplace models in the P2P industry include peer-to-peer lending platforms like LendingClub and Prosper, where borrowers and lenders connect directly, and crowdfunding platforms like Kickstarter and Indiegogo, where project creators and backers interact. These platforms enable individuals to access financing or support directly from a community of lenders or backers.

Collaborative Consumption Model

The collaborative consumption model, also known as the sharing economy model, revolves around individuals sharing underutilized assets or resources with others in exchange for monetary compensation. P2P platforms play a crucial role in facilitating these exchanges by providing a platform for individuals to list and offer their assets or services.

Platforms like Airbnb and Uber exemplify the collaborative consumption model. Homeowners can rent out their spare rooms or properties to travelers, and individuals with vehicles can provide transportation services to passengers. The platform acts as an intermediary, handling the payment process and ensuring trust and safety between participants.

Sharing Economy Model

The sharing economy model takes the collaborative consumption model further by focusing on sharing assets and resources without a monetary exchange. Instead of monetary compensation, individuals engage in non-monetary exchanges, such as sharing goods, services, or skills.

For example, platforms like Freecycle and Shareable enable individuals to give away or share items they no longer need, promoting sustainability and reducing waste. Skill-sharing platforms like TaskRabbit and Upwork allow individuals to offer their skills and services to others in exchange for reciprocal services or favors.

Blockchain and Decentralized Models
With the advent of blockchain technology, new P2P business models have emerged that leverage the decentralized nature of blockchain networks. These models aim to eliminate the need for intermediaries entirely, enabling direct peer-to-peer transactions with increased security, transparency, and efficiency. Decentralized finance (DeFi) platforms, built on blockchain networks like Ethereum, facilitate P2P lending, borrowing, and trading of digital assets without relying on traditional financial institutions. Smart contracts, powered by blockchain technology, automate and enforce the terms of transactions, removing the need for intermediaries. Additionally, decentralized marketplaces built on blockchain, such as OpenBazaar, enable individuals to buy and sell goods directly, with transactions recorded on the blockchain for transparency and trust.

Risks of P2P Industry

While the P2P industry offers significant benefits, it is important to consider the risks associated with P2P activities. P2P lending carries the risk of borrower defaults, which can result in the loss of capital for lenders. Even with risk assessment models in place, there is no guarantee that borrowers will repay their loans. Lenders must carefully evaluate the creditworthiness of borrowers and diversify their investments to mitigate the risk of default. Unlike traditional financial institutions, P2P platforms may not offer the same level of regulatory protections. In some jurisdictions, P2P lending and crowdfunding may not be subject to the same regulations and oversight as traditional lending institutions. This can expose participants to potential risks and scams. P2P platforms face the risk of fraudulent activities, including identity theft, fake listings, and misleading information. Platforms must implement robust security measures to protect user data and establish mechanisms to detect and prevent fraudulent behavior. However, fraudulent activities can still occur, posing risks to both borrowers and lenders. P2P investments can be subject to market volatility and economic conditions. Economic downturns or disruptions in specific industries can impact borrower repayment rates and the value of investments. Lenders must be prepared for potential fluctuations and assess the risks associated with different loan categories and industries. Unlike traditional investment options, such as stocks or bonds, P2P investments may lack liquidity. Once funds are invested, they are typically tied up for the duration of the loan term. This means that lenders may not have immediate access to their invested capital if they need it urgently. P2P platforms may face operational challenges or even closure. Participants must consider the reliability and reputation of the platform they choose. If a platform shuts down or faces financial difficulties, it can impact the funds and investments of users. It is crucial to conduct due diligence and choose platforms with a solid track record and an established reputation.

Robo-Advisory

Origins of Robo-Advisory

Robo-advisory has emerged as a significant innovation within the financial services industry, revolutionizing the way individuals and institutions approach investment management. The origins of robo-advisory can be traced back to the aftermath of the 2008 financial crisis. The crisis exposed the shortcomings of traditional investment management models, leading to a demand for more accessible, transparent, and cost-effective solutions. Fueled by advancements in FinTech, the concept of robo-advisory emerged as a disruptive alternative.

Early adopters of robo-advisory were primarily FinTech startups seeking to bridge the gap between professional investment advice and individual investors with limited assets. Technological enablers such as artificial intelligence (AI), machine learning, and big data analytics played a crucial role in the development and growth of robo-advisory platforms. These technologies allowed for automated data analysis, personalized portfolio construction, and efficient investment strategies.

The early 2010s witnessed the emergence of standalone robo-advisory startups, such as Betterment and Wealthfront, that offered automated investment services directly to retail investors. These platforms utilized algorithms to create diversified portfolios based on individual risk profiles and financial goals, disrupting the traditional advisor-client relationship.

Recognizing the potential of robo-advisory, traditional financial institutions began entering the market. Companies like Vanguard, Charles Schwab, and Fidelity introduced their own robo-advisory platforms, combining the trust and brand recognition of established institutions with the technological capabilities of robo-advisors.

As robo-advisory gained traction, platforms expanded their services beyond basic portfolio management. They began offering features such as tax-loss harvesting, retirement planning, and socially responsible investing. Additionally, hybrid models emerged, blending automated portfolio management with access to human advisors for more complex financial planning needs.

Robo-Advisory Business Model

The robo-advisory business model leverages technology and algorithms to provide automated investment management services to clients. The primary objectives are to democratize access to investment advice, enhance portfolio performance, lower costs, and improve the overall client experience. Robo-advisory platforms typically target retail investors, including millennials, who seek simplified and cost-effective investment solutions. However, some platforms have expanded their offerings to accommodate high-net-worth individuals and institutional investors.

Robo-advisory platforms rely on advanced technology infrastructure, including AI, machine learning, big data analytics, and cloud computing. These technologies enable efficient data processing, algorithm-driven portfolio construction, and personalized investment recommendations. Robo-advisory platforms employ digital onboarding processes to gather client information, assess risk tolerance, and determine investment objectives. Through online questionnaires and algorithms, the platforms determine suitable asset allocations based on risk profiles. Robo-advisors utilize algorithms to construct and manage client portfolios based on factors such as risk tolerance, time horizon, and financial goals. These algorithms consider various asset classes, diversification, and rebalancing strategies to optimize portfolio performance. Robo-advisory platforms automatically rebalance client portfolios to maintain the desired asset allocations. When market fluctuations cause deviations, the algorithms trigger trades to realign the portfolio with the target allocation, ensuring adherence to the investment strategy. Some robo-advisors offer tax optimization strategies, including tax-loss harvesting, to minimize the impact of taxes on investment returns. Algorithms identify opportunities to offset capital gains with capital losses, reducing tax liabilities for clients. Robo-advisory platforms provide clients with real-time performance reporting and portfolio monitoring. Clients can access detailed information on their investments, including asset allocation, returns, and fees, through intuitive online dashboards or mobile applications.

The primary revenue source for robo-advisory platforms is asset-based fees, charged as a percentage of the client's portfolio value. These fees typically range from 0.20% to 1% of assets under management (AUM), depending on the platform and the level of services provided. Robo-advisory platforms may generate additional revenue by offering value-added services, such as financial planning, access to premium investment products, or customized portfolios for high-net-worth clients. These services often carry separate fees or are bundled into premium tiers (Fig. 3.1).

RegTech

In today's rapidly evolving business landscape, regulatory compliance has become increasingly complex and demanding. Organizations across various industries face the challenge of adhering to a plethora of laws, regulations, and standards set by governing bodies. Failure to comply with these requirements can result in severe consequences, including financial penalties, reputational damage, and legal implications. To tackle the growing compliance burden, a new field of technology has emerged: RegTech, short for Regulatory Technology. RegTech refers to the use of advanced technologies to streamline and automate regulatory compliance processes. By leveraging innovative solutions, RegTech aims to enhance the efficiency, accuracy, and effectiveness of compliance operations while reducing costs and mitigating risks.

An Overview of RegTech Growth

The evolution of RegTech can be traced back to the aftermath of the 2008 global financial crisis. The crisis exposed significant weaknesses in regulatory oversight and compliance processes, prompting regulators and financial institutions to seek more robust and efficient solutions to address

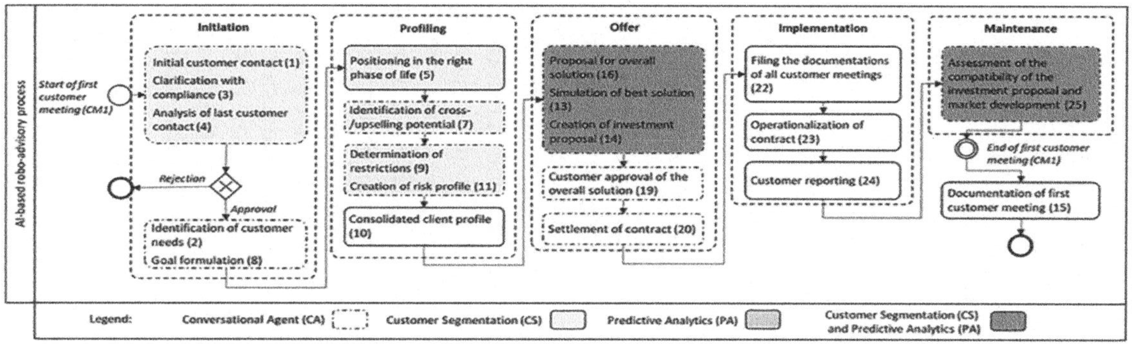

Fig. 3.1 Robo-advisory process in banking sector (*Source* Dietzmann et al. [2022])

compliance challenges. The emergence of RegTech can be understood through the following stages of its evolution:

Early Stage: Post-Financial Crisis (2008–2010)

In the wake of the financial crisis, regulators and financial institutions recognized the need for improved compliance systems. This led to the initial exploration of technology-driven solutions to enhance regulatory compliance. The focus was primarily on addressing risk management, reporting, and data analytics. During this stage, RegTech solutions began to leverage existing technologies, such as data management systems, business intelligence tools, and risk management software, to streamline compliance processes. However, the adoption of these solutions was relatively limited, primarily confined to large financial institutions due to high implementation costs and limited awareness.

Expansion and Diversification (2011–2015)

In the subsequent years, RegTech gained momentum and expanded beyond the financial sector to other regulated industries, including healthcare, energy, telecommunications, and data privacy. The increasing regulatory burden across sectors drove the demand for technology-enabled compliance solutions. Regulatory reporting emerged as a significant area of focus during this stage. RegTech solutions aimed at automating data collection, aggregation, and reporting processes, reducing manual efforts and improving accuracy. Risk management and monitoring capabilities were also enhanced, with the adoption of advanced analytics, machine learning, and real-time transaction monitoring tools. Additionally, identity verification and customer due diligence became prominent components of RegTech, driven by the need for efficient and secure customer onboarding processes. Electronic Know Your Customer (e-KYC) solutions, leveraging biometric authentication and digital signatures, gained traction, enabling organizations to streamline identity verification while ensuring compliance.

Maturation and Technological Advancements (2016–2020)

RegTech matured further during this stage, driven by rapid advancements in technology and increased collaboration between regulators, financial institutions, and technology firms. Regulators recognized the potential of technology to improve compliance and actively supported the development and adoption of RegTech solutions.

Artificial intelligence (AI), machine learning (ML), big data analytics, and blockchain technology emerged as key enablers of RegTech innovation. These technologies enabled more sophisticated risk assessment, real-time monitoring, and automation of compliance processes. Advanced analytics tools empowered organizations to analyze large volumes of structured and unstructured data for identifying compliance risks, patterns, and anomalies.

Regulatory sandboxes were established in several jurisdictions, providing a controlled environment for testing and validating RegTech solutions. Collaboration between regulators and market participants facilitated knowledge exchange, standardization of best practices, and the development of interoperable RegTech solutions.

Current and Future Trends

RegTech continues to evolve rapidly, fueled by ongoing advancements in technology and the need for efficient compliance processes in the face of evolving regulations. Several trends are shaping the future of RegTech. For example, AI and ML technologies will play an increasingly significant role in RegTech, enabling organizations to automate compliance checks, enhance risk assessment capabilities, and improve anomaly detection. Blockchain technology holds great potential in ensuring secure data sharing, identity verification, and creating immutable audit trails. Its integration with RegTech solutions can enhance data integrity, transparency, and security. The emergence of Regulatory Compliance as a Service (RCaaS) models allows organizations to outsource their regulatory compliance functions to specialized RegTech providers. This model offers cost-effective solutions, expertise, and scalability, particularly beneficial for small and medium enterprises (SMEs) with limited resources. RegTech solutions are becoming more sophisticated in the area of regulatory reporting. They offer automated data collection, integration, and analysis, enabling organizations to generate accurate and timely reports for regulatory authorities. Compliance analytics tools are also evolving to provide advanced insights and predictive analytics for better risk management. The growing emphasis on sustainability and environmental, social, and governance (ESG) factors is driving the need for RegTech solutions to address ESG compliance requirements. RegTech tools are being developed to help organizations monitor, report, and ensure compliance with environmental and social regulations, as well as governance standards.

RegTech Business Models

The RegTech business model encompasses various approaches and strategies that RegTech companies adopt to deliver their solutions and generate revenue. While specific business models may vary depending on the company's target market, technology offerings, and value proposition, the following are some common elements and models within the RegTech industry:

Software-as-a-Service (SaaS) Model

Many RegTech companies operate on a SaaS model, where they provide their compliance software solutions as a subscription-based service. Customers access the software through the cloud, eliminating the need for upfront infrastructure investments and reducing maintenance and upgrade costs. The SaaS model allows for scalability, flexibility, and ease of adoption, making it popular among businesses of all sizes.

Customization and Consulting Model

Some RegTech companies offer customized solutions and consulting services tailored to the specific compliance needs of their clients. These companies work closely with organizations to understand their unique compliance requirements and to develop customized software solutions. This model often involves a combination of software licensing, consulting fees, and ongoing support and maintenance contracts.

Regulatory Data and Analytics Model

RegTech companies specializing in data management and analytics may focus on providing comprehensive and up-to-date regulatory data and analytics platforms. These platforms aggregate regulatory information from various sources, analyze it, and provide actionable insights to businesses. Companies adopting this model often generate revenue through subscription fees, licensing of data, or consultancy services based on data analytics.

Regulatory Compliance as a Service (RCaaS) Model

The RCaaS model involves providing end-to-end regulatory compliance services to businesses. RegTech companies offer a suite of integrated compliance solutions, including software, data analytics, reporting tools, and consultancy services. Clients outsource their compliance functions to the RegTech provider, allowing them to focus on their core business activities. Revenue is generated through service fees or subscription-based models.

Partnership and Integration Model

RegTech companies may collaborate with established technology providers, such as financial software vendors or data providers, to integrate their solutions into existing platforms or systems. By leveraging partnerships and integrations, RegTech companies can tap into existing customer bases and expand their reach. Revenue is often generated through licensing fees or revenue-sharing agreements with the partner companies.

Regulatory Sandbox Model

Regulatory sandboxes, established by regulators in some jurisdictions, allow RegTech companies to test and validate their solutions in a controlled environment. Companies participating in regulatory sandboxes can refine their offerings, gain regulatory approval, and demonstrate their value to potential customers and investors. The revenue generation in this model typically occurs after successful testing, with companies commercializing their solutions through licensing or subscription-based models.

Data Security and Compliance Model

RegTech companies focusing on data security and compliance offer solutions that help organizations protect sensitive data, ensure regulatory compliance, and meet privacy requirements. These companies may provide tools for encryption, data access control, identity verification, and secure communication. Revenue is often generated through subscription fees, licensing, or consulting services related to data security and compliance.

Insurtech

Insurtech, a portmanteau of "insurance" and "technology," refers to the application of technological innovations and digital transformation within the insurance industry. It encompasses the use of advanced technologies, data analytics, automation, artificial intelligence (AI), machine learning, and blockchain to enhance and revolutionize various aspects of the insurance value chain, including product development, distribution, underwriting, claims management, risk assessment, customer experience, and operational efficiency. Insurtech companies leverage technology-driven solutions and disruptive business models to address traditional challenges and inefficiencies in the insurance industry. By harnessing the power of technology, Insurtech aims to improve customer engagement, increase transparency, enhance risk assessment accuracy, streamline processes, reduce costs, and provide more tailored and flexible insurance products and services.

Impact of Insurtech on the Insurance Value Chain

The impact of Insurtech on the insurance value chain has been significant, transforming traditional processes and improving efficiency, customer experiences, and risk management. Insurtech has revolutionized the way insurance products are distributed and purchased. Digital platforms and mobile apps have made insurance accessible to customers anytime, anywhere. Insurtech companies provide user-friendly interfaces, allowing customers to compare policies, receive instant quotes, and make purchases online. This direct-to-consumer approach eliminates the need for intermediaries, reduces distribution costs, and enhances transparency. Moreover, Insurtech has improved customer experiences by offering personalized recommendations, simplified processes, and enabling self-service functionalities through intuitive interfaces and chatbots.

Insurtech has transformed the underwriting process through advanced data analytics and AI. Insurtech companies leverage vast amounts of data from various sources, including customer data, external databases, and IoT devices, to assess risks accurately. AI algorithms analyze data patterns, identify correlations, and make predictions, enabling insurers to make more informed underwriting decisions. This leads to improved risk selection, more accurate pricing, and the ability to tailor policies to individual customers' needs. Insurtech also facilitates automated underwriting processes, reducing manual intervention and streamlining policy issuance.

Insurtech has streamlined the claims management process, making it faster and more efficient. Insurtech companies utilize automation, digital documentation, and AI-powered algorithms to expedite claims processing. Customers can submit claims electronically, along with supporting documents, through online portals or mobile apps. AI algorithms analyze claims data, identify patterns, and detect potential fraud, enabling insurers to detect and prevent fraudulent activities more effectively. This reduces claim settlement time, enhances customer satisfaction, and ensures accurate claims payouts.

Insurtech has facilitated the development of personalized and usage-based insurance products. By leveraging data from IoT devices, telematics, and other sources, insurers can gather real-time information on customers' behaviors, usage patterns, and risks. This enables the offering of usage-based insurance (UBI) products, where premiums are based on actual usage or specific risk factors. Insurtech companies provide customers with feedback on their behaviors, incentivizing safer practices and potentially reducing premiums. Personalized insurance offerings cater to individual needs, allowing customers to choose coverage options that align with their specific requirements.

Insurtech has transformed customer engagement and communication in the insurance industry. Chatbots, virtual assistants, and AI-powered customer service platforms provide real-time support and assistance to customers, answering inquiries, providing policy information, and guiding them through the insurance process. Insurtech companies utilize personalized dashboards and mobile apps, allowing customers to manage their policies, access documents, make payments, and initiate claims conveniently. These digital touchpoints enhance customer experiences, foster engagement, and enable insurers to build stronger relationships with their policyholders.

Insurtech has also improved operational efficiency within insurance companies. Automation, digitalization, and streamlined processes have reduced manual tasks, minimized paperwork, and optimized resource allocation. Insurtech solutions enable the automation of routine tasks such as data entry, policy generation, and claims processing, freeing up valuable human resources to focus on more complex and value-added activities. This leads to cost savings, increased productivity, and improved operational performance for insurers.

Role of FinTech in Covid-19 Era

The Covid-19 pandemic has disrupted the world in ways we could not have imagined, and the impact of the virus has been felt across all sectors of the economy. The pandemic has forced many businesses to close, and many people have lost their jobs. However, the FinTech industry has emerged as a bright spot amid the chaos caused by the pandemic. FinTech has played a critical role in the Covid-19 era, helping people and businesses to adapt to the new normal. This section briefly discusses the role of FinTech in the Covid-19 era and how it has helped individuals and businesses navigate the pandemic.

Contactless Payments

The Covid-19 pandemic has accelerated the adoption of contactless payments, as people have become more conscious of the need for hygiene and reducing physical contact. FinTech companies have played a significant role in this transformation, providing the infrastructure for contactless payments. With the help of FinTech, businesses can now offer contactless payment options such as mobile wallets, QR codes, and other digital payment solutions, reducing the need for physical cash and contact.

Digital Banking

The Covid-19 pandemic has also highlighted the need for digital banking solutions, as people are unable or unwilling to visit bank branches due to the risk of infection. FinTech companies have been at the forefront of developing digital banking solutions that allow customers to carry out transactions from the comfort of their homes. Digital banking has become the new normal, with FinTech companies providing online banking, mobile banking, and other digital solutions that offer convenience and safety. Chapter 6 provides an in-depth description of digital banks and their functions.

Remote Work

The Covid-19 pandemic has forced many businesses to adopt remote work arrangements, which have presented new challenges for managing financial transactions. FinTech has played a significant role in enabling remote work, providing solutions for managing payroll, invoicing, and other financial operations remotely. FinTech has also facilitated remote lending, allowing businesses to access funds without having to physically visit a bank.

Financial Inclusion

The Covid-19 pandemic has highlighted the importance of financial inclusion, as many people have been left vulnerable due to the economic impact of the pandemic. FinTech has played a critical role in promoting financial inclusion, providing solutions that enable people to access financial services, including loans and insurance, remotely. FinTech has also enabled people to access financial education, improving financial literacy and promoting responsible financial behavior.

Data Analytics

The Covid-19 pandemic has highlighted the importance of data analytics, as businesses seek to understand the impact of the pandemic on their operations. FinTech companies have played a critical role in providing data analytics solutions that enable businesses to monitor their financial performance, identify trends, and make informed decisions. FinTech has also facilitated the use of data analytics in risk management, helping businesses to identify and mitigate financial risks.

Financial Planning

The Covid-19 pandemic has disrupted financial planning, as businesses and individuals struggle to predict the future in the face of unprecedented uncertainty. FinTech has played a significant role in facilitating financial planning, providing solutions that enable businesses and individuals to forecast and manage their finances in the face of uncertainty. FinTech has also enabled businesses to access financing options that offer flexibility and help them manage cash flow.

References

Acunto, F. D., & Rossi, A. G. (2020). *Robo-advising* (Issue 8225, pp. 1–30).

Anagnostopoulos, I. (2018). FinTech and regtech: Impact on regulators and banks. *Journal of Economics and Business, 100*, 7–25. https://doi.org/10.1016/j.jeconbus.2018.07.003

Arner, D., Buckley, R., & Zetzsche, D. (2022). Governing FinTech 4.0: BigTech, platform finance, and sustainable development. *Fordham Journal of Corporate & Financial Law, 27*(1), 1–71.

Arner, D. W., Barberis, J., & Buckley, R. P. (2017). FinTech, RegTech, and the reconceptualization of financial regulation. *Northwestern Journal of International Law & Business, 37*(3), 1–44.

Assadi, D. (2016). *In search of crowdfunding business models*. IGI Global.

Beaulieu, T., & Beaulieu, T. (2016). *A conceptual framework for understanding crowdfunding: A conceptual framework for understanding crowdfunding. January 2015.*

Berger, S. C., & Gleisner, F. (2009). Emergence of financial intermediaries in electronic markets: The Case of online P2P lending. *German Academic Association of Business Research, 2*(1), 39–65.

Bettinger, A. (1972). *FinTech: A series of 40 time shared models used at manufacturers hanover trust company* (pp. 62–63). Interfaces.

Bian, W., & Cong, L. W. (2023). The rise of e-wallets and buy-now-pay-later. In *NBER working papers.*

Bouhsine, T. (2020, August). *Design and full stack development of a crowd-funding platform Sahem ´ par: Dr . BELAQZIZ Salwa Encadr e*. https://doi.org/10.13140/RG.2.2.15052.33926

Brenner, L. (2019). *Robo-advisors: A substitute for human financial advice? Robo-advisors: A substitute for human financial*. Leibniz Information Centre for Economics. https://doi.org/10.2139/ssrn.3414200

Buckley, R. P., Arner, D. W., Zetzsche, D. A., & Weber, R. H. (2020). The road to RegTech: The (astonishing) example of the European Union. *Journal of Banking Regulation, 21*(1), 26–36. https://doi.org/10.1057/s41261-019-00104-1

C, P. P. P. (2021). Understanding the implications of FinTech Peer-to- Peer (P2P) lending during the COVID-19 pandemic understanding the implications of FinTech understanding the implications of FinTech Peer-to- Peer (P2P) lending during the COVID-19 pandemic. *Journal of Sustainable Finance & Investment, 1–16*. https://doi.org/10.1080/20430795.2021.1917225

Candy, C., Robin, R., Sativa, E., Septiana, S., Can, H., & Alice, A. (2022). FinTech in the time of COVID-19: Conceptual overview. *Jurnal Akuntasi Keuangan Dan Manajemen, 3*(3), 253–262.

Carstens, A. (2021). *Public policy for big techs in finance*. Bank for International Settlement.

Cicchiello, A. (2019). Harmonising the crowdfunding regulation in Europe: Need, challenges, and risks. *Journal of Small Business & Entrepreneurship, 32*(6), 585–606. https://doi.org/10.1080/08276331.2019.1603945

Dietzmann, C., Jaeggi, T., & Alt, R. (2023). Implications of AI-based robo-advisory for private banking investment advisory. *Journal of Electronic Business & Digital Economics, 2*(1), 3–23. https://doi.org/10.1108/JEBDE-09-2022-0037

Dorfleitner, G., & Hornuf, L. (2019). *FinTech and data privacy in Germany*. Springer.

Ehrentraud, J., Prenio, J., Boar, C., Lawson, A., & Janfils, M. (2021). FinTech and payments: Regulating digital payment services and e-money. In *FSI Insights on policy implementation*. Bank for International Settlements, Basel. https://www.bis.org/fsi/publ/insights33.pdf

Emekter, R., Tu, Y., Jirasakuldech, B., & Lu, M. (2015). Evaluating credit risk and loan performance in online Peer-to-Peer (P2P) lending. *Applied Economics, 47*(1), 54–70. https://doi.org/10.1080/00036846.2014.962222

Faruk, A., & Musa, I. (2021). A bibliometric analysis of FinTech and blockchain in Islamic finance. In *MPRA* (Issue 109712).

Fisch, J. E., Labouré, M., & Turner, J. A. (2018). *The emergence of the Robo-advisor* (Wharton Pension Research Council Working Papers).

Goyal, A. (2022). *E Wallet app development—Cost & key features*. Octal IT Solution.

Havrylchyk, O., & Verdier, M. (2019). The financial intermediation role of the P2P lending platforms. *Comparative Economic Systems, 60*, 115–130. https://doi.org/10.1057/s41294-017-0045-1

Hemer, J. (2011). A snapshot on crowdfunding. In *Arbeitspapiere Unternehmen und Region, No. R2/2011, Fraunhofer-Institut für System- und Innovationsforschung ISI, Karlsruhe.*

Hollanders, M., & Natarajan, H. (2020). Payment aspects of financial inclusion in the FinTech era. In *Committee on payments and market infrastructures World Bank Group* (pp. 1–80). World Bank Group.

Huang, R. H. (2018). Online P2P lending and regulatory responses in China : Opportunities and challenges. *European Business Organization Law Review, 19*(1), 63–92. https://doi.org/10.1007/s40804-018-0100-z

InfoDev. (2013). *Crowdfunding's potential for the developing world: Finance and private sector development department*. World Bank.

Kaili, E., & Psarrakis, D. (2021). *Disintermediation economics: The impact of blockchain on markets and policies* (pp. 1–336). Palgrave Macmillan.

Lee, E. (2019). Equity crowdfunding in Hong Kong: Potential, challenges and investor protection. *Journal of Corporate Law Studies, 19*(2), 277–302. https://doi.org/10.1080/14735970.2017.1369235

Leone, D., Cristina, M., Gabteni, H., & Rosaria, M. (2023). Reward-based crowdfunding for building a valuable circular business model. *Journal of Business Research, 157*(December 2022), 113562. https://doi.org/10.1016/j.jbusres.2022.113562

Lopez Nino, J., Langthaler, J., Fabian, M., & Mayorga, J. (2017). *An overview of FinTechs: Their benefits and risks*. Association of Supervisors of Banks of the Americas.

Lynn, T., Mooney, J. G., Rosati, P., & Cummins, M. (2019). *Disrupting Finance: FinTech and strategy in the 21st century*. Springer.

Melanie, F. (2015). Robo-Advisors: A closer look. *Leibniz Information Centre for Economics*. https://doi.org/10.2139/ssrn.2658701

Meyer, T. (2007). *The power of people: Online P2P lending nibbles at banks' loan business*. Deutsche Banks' Research.

Mohamed, H., & Ali, H. (2022). Chapter 2 FinTech—Definition, history, and global landscape. In *Blockchain, FinTech, and Islamic Finance*. https://doi.org/10.1515/9781547400966-002

Mu, C., & Frost, J. (2022). *FinTech and market structure in the COVID-19 pandemic*. Financial Stability Board.

Payments, C., & Infrastructures, M. (2014). *Committee on payments and market infrastructures non-banks in retail payments*.

Perini, F., Schwarten, G., & Comolli, L. (2013, May). *The power of sharing: Exploring the digital sharing economy at the base of the Pyramid*. NEST.

Phoon, K. F., Chiew, C., & Koh, F. (2018). Robo-advisors and wealth management. *Institutional Knowledge at Singapore Management University, 20*(3), 79–94. https://doi.org/10.3905/jati.201

Pierrakis, Y., & Catalunya, U. I. D. (2018). Crowdfunding: A new innovative model of providing funding to projects and Business. In *SSRN Electronic Journal* (Issue November). https://doi.org/10.2139/ssrn.2395226

Pinem, N. A., Sulistyawati, F., Nifati, E., Gulo, P., & Buana, U. M. (2023). Analysis of business implementation on shippepay digital wallet. *Jurnal Impresi Indonesia, 2*(1), 71–82. https://doi.org/10.58344/jii.v2i1.2042

Reyes-Mercado, P. (2021). *FinTech strategy: Linking entrepreneurship, finance, and technology*. Palgrave Macmillan.

Sabie, A., Moisa, B., & van Stiphout, M. (2018). Payment methods report 2018 innovations in the way We Pay. In *The Paypers*.

Schriftenreihe, I. V. W. H. S. G., & Braun, A. (2017). The current InsurTech Landscape: Business models and disruptive potential. In Institute of Insurance Economics I.VW-HSG, University of St. Gallen (Issue 62, pp. 1–195).

Sharma, S., & Lertnuwat, N. (2016). The financial crowdfunding with diverse business models. *Journal of Asian and African Social Science and Humanities, 2*(2), 74–89.

Sikri, A., Dalal, S., Singh, N. P., & Le, D. (2019). Mapping of e-wallets with features. In *Cyber Security in parallel and distributed computing* (pp. 245–262). Wiley.

Stoeckli, E., Dremel, C., & Uebernickel, F. (2018). Exploring characteristics and transformational capabilities of InsurTech innovations to understand insurance value creation in a digital world. *Electronic Markets, 28*, 287–305.

Suryono, R. R., Purwandari, B., & Budi, I. (2019). Peer to Peer (P2P) lending problems and potential solutions: A systematic literature review systematic literature review. *Procedia Computer Science, 161*, 204–214. https://doi.org/10.1016/j.procs.2019.11.116

Tut, D. (2023). FinTech and the COVID-19 pandemic: Evidence from electronic payment systems. *Emerging Markets Review, 54*(December 2022), 100999. https://doi.org/10.1016/j.ememar.2023.100999

van Stiphout, M., & Mual, M. (2017). Payment methods report 2017 insights into the e-wallets landscape. In *The Paypers.*

Veretennikova, L. (2023). *E-wallet development: A vital step for any business of the future*. Star Global.

Wang, H., Chen, K., Zhu, W., & Song, Z. (2015). A process model on P2P lending. *Financial Innovation, 1*(3), 1–8. https://doi.org/10.1186/s40854-015-0002-9

World Bank, C., & Economic Forum, W. (2020). *The global Covid-19 FinTech market rapid assessment study*. University of Cambridge, World Bank Group and the World Economic Forum.

Zhang, B., & Thorp, S. (2016). *Harnessing potential.* Cambridge Centre for Alternative Finance (Issue March, pp. 1–96).

Zhao, H., Ge, Q., YongLiu, W., & G., Chen, E., & Zhang, H. (2017). P2P lending survey: Platforms, recent advances and prospects. *ACM Transactions on Intelligent Systems and Technology, 8*(6), 1–28.

Ziegler, T., Shneor, R., Wenzlaff, K., & Suresh, K. (2021). *The second global alternative finance market benchmarking*. Cambridge Centre for Alternative Finance.

Ziegler, T., & Shnoer, R. (2020). *The global alternative finance market benchmarking report*. Cambridge Centre for Alternative Finance.

CHAPTER 4

Cryptocurrency

Introduction

This chapter presents insights, facts, and data to familiarize the reader with the concept of cryptocurrency. For this purpose, first a brief overview of the history underlying the concepts of blockchain and cryptocurrency is provided; this will be followed by an introduction on technical advancements supporting its developments in the market. Focusing on cryptocurrency as a payment method, this chapter elaborates on the cryptocurrency wallets and the exchange methods. A brief introduction to the process of cryptocurrency mining is provided, followed by issues related to data privacy. To distinguish various types of digital assets, this chapter also presents basic information on the stablecoins and their functions. Finally, this chapter provides a concise overview of current most prominent cryptocurrencies based on their market capitalization and reliability.

Genesis of Cryptography and Cryptocurrency

Cryptography has been around for centuries and has been used in various ways to protect confidential information from unauthorized access. It is the practice of converting information into a code that only authorized individuals can decode. Over the years, cryptography has evolved from the use of simple codes to complex algorithms that are almost impossible

B. Naysary and A. Tarazi, *The Digital Finance Era*,
https://doi.org/10.1007/978-981-97-3970-7_4

to crack. The invention of the internet has revolutionized communication and information sharing, but it has also brought about new challenges in securing confidential information. In recent years, the concept of cryptocurrency has emerged, which utilizes cryptography to secure financial transactions and provides a decentralized system of financial exchange. In this section, we explore the genesis of cryptography and cryptocurrency, and how they have evolved over time.

The earliest evidence of cryptography dates back to ancient times. The Egyptians used hieroglyphics to encode secret messages, and Julius Caesar used a simple substitution cipher to protect military communications. However, the true origins of modern cryptography can be traced back to the Middle Ages. In the Middle Ages, cryptography was used primarily for military and diplomatic purposes. During this time, secret messages were often encoded using simple substitution ciphers, which involved replacing each letter in the message with another letter or symbol. These ciphers were relatively easy to break, and as a result, more complex ciphers were developed. In the sixteenth century, the Italian polymath, Girolamo Cardano, published a book called *Ars Magna*, which contained the first published description of a polyalphabetic cipher. This cipher used multiple alphabets to encrypt messages, making it much more difficult to break than previous ciphers. During the Renaissance period, cryptography continued to evolve, and new ciphers were developed to protect confidential information. The most famous of these ciphers was the *Vigenère cipher*, which was invented by the French cryptographer, Blaise de Vigenère. This cipher used a keyword to encrypt messages, and it was considered unbreakable until the nineteenth century. The twentieth century saw a rapid expansion in the field of cryptography. With the advent of computers, new algorithms were developed to provide more secure methods of encryption. In 1976, two American cryptographers, Whitfield Diffie and Martin Hellman, published a paper on public-key cryptography, which revolutionized the field of cryptography. Public-key cryptography utilizes two keys, a public key and a private key, to encrypt and decrypt messages. The public key is available to everyone, while the private key is kept secret. This method of encryption made it possible for individuals to communicate securely over the internet, and it paved the way for the development of modern encryption algorithms.

Cryptocurrency, as we know it today, has its roots in the early 2000s. In 2008, an unknown person or group of people using the pseudonym Satoshi Nakamoto published a white paper titled "Bitcoin: A Peer-to-Peer

Electronic Cash System." This white paper proposed a new type of digital currency that utilized cryptography to secure transactions and eliminate the need for intermediaries like banks. Bitcoin was the first decentralized cryptocurrency, and it quickly gained popularity among enthusiasts who saw it as a revolutionary new form of currency. Bitcoin transactions were verified by a network of computers, known as nodes, that used complex algorithms to ensure the integrity of the system. In 2011, a new cryptocurrency called Litecoin was introduced, which was based on the Bitcoin protocol but with some modifications. Litecoin was designed to be faster and more efficient than Bitcoin, with shorter transaction times and a larger supply of coins. Since then, hundreds of new cryptocurrencies have been developed, each with its own unique features and advantages. Some cryptocurrencies, like Ethereum, are designed to be more versatile than Bitcoin and can be used to develop decentralized applications.

Cryptography plays a critical role in the security and integrity of cryptocurrencies. The decentralized nature of cryptocurrency means that there is no central authority responsible for verifying transactions or keeping track of the ledger. Instead, the ledger is maintained by a network of nodes that uses complex algorithms to verify and record transactions. Each transaction in a cryptocurrency network is verified using cryptography. When a user initiates a transaction, they create a digital signature using their private key. This signature is then broadcast to the network, and the nodes use the sender's public key to verify the transaction and ensure that it is legitimate. Once the transaction is verified, it is added to the blockchain, which is a public ledger that contains a record of all transactions on the network. The blockchain is secured using cryptography, which ensures that the ledger cannot be tampered with or altered. The nodes on the network use complex algorithms to verify each transaction and add it to the blockchain in a secure and transparent manner.

Blockchain

Blockchain technology is a revolutionary concept that has transformed the way we think about security, transparency, and financial transactions. It was first introduced in 2008 as the underlying technology behind the cryptocurrency Bitcoin, but it has since been adopted by a wide range of industries for its many benefits. This section explores the basics of blockchain technology, its advantages and disadvantages, and its potential applications in various industries. At its core, blockchain technology is a decentralized ledger that records transactions in a secure and transparent manner. It consists of a network of nodes that work together to verify and record transactions, with each node having a copy of the entire ledger. This decentralized nature of the blockchain makes it more secure, as there is no central authority controlling the ledger. In a blockchain network, each transaction is verified using complex algorithms and cryptographic protocols, ensuring that only legitimate transactions are recorded. Once a transaction is verified, it is added to the blockchain as a new block, and it becomes part of a permanent and unalterable record. The blockchain is maintained by the network of nodes, and each node is responsible for verifying transactions and adding them to the ledger.

Distributed Ledger

A distributed ledger is a database that is spread across a network of computers or nodes. Each node on the network contains a copy of the ledger, and any changes made to the ledger are updated on all nodes in real time. The ledger is maintained through a consensus mechanism, which allows nodes on the network to reach agreement on the validity of transactions and update the ledger accordingly. Distributed ledgers provide a number of benefits over traditional, centralized databases. One of the main advantages is that they are more secure and resistant to tampering. Since the ledger is spread across multiple nodes, it is much harder for any one party to make unauthorized changes to the data. Additionally, distributed ledgers are more transparent, as all participants on the network have access to the same information and can verify the accuracy of the ledger in real time. Distributed ledgers are most commonly associated with blockchain technology, but they can also be implemented using other technologies, such as distributed databases or peer-to-peer networks. The key to a distributed ledger is that it is decentralized, meaning that there is no single point of control or authority.

Nodes

A node in a blockchain network is a computer or device that runs software that allows it to participate in the network. Nodes play a crucial role in the operation of blockchain systems by verifying transactions, storing the blockchain ledger, and communicating with other nodes to keep the network synchronized and secure. In a blockchain network, every node has a copy of the blockchain ledger. Each block in the blockchain contains a set of transactions, a timestamp, and a unique cryptographic hash that links it to the previous block in the chain. This creates a chronological and tamper-evident record of all the transactions on the network. Nodes are responsible for validating new transactions and adding them to the blockchain. When a user initiates a transaction, it is broadcast to the network and propagated to all the nodes. Each node checks the transaction to make sure it is valid, by checking the sender's balance, verifying the digital signature, and confirming that the transaction follows the rules of the protocol. If the transaction is valid, the node adds it to its copy of the blockchain ledger. Once a block of transactions has been added to the blockchain, it is propagated to all the nodes in the network. Each node checks the block's hash to confirm that it is valid and then adds it to its copy of the blockchain. This creates a consensus among the nodes about the state of the blockchain and ensures that all the nodes have an identical copy of the ledger. Nodes communicate with each other using a peer-to-peer network protocol. This means that each node can send and receive data directly with any other node on the network, without the need for a central server or intermediary. Nodes use a protocol called gossip to share information about transactions and blocks with each other. When a node receives a new block, it sends it to its neighbors, who in turn send it to their neighbors, and so on, until all the nodes in the network have received it. Nodes can be categorized into different types depending on their role in the network. For example, full nodes store a complete copy of the blockchain and participate in the validation of transactions and the creation of new blocks. Light nodes, on the other hand, only store a subset of the blockchain and rely on other nodes to provide them with information about transactions and blocks. In addition to validating transactions and adding them to the blockchain, nodes also play a crucial role in the security of the network.

Transactions

A transaction in a blockchain network is a record of a transfer of value from one party to another. Transactions are the building blocks of the blockchain, and they create a tamper-evident and immutable record of all the activity on the network. Transactions can involve the transfer of cryptocurrencies, digital assets, or any other form of digital representation of value. When a user initiates a transaction, they create a digital message that includes the recipient's address, the amount of value being transferred, and any additional data or instructions related to the transaction. This message is signed with the sender's private key, which ensures that only the sender can initiate the transaction and prevent any tampering or alteration of the message. Once the transaction is created, it is broadcast to the network and propagated to all the nodes. Each node checks the transaction to ensure that it is valid. If the transaction is valid, it is added to the next block in the blockchain. Each block contains a set of transactions, and once a block is added to the blockchain, it is propagated to all the nodes in the network. This creates a consensus among the nodes about the state of the blockchain and ensures that all the nodes have an identical copy of the ledger. Once a transaction is added to the blockchain, it becomes a permanent and immutable part of the network's history. Transactions can be traced back to their origin and verified by anyone on the network, creating a transparent and auditable record of all the activity on the blockchain. Transactions in blockchain networks are often processed using a fee-based system, where users pay a small amount of cryptocurrency to the network as a transaction fee. These fees incentivize miners and nodes to validate and process transactions by compensating them for the resources and energy required to maintain the network.

Consensus Mechanism

Consensus mechanism is a critical component of blockchain technology that enables nodes in the network to agree on the state of the blockchain without the need for a central authority. In a blockchain network, consensus refers to the process of reaching an agreement among nodes about the validity of new transactions and blocks. The consensus mechanism ensures that all nodes on the network maintain a consistent and synchronized copy of the blockchain. There are several consensus mechanisms used in blockchain networks, each with its own strengths and weaknesses. Some of the most common consensus mechanisms include Proof-of-Work (PoW), Proof-of-Stake (PoS), Delegated Proof-of-Stake (DPoS), and Byzantine Fault Tolerance (BFT). Proof-of-Work is the most widely used consensus mechanism in blockchain networks, and it is used by popular cryptocurrencies like Bitcoin and Ethereum. In PoW, nodes called miners compete to solve a complex mathematical problem to validate transactions and add new blocks to the blockchain. The first miner to solve the problem is rewarded with newly minted cryptocurrency, and the block is added to the blockchain. Proof-of-Stake is an alternative consensus mechanism that is gaining popularity in blockchain networks. In PoS, nodes are chosen to validate transactions and add new blocks based on the amount of cryptocurrency they hold, rather than their computational power. Nodes that hold a larger amount of cryptocurrency have a higher chance of being selected to validate transactions and earn rewards. Delegated Proof-of-Stake is a variant of PoS where a small group of nodes are chosen to validate transactions and create new blocks on behalf of the network. This reduces the computational and energy requirements of the consensus mechanism, as the nodes are selected based on their reputation and trustworthiness. Byzantine Fault Tolerance is a consensus mechanism used in distributed systems that allows the network to continue operating even if some nodes are malicious or fail. In BFT, nodes communicate with each other to verify transactions and create new blocks, and the network requires a certain number of nodes to agree on each transaction before it is added to the blockchain.

Cryptography

Cryptography is a fundamental aspect of blockchain technology that is used to secure and protect the data stored in the blockchain. Cryptography involves the use of mathematical algorithms to encrypt data and ensure its confidentiality, integrity, and authenticity. In a blockchain network, cryptography is used in several ways. One of the most important uses of cryptography is to protect the privacy and security of user data. When a user initiates a transaction on the blockchain, their data is encrypted using public-key cryptography. This involves the use of two keys, a public key and a private key. The public key is used to encrypt the data, while the private key is used to decrypt it. Only the owner of the private key can decrypt the data, ensuring that the transaction is secure and private. Another important use of cryptography in blockchain technology is to ensure the integrity and authenticity of data. Any attempt to alter the data in the blockchain would change the hash of the block, making it invalid and easily detectable. Cryptography is also used in the consensus mechanism of the blockchain network. In Proof-of-Work, miners compete to solve a complex mathematical problem, which involves the use of cryptographic algorithms.

Blocks

A block in a blockchain network is essentially a digital ledger that records a set of transactions. Each block contains a header and a body. The header contains information about the block, such as the hash of the previous block in the chain, the timestamp of the block, and the nonce (a randomly generated number, and it is used to verify transactions or perform security checks). The body of the block contains a set of transactions that have been validated and added to the block. The process of creating a block in a blockchain network involves several steps. First, transactions are broadcast to the network and collected by the nodes in the network. The nodes verify the transactions to ensure that they are valid and comply with the rules of the network. Once the transactions are validated, they are added to a block along with the header information. The header of the block includes the hash of the previous block in the chain. This creates a chain of blocks, where each block is linked to the previous block through its hash value. This chain of blocks creates a tamper-proof and immutable record of all the transactions that have occurred on the blockchain. The header also includes a timestamp, which records the time when the block was created, and a nonce. The nonce is a random number that is added to the header, and miners must find a specific value for the nonce that makes the hash of the block meet a certain difficulty level. This is known as the Proof-of-Work mechanism, and it ensures that the creation of new blocks on the blockchain requires significant computational power and energy. Once a miner finds a value for the nonce that satisfies the difficulty level, they broadcast the new block to the network. The other nodes in the network verify the block and add it to their local copy of the blockchain. Once the block is added to the blockchain, the transactions it contains are considered confirmed and cannot be altered or deleted.

Hashing

A hash function is a mathematical algorithm that takes input data of any size and produces a fixed-size output, known as a hash. The hash value is unique to the input data, and any change in the input data results in a different hash value. In a blockchain network, hashing is used to create a unique digital fingerprint for each block in the blockchain. The header in each block includes a hash of the previous block in the chain. This creates a chain of blocks, where each block is linked to the previous block through its hash value. The process of hashing in a blockchain network involves several steps. First, the data to be hashed, which could be a transaction or a block, is passed through a hash function. The hash function produces a unique hash value that represents the data. This hash value is added to the block header, along with other information, such as the hash of the previous block, a timestamp, and a nonce. Once the block header is complete, the entire block is hashed again. This creates a new hash value that represents the entire block, including the hash value of the previous block. This hash value is then added to the blockchain, and the process repeats for each subsequent block. If any part of the data in a block is altered, the hash value of the block changes, making it easy to detect any attempt to tamper with the data.

Smart Contracts

Smart contracts are self-executing contracts that are stored on a blockchain network. They allow for the automation of contractual agreements between parties, without the need for intermediaries such as lawyers or banks. Smart contracts are a key feature of blockchain technology and have the potential to revolutionize the way we conduct business and manage transactions. Smart contracts are computer programs that are stored on a blockchain network and can be programmed to execute specific actions automatically when certain conditions are met. These conditions are predefined in the code of the smart contract, and when they are met, the contract is automatically executed. Smart contracts are designed to operate in a trustless environment, where parties do not need to trust each other or a central authority to execute the contract. Smart contracts work by using a combination of cryptographic protocols and blockchain technology to ensure that the contract is executed as programmed. When a smart contract is created, it is stored on the blockchain network, and each node on the network has a copy of the contract. When a party wishes to enter into a contract, they send a transaction to the smart contract, which is then stored on the blockchain. The contract is then executed automatically when the predefined conditions are met. Traditional contracts often require intermediaries to enforce the terms of the contract and ensure that parties are meeting their obligations. Smart contracts, on the other hand, are self-executing, and the terms of the contract are enforced automatically. Smart contracts can be used in a wide range of industries, including finance, real estate, and supply chain management. For example, in finance, smart contracts can be used to automate the settlement of trades, reducing the time and costs associated with traditional settlement processes. In real estate, smart contracts can be used to automate the transfer of property ownership, making the process more efficient and secure. In supply chain management, smart contracts can be used to automate the tracking of goods and ensure that they are delivered to the correct location at the right time. Smart contracts are also transparent, and the terms of the contract are visible to all parties on the blockchain network. This transparency helps to ensure that parties are held accountable for their actions and that the terms of the contract are enforced fairly. However, there are some limitations to smart contracts. Smart contracts are only as good as the code they are written in, and errors in the code can result in significant problems. Additionally, smart contracts cannot handle complex legal agreements that require human interpretation or judgment. Smart contracts are also limited by the capabilities of the blockchain network, and as such, they may not be suitable for all types of contracts.

In order to understand how blockchain works, it is helpful to look at an example. Let's say that person A wants to transfer some money to person B using a distributed ledger. Person A initiates the transaction by creating a new record on the ledger, which includes the amount of money he/she wants to transfer and person B's public key (an identifier that uniquely identifies person B on the ledger). This transaction is broadcast to all nodes on the network. Once the transaction is received by the nodes on the network, a consensus mechanism is used to validate the transaction. Depending on the specific consensus mechanism being used, this may involve a vote by nodes on the network, or it may involve a complex mathematical puzzle that must be solved by a node in order to validate the transaction. Once the transaction has been validated, it is added to the ledger as a new block. The block is given a unique identifier (the block hash) and is linked to the previous block in the chain.

Pros and Cons of Blockchain

Blockchain technology has gained significant attention in recent years due to its potential to transform various industries, from finance and banking, to supply chain management and voting systems. While blockchain offers several advantages, it also has limitations and challenges that must be carefully considered.

One of the most significant advantages of blockchain technology is its security features. Blockchain uses cryptographic algorithms to secure data, making it almost impossible for hackers to tamper with or alter the data. The data in each block is secured using complex cryptographic algorithms, and each block is linked to the previous block in the chain, creating an unbreakable chain of blocks. This makes it highly resistant to tampering and hacking attempts. Blockchain technology allows for a transparent and publicly auditable ledger of all transactions. The decentralized nature of blockchain allows anyone to view the transactions on the network, providing greater transparency and accountability in various industries and applications. This transparency can enhance trust and accountability among stakeholders, and can also reduce fraud and corruption. Another significant advantage of blockchain technology is its decentralization. Blockchain eliminates the need for intermediaries, such as banks, governments, and other third-party intermediaries, in various applications. This reduces costs, eliminates the need for trust in intermediaries, and provides greater autonomy to individuals. Decentralization can also enhance privacy and security, as users have greater control over their data and assets. Blockchain technology can significantly reduce the time and costs associated with processing and settling transactions, compared to traditional systems that rely on intermediaries. Blockchain transactions can be processed and settled within minutes, compared to several days for traditional systems. This can result in significant cost savings, faster transaction times, and improved efficiency for businesses and individuals. The decentralized nature of blockchain makes it highly resistant to attacks and system failures, making it more resilient and reliable than centralized systems. The data in the blockchain is stored on multiple nodes, making it virtually impossible to destroy or corrupt the data. Blockchain provides new opportunities for innovation and creativity, and can drive the development of new applications and business models.

One of the biggest challenges facing blockchain technology is scalability (the ability to continue to function properly when changed in size or volume). The current limitations of blockchain technology in terms of processing speed and capacity may make it difficult to scale up to support large-scale applications, such as those in the financial sector. This can lead to slow transaction times and high transaction fees, which can limit the adoption of blockchain in certain industries. The computational power required for blockchain transactions can be energy intensive, resulting in significant carbon emissions and environmental impacts. The energy consumption associated with blockchain transactions can be a significant barrier to adoption, particularly in industries that are focused on sustainability and reducing carbon emissions. The lack of a clear regulatory framework for blockchain technology creates uncertainty for businesses and investors, and may impede the adoption of blockchain in certain industries. The lack of regulation can also lead to legal and ethical concerns, particularly with regard to privacy and security. The complexity of blockchain technology, including its cryptographic algorithms and decentralized network architecture, can be a barrier to entry for many users and developers. The learning curve associated with blockchain technology can be steep, and many users may struggle to understand how to use and interact with blockchain applications. While blockchain technology is generally considered to be highly secure, there are still risks associated with the storage and management of private keys, which are essential for accessing and managing blockchain assets. If private keys are lost or stolen, it can result in the loss of assets or data, and there is no way to recover them. Blockchain technology is dependent on internet connectivity, which can be a challenge in areas with poor internet infrastructure or in situations where the internet is not accessible, such as during natural disasters. The lack of interoperability between different blockchain networks and applications can limit the potential for blockchain to be used in various industries and applications.

Applications of Blockchain

The unique features of blockchain have made it an attractive technology for various applications in different industries. This section provides an overview of some of these industries and how they can utilize blockchain.

Cryptocurrency

Cryptocurrency is the most well-known application of blockchain technology. It is a digital asset that uses cryptography to secure its transactions and to control the creation of new units. Blockchain technology is used to maintain a distributed ledger of all cryptocurrency transactions. Bitcoin, the first cryptocurrency, was created in 2009, and since then, several other cryptocurrencies have emerged, such as Ethereum, Ripple, Litecoin, and more. Blockchain technology has transformed the way people transact and exchange value, offering a decentralized and secure way to transfer funds without the need for intermediaries like banks or financial institutions.

Cryptocurrencies have also enabled cross-border transactions, making it easier and cheaper to send money across different countries.

Supply Chain Management
Supply chain management involves the management of the flow of goods and services from the point of origin to the point of consumption. Blockchain technology can be used to improve supply chain management by providing transparency and traceability of the products as they move through the supply chain. By using blockchain technology, companies can track the movement of goods and services from the supplier to the manufacturer, to the distributor, and finally to the end consumer. This can help reduce the time and cost of the supply chain process, prevent fraud and counterfeit products, and improve the overall quality of products.

Digital Identity Management
Digital identity management involves the management of digital identities, including personal data and credentials. Blockchain technology can be used to create a decentralized and secure system for managing digital identities. By using blockchain technology, users can create a digital identity that is secured by cryptography, and this identity can be used for various purposes, such as voting, online transactions, and more. Decentralized identity management can also help protect users' privacy by giving them more control over their personal data.

Voting Systems
Blockchain technology can be used to create a secure and transparent voting system. By using blockchain technology, voters can cast their vote anonymously, and the results can be verified by anyone on the blockchain network. This can help prevent fraud and ensure that the voting process is fair and transparent. Blockchain-based voting systems can also increase voter participation, reduce the cost of elections, and make the process more efficient.

Healthcare
Blockchain technology can be used to improve the healthcare industry by providing a secure and transparent system for managing medical records. By using blockchain technology, medical records can be stored securely and accessed only by authorized parties. This can help prevent medical identity theft and improve the overall quality of healthcare. Blockchain

technology can also be used to track the supply of medicines and prevent counterfeit drugs from entering the market.

Real Estate
Real estate is another industry that can benefit from blockchain technology. By using blockchain technology, real estate transactions can be made more secure and transparent. Blockchain-based systems can be used to store and manage property records, reducing the risk of fraud and errors. By using blockchain technology, real estate transactions can also be completed more quickly and efficiently, reducing the time and cost of the process. Blockchain-based systems can also provide a more transparent and efficient way of managing property rental agreements.

Intellectual Property
Blockchain technology can be used to protect intellectual property rights by providing a secure and transparent way of managing copyrights, trademarks, and patents. By using blockchain technology, intellectual property rights can be registered and verified, making it easier to protect and monetize intellectual property. Blockchain technology can also be used to track the use of intellectual property and ensure that royalties and licensing fees are paid to the rightful owners.

Gaming
Blockchain technology can be used to create decentralized gaming platforms that provide a more transparent and fair gaming experience. By using blockchain technology, players can verify the fairness of the game and ensure that the game is not rigged. Blockchain-based gaming platforms can also provide a more secure way of storing and transferring in-game assets, such as virtual currency, weapons, and items.

Education
Blockchain technology can be used to create a decentralized and secure system for managing educational records. By using blockchain technology, educational records can be stored securely and accessed only by authorized parties. This can help prevent fraud and ensure that educational records are accurate and up to date. Blockchain-based systems can also provide a more efficient way of verifying educational credentials, such as degrees and certifications.

Cryptocurrency Wallets

Cryptocurrencies operate independently of a central bank and are decentralized, which means they are not governed by any central authority. Cryptocurrency wallets are essential tools for storing, managing, and transacting digital currencies. A cryptocurrency wallet is a digital wallet that stores a user's private and public keys. Private keys are secret codes that allow access to a user's cryptocurrency holdings, while public keys are the user's address on the blockchain, allowing them to send and receive cryptocurrencies. Cryptocurrency wallets enable users to manage their digital currency holdings, send and receive cryptocurrencies, and track their transactions. When a user sends cryptocurrency to another user, they are sending a message that includes a digital signature of the transaction. The digital signature is created using the sender's private key, which is then verified using the sender's public key. The transaction is broadcasted to the cryptocurrency network and confirmed by the network's nodes and then added to the blockchain ledger. When receiving cryptocurrency, the wallet generates a unique public key that is shared with the sender to receive the cryptocurrency. The wallet also stores a record of all the user's transactions, allowing them to track their digital currency holdings.

In the world of cryptocurrency, public and private keys are essential concepts that every user must understand. These keys play a crucial role in ensuring the security and privacy of a user's digital currency holdings.

Public Key

A public key is a cryptographic code that is shared with others in the cryptocurrency network to receive digital currency payments. It is essentially an address that is publicly visible on the blockchain, allowing other users to send cryptocurrency to that address. A public key is also referred to as a "wallet address" or a "public address." A public key is a long string of alphanumeric characters that is generated by a user's cryptocurrency wallet. It is derived from the user's private key using complex mathematical algorithms. A public key is used to encrypt the message that is sent to a user's wallet, ensuring that only the owner of the private key can access the message.

Private Key

A private key is a secret code that is used to access a user's digital currency holdings. It is essentially the key to the user's wallet, allowing them to send and receive digital currency payments. A private key is also referred to as a "secret key" or a "seed phrase." A private key is a long string of alphanumeric characters that is generated by a user's cryptocurrency wallet. It is derived from a random number using complex mathematical algorithms. A private key is kept secret by the user and should never be shared with anyone else. If a user's private key is lost or stolen, they will lose access to their digital currency holdings permanently.

Types of Cryptocurrency Wallets

There are various types of cryptocurrency wallets available, each with its unique features and security levels:

Hardware Wallets
Hardware wallets are physical devices that store a user's private keys offline. They are considered one of the most secure options for storing cryptocurrencies as they are not connected to the internet and cannot be hacked remotely. Hardware wallets are often shaped like USB drives and require a user to enter a PIN to access their private keys. Some popular hardware wallets include Ledger Nano S, Trezor, and KeepKey. Unlike software wallets that are stored on a computer or mobile device, hardware wallets are designed to be offline and provide a high level of security against hacking and theft. They are small devices that can fit in the palm of your hand and is typically connected to a computer or mobile device using a USB or Bluetooth connection. Hardware wallets are designed to be offline, meaning that they are not connected to the internet or other networks. Hardware wallets come with a small display screen and buttons that allow users to confirm transactions and manage their digital currency holdings. They are designed to be user-friendly and easy to use, even for beginners. A hardware wallet works by storing a user's private keys offline, making it more difficult for hackers to access them. When a user wants to send or receive digital currency, they connect the hardware wallet to a computer or mobile device and enter their PIN code or password to unlock the device. Once the hardware wallet is unlocked,

the user can access their digital currency holdings and confirm transactions using the device's display screen and buttons. The hardware wallet generates a unique digital signature for each transaction, which is verified by the network's nodes to ensure that the transaction is legitimate. After the transaction is confirmed, the hardware wallet disconnects from the computer or mobile device, ensuring that the private keys remain secure and offline.

Hardware wallets are important in cryptocurrency because they provide a high level of security against hacking and theft. Since private keys are stored offline, it is more difficult for hackers to access them compared to software wallets that are stored on a computer or mobile device. Hardware wallets are also important for protecting against physical theft. If a user's computer or mobile device is stolen, their software wallet could be compromised, allowing a thief to access their digital currency holdings. However, a hardware wallet would be useless to a thief without the PIN code or password to unlock the device. Finally, hardware wallets are important for providing peace of mind to cryptocurrency holders.

Software Wallets

Software wallets are digital wallets that can be accessed through a desktop or mobile application. They are connected to the internet and offer a more convenient way to manage cryptocurrency holdings. Software wallets can be further divided into two categories:

- Desktop Wallets, which are installed on a user's computer, and the private keys are stored locally. They offer a high level of security as the private keys are stored offline, but they are susceptible to malware attacks. Some popular desktop wallets include Electrum, Exodus, and Atomic Wallet.
- Mobile Wallets, which are applications that can be downloaded on a user's smartphone. They offer a convenient way to manage cryptocurrency holdings, and some even offer contactless payment options. However, mobile wallets are susceptible to malware attacks, and users must ensure their devices are secure. Some popular mobile wallets include Mycelium, Breadwallet, and Coinbase Wallet.

Unlike hardware wallets, software wallets are connected to the internet and rely on software security measures to protect user's cryptocurrency holdings. It works by storing a user's private keys and using them to sign transactions when sending or receiving cryptocurrency. To use a software wallet, a user must first download and install the application on their computer or smartphone. They must then create a new wallet or import an existing wallet by entering their private keys. Once the wallet is set up, a user can send and receive cryptocurrency using the application's interface. Software wallets are important in cryptocurrency because they provide easy access to digital currency holdings and allow users to send and receive cryptocurrency on-the-go. They are also easy to use and require minimal technical expertise. Software wallets are important for the growth and adoption of cryptocurrency, as they make it easier for users to store, send, and receive digital currency. By eliminating the need for physical storage and traditional banking systems, software wallets provide a more efficient and secure way to manage digital currency holdings. However, software wallets also have some drawbacks that users need to be aware of. Because they are connected to the internet, software wallets are more vulnerable to hacking, phishing attacks, and other security breaches. Users need to take extra care to ensure that their private keys are stored securely and that their wallets are protected with strong passwords and two-factor authentication.

Paper Wallets

A paper wallet is a form of cold storage for cryptocurrencies, where a user's private keys are written down on a piece of paper and stored offline. Paper wallets are a simple and inexpensive way to store cryptocurrencies and provide a high level of security. A paper wallet is a physical document that contains a user's public and private keys. Public keys are used to receive cryptocurrency, while private keys are used to access and authorize transactions. The paper wallet is generated using an open-source software program that creates a unique public address and private key pair. Once the wallet is generated, the user can print the paper wallet and store it in a safe place. Paper wallets are considered a form of cold storage because they are not connected to the internet and are therefore less susceptible to hacking and other forms of cybercrime. The public address is also printed on the paper wallet, which can be used to receive cryptocurrency. When sending cryptocurrency from a paper wallet, the user must import the private keys into a software wallet or a hardware wallet. This process involves scanning the QR code on the paper wallet, which contains the private keys. Once the private keys are imported, the user can sign transactions and send cryptocurrency. Paper wallets are important in cryptocurrency because they provide a high level of security and are relatively easy to use. Unlike software wallets, which are connected to the internet and therefore more susceptible to hacking and other forms of cybercrime, paper wallets are offline and are not vulnerable to these types of attacks. Paper wallets also provide a low-cost and accessible way for users to store their cryptocurrency holdings. Users can create a paper wallet for free using an open-source software program and can print the paper wallet using any printer. This makes paper wallets a good option for users who do not want to invest in expensive hardware wallets or pay fees for software wallets. However, paper wallets also have some drawbacks that users need to be aware of. One of the major drawbacks of paper wallets is that they are vulnerable to physical damage and loss. If a paper wallet is lost or destroyed, the user may lose access to their cryptocurrency holdings permanently. Paper wallets are also less convenient than software wallets or hardware wallets, as they require the user to manually enter the private keys into a software wallet or hardware wallet to send cryptocurrency. This can be time-consuming and may increase the risk of errors.

Choosing a Cryptocurrency Wallet

When choosing a cryptocurrency wallet, users must consider their security needs and the convenience of the wallet. Hardware wallets offer the highest level of security, while software wallets offer convenience. However, users must ensure they are using a reputable wallet provider and keep their devices secure to prevent hacking and theft. Here are some factors to consider when choosing a cryptocurrency wallet:

- The security of a cryptocurrency wallet should be the primary concern when choosing a wallet. Hardware wallets are considered the most secure option, as they store private keys offline and cannot be hacked remotely.
- Users should also consider the convenience of the wallet. Software wallets offer more convenience than hardware wallets, but they are less secure. Mobile wallets are the most convenient as they can be accessed on-the-go, but they are susceptible to malware attacks.
- Users should ensure that their chosen wallet is compatible with the cryptocurrencies they wish to store. Some wallets support only

specific cryptocurrencies, while others support a range of cryptocurrencies.
- The user interface of a cryptocurrency wallet should be user-friendly and easy to navigate. A complicated interface can lead to mistakes and potential loss of funds.
- Users should choose a wallet provider with an excellent reputation in the cryptocurrency community. A reputable provider will offer better security and customer support.

Cryptocurrency Exchange

A cryptocurrency exchange is a platform that allows users to buy and sell cryptocurrencies for other cryptocurrencies or fiat currency (such as US dollars, Euros, or Japanese Yen). Cryptocurrency exchanges provide a marketplace where buyers and sellers can come together to trade cryptocurrencies at agreed-upon prices. Here's how a cryptocurrency exchange works:

- Registration: Users are required to register on the exchange platform and complete a Know Your Customer (KYC) process. This process includes providing identification documents and other personal information to comply with anti-money laundering regulations.
- Funding: Users must deposit funds into their exchange account in order to start trading. They can deposit fiat currency or cryptocurrency, depending on the exchange's policies.
- Placing Orders: Users can place different types of orders on the exchange platform. The most common types of orders are buy-and-sell orders. A buy order is an instruction to buy a cryptocurrency at a specified price, while a sell order is an instruction to sell a cryptocurrency at a specified price.
- Matching Orders: The exchange platform matches buy and sell orders from users. When a buy order is matched with a sell order, a trade occurs. The exchange platform facilitates the trade by transferring the cryptocurrency from the seller's account to the buyer's account.

- Fees: Cryptocurrency exchanges charge fees for each trade that occurs on their platform. The fees vary depending on the exchange and can be a flat fee or a percentage of the transaction amount.
- Withdrawals: Users can withdraw their funds from the exchange once they have completed the trading process. They can withdraw cryptocurrency to their personal wallets or fiat currency to their bank accounts.

Some exchanges also offer additional features, such as margin trading, lending, and staking. Margin trading allows users to trade cryptocurrencies with borrowed funds, while lending allows users to earn interest on their cryptocurrency holdings. Staking involves holding cryptocurrency in a wallet to support the network and receive rewards. While cryptocurrency exchanges play a vital role in the cryptocurrency ecosystem, users should be aware of the risks involved in trading on an exchange, such as hacking, regulatory risks, and market volatility. It is important to research and choose a reputable and secure exchange platform before making any trades.

Cryptocurrency as a Payment Mode

Cryptocurrencies are known for their volatility, which means that their value can fluctuate rapidly. This can make it challenging to use cryptocurrency as a mode of payment, as the value of the cryptocurrency at the time of the transaction may be different from the value at the time the merchant receives the payment.

The legality of cryptocurrency as a form of legal tender varies by country. Legal tender is a term that refers to the official currency that must be accepted as payment for debts and taxes. Some countries have recognized cryptocurrency as legal tender, and most have not. While in most countries, cryptocurrency is not recognized as a legal tender, it is still legal to buy, sell, and hold cryptocurrency. In these countries, cryptocurrency is treated as property or an asset for tax and legal purposes. It is important to note that even in countries where cryptocurrency is not recognized as a legal tender, it can still be used as a mode of payment unless it is recognized as illegal by the country's law. Merchants can choose to accept cryptocurrency as a form of payment, and individuals can use cryptocurrency to buy goods and services online or in person.

Cryptocurrency Mining

Cryptocurrency mining is the process by which new units of cryptocurrency are created and validated. Mining is essential to the operation of many cryptocurrencies. In this process, miners compete to solve complex mathematical problems, which allows them to add new blocks to the blockchain, and in turn, earn rewards in the form of cryptocurrency. Followings are essential components and concepts while considering cryptocurrency mining:

Mining Equipment

Cryptocurrency mining is the process of validating transactions and adding new blocks to the blockchain. This process requires significant computing power, which is provided by specialized equipment known as mining rigs. In the early days of cryptocurrency, miners could use their computer's CPU (central processing unit) to mine cryptocurrency. However, as the difficulty of mining increased, CPUs became less effective. GPUs (graphics processing units) are specialized hardware that is designed to perform complex calculations quickly and efficiently. These devices are significantly faster than CPUs and can be used to mine cryptocurrency. ASICs (application-specific integrated circuits) are specialized mining devices that are designed to perform mining cryptocurrency. These devices are significantly faster and more efficient than GPUs and CPUs and are the most commonly used type of mining equipment for Bitcoin. FPGAs (field-programmable gate arrays) are specialized hardware that can be programmed to perform specific tasks. FPGAs are more flexible than ASICs and can be reprogrammed for other tasks, making them useful for miners who want to switch between different cryptocurrencies. Mining rigs are specialized computer systems that are designed for cryptocurrency mining. These systems are typically made up of multiple GPUs or ASICs, which are connected to a power supply and a motherboard. Mining rigs can be assembled by miners themselves or purchased from manufacturers. Mining rigs generate a significant amount of heat, which can cause the hardware to malfunction or fail. To prevent this, miners use specialized cooling systems, such as fans or liquid cooling, to keep the temperature of the hardware under control. Mining rigs require a significant amount of power to operate, which can be a significant expense for miners. To power their mining rigs, miners use specialized power supplies that are designed to handle the high-power requirements of the hardware.

Mining Software

Once a miner has assembled their mining rig, they need to install mining software that enables the rig to connect to the blockchain network and participate in the mining process. Mining software communicates with other nodes on the network, receives new transaction data, and validates new blocks. Mining software is designed to control and monitor the mining hardware, connect to the mining pool, and interact with the blockchain. Here we explore some of the popular and most widely used mining software. CGMiner is one of the most popular mining software available. It is open-source software and is compatible with ASICs and FPGAs. CGMiner supports multiple mining pools and can control multiple mining devices at once. It also includes features such as fan speed control and temperature monitoring. BFGMiner is another popular mining software that is designed for ASICs and FPGAs. It is also open-source software and includes features such as dynamic clocking, remote interface capabilities, and fan control. BFGMiner is compatible with multiple operating systems, including Windows, macOS, and Linux. EasyMiner is a graphical user interface (GUI) mining software that is designed for beginners. It is compatible with both GPUs and ASICs and supports multiple mining pools. EasyMiner also includes features such as fan speed control and temperature monitoring. Claymore's Dual Miner is a mining software that is designed for both AMD and Nvidia GPUs. It is a closed-source software and includes features such as automatic fan control, temperature monitoring, and dual mining capabilities. Claymore's Dual Miner also supports multiple operating systems, including Windows and Linux. NiceHash Miner is a mining software that is designed for both CPUs and GPUs. It is a closed-source software and includes features such as automatic switching between mining algorithms, automatic optimization, and real-time statistics. NiceHash Miner also includes a built-in marketplace that allows miners to buy and sell hash power. Cudo Miner is a mining software that is designed for both CPUs and GPUs. It includes features such as automated mining and mining profitability switching. Cudo Miner also includes a built-in benchmarking tool that allows miners to optimize their mining settings for maximum profitability. Awesome Miner is a mining software that is designed for both ASICs and GPUs. It is a closed-source software and includes features such as automatic profit switching, remote management, and temperature monitoring. Awesome Miner also supports multiple mining pools and multiple mining algorithms.

Validation

Miners compete to validate new transactions and add them to the blockchain. To do this, they must solve complex mathematical problems that require significant computing power. The first miner to solve the problem and validate the block receives a reward in the form of new cryptocurrency. Cryptocurrency mining validation is the process of verifying transactions on the blockchain and adding them to the distributed ledger.

Mining Difficulty

The difficulty of mining cryptocurrency is adjusted over time to ensure that new blocks are added to the blockchain at a consistent rate. This means that as more miners join the network, the difficulty of the mathematical problems increases, making it more difficult to mine cryptocurrency. Cryptocurrency mining difficulty refers to the level of difficulty involved in solving the cryptographic puzzles required to validate transactions on a particular blockchain. Mining difficulty is a measure of how difficult it is to find a hash that is less than or equal to the target hash. The target hash is a value that is set by the network and is adjusted periodically to maintain a consistent block time. The target hash is calculated by taking the maximum hash value and dividing it by the current difficulty level. The difficulty level is adjusted every block based on the number of miners on the network and the total hash rate. The goal of adjusting the difficulty level is to ensure that the block time remains constant. If the hash rate on the network increases, the difficulty level will increase, making it more difficult to find a valid hash. If the hash rate on the network decreases, the difficulty level will decrease, making it easier to find a valid hash. The formula for calculating mining difficulty varies depending on the blockchain, but it generally involves taking the current difficulty level and adjusting it based on the time it took to mine the previous block. If the previous block was mined faster than the target block time, the difficulty level will increase. If the previous block was mined slower than the target block time, the difficulty level will decrease.

There are several factors that can influence mining difficulty. Some of these factors include:

- Hash rate: The hash rate is the number of hashes per second that a miner can produce. The higher the hash rate, the more difficult it is to find a valid hash.
- Number of miners: The number of miners on the network can also influence mining difficulty. If there are more miners on the network, it will be more difficult to find a valid hash.
- Block time: The block time is the amount of time it takes to mine a block. If the block time is shorter than the target block time, the difficulty level will increase.
- Network participation: The level of participation on the network can also influence mining difficulty. If there are more nodes on the network, it will be more difficult to find a valid hash.
- Mining rewards: The mining rewards can also affect mining difficulty. If the rewards are high, more miners will participate in the network, increasing the difficulty level.

The mining difficulty has several implications for the cryptocurrency ecosystem. First, it can influence the profitability of mining. As the difficulty level increases, it becomes more difficult to find a valid hash, reducing the rewards for miners. This can make mining less profitable, resulting in fewer miners on the network. Second, mining difficulty can also influence the security of the blockchain. If the difficulty level is too low, it becomes easier for attackers to launch a 51% attack on the network. A 51% attack is when an attacker controls more than 50% of the network hash rate, giving them the ability to control the blockchain and double-spend coins. Lastly, mining difficulty can also influence the speed of transaction confirmations. If the difficulty level is too high, it may take longer for transactions to be confirmed on the network, resulting in slower transaction times.

Rewards

Miners receive rewards for validating new blocks and adding them to the blockchain. The rewards are in the form of newly minted cryptocurrency and transaction fees paid by users who are sending transactions on the network. Cryptocurrency mining rewards are the incentives provided to miners for validating transactions and adding them to the blockchain. The amount of the mining reward varies depending on the cryptocurrency being mined and the current block reward. Block rewards are the primary source of mining rewards. When a miner successfully validates a block of transactions, they are rewarded with a certain amount of newly minted coins. The block reward is usually fixed for a given cryptocurrency and is designed to decrease over time as the total supply of the cryptocurrency increases. Transaction fees are another source of mining rewards. When a transaction is submitted to the blockchain, a small fee is attached to it. This fee is paid to the miner, who validates the transaction and adds it to the blockchain. Transaction fees are optional, but they incentivize miners to prioritize transactions with higher fees to maximize their rewards. Mining rewards have several impacts on the cryptocurrency ecosystem. First, they incentivize miners to participate in the network and validate transactions. Without mining rewards, there would be no incentive for miners to dedicate their computing power to validate transactions. Second, mining rewards affect the supply of the cryptocurrency. As the block reward decreases over time, the total supply of the cryptocurrency increases at a slower rate. This can result in a decrease in inflation and an increase in scarcity, potentially driving up the value of the cryptocurrency. Lastly, mining rewards can also have an impact on transaction fees. As the block reward decreases, miners may rely more heavily on transaction fees to compensate for the decrease in their rewards. This can lead to higher transaction fees, making it more expensive to send transactions on the network.

Mining Pool

Mining can also be done through mining pools, where multiple miners join together to combine their computing power and share the rewards. Here, the rewards are distributed among the members of the pool based on their contribution to solving the mathematical problem. Instead of competing against each other, pool miners work together to solve complex mathematical equations, and once a block is found, the reward is distributed among the members of the pool based on their contribution. In the mining pool, the operator manages the pool and collects a fee for their services. The operator handles the distribution of rewards, manages the mining software, and provides support to members of the pool. The fee is usually a percentage of the rewards earned by the pool members. To participate in pool mining, miners need to connect their mining hardware to the pool's mining software. The software then coordinates the mining activities of all the miners in the pool, making sure that everyone is working on the same problem. When a block is found, the pool software distributes the reward among the pool members based on their contribution. There are different methods of distributing the rewards among pool members. The most common method is the proportional method, in which each miner is rewarded based on their share of the pool's computing power. Another method is the pay-per-share method, in which miners are rewarded based on the number of shares they submit to the pool. Each share represents a portion of the solution to the mathematical equation that the pool is trying to solve.

One of the main benefits of pool mining is the increased probability of finding a block and earning a reward. Mining on your own can be challenging because the probability of finding a block is low, and the reward is distributed only to the miner who finds the block. By pooling resources, miners can increase their chances of finding a block and earning a reward, even if it is distributed among several miners. Another benefit of pool mining is the reduced variance in rewards. Mining on your own can be unpredictable, and you may go long periods without finding a block. This can be challenging for small-scale miners who rely on mining as a source of income. Pool mining helps to reduce the variance in rewards, ensuring that miners earn a more stable income. Additionally, pool mining allows for a more equitable distribution of rewards. In solo mining, those with more powerful mining equipment have an advantage over those with less powerful equipment. In pool mining, everyone has an equal chance of earning rewards, regardless of the power of their mining equipment.

While there are many benefits to pool mining, there are also some drawbacks to consider. One potential drawback is the fee charged by the pool operator. The fee is typically a percentage of the rewards earned by the pool members, and it can add up over time. Miners need to weigh the benefits of pool mining against the fees charged by the operator to determine if it is a viable option for them. Another potential drawback of pool mining is the increased complexity of setup and maintenance. Miners need to have a basic understanding of mining software and hardware, as well as networking and security. Additionally, pool mining requires a stable internet connection and reliable mining hardware, which can be costly.

Cryptocurrency and Data Privacy

Cryptocurrencies are often associated with anonymity or privacy due to the fact that they operate on a decentralized blockchain network. While cryptocurrencies do offer some level of privacy, it is important to understand that they are not completely anonymous. The anonymity of cryptocurrency transactions is ensured by the use of public and private keys. Every cryptocurrency user has a public key that is used to receive cryptocurrency and a private key that is used to send cryptocurrency. When a user sends cryptocurrency to another user, they broadcast a transaction to the network that includes the recipient's public key and the amount of cryptocurrency being sent. The transaction is then verified by miners on the network and added to the blockchain. The use of public and private keys means that cryptocurrency transactions are pseudonymous rather than completely anonymous. While a user's identity is not directly tied to their public key, it is still possible to trace transactions through the blockchain and potentially identify a user based on patterns of transactions. However, it is much more difficult to link a specific identity to a public key than it is to link a bank account to a traditional financial transaction. In addition to the use of public and private keys, some cryptocurrencies offer additional features to ensure anonymity. For example, the cryptocurrency Monero uses ring signatures to mix transactions together, making it difficult to trace a transaction to a specific user. This process, called "ringCT," combines multiple inputs and outputs from different users into a single transaction, obscuring the true sender and recipient. Another example is Zcash, which uses a form of encryption called "zk-SNARKs" to shield transaction information from public view. Despite these measures, it is important to note that cryptocurrency transactions are not completely anonymous. While it may be difficult to trace a transaction to a specific user, it is still possible for determined individuals or organizations to analyze the blockchain and uncover information about the parties involved. Additionally, many cryptocurrency exchanges and wallets require users to verify their identity in order to comply with anti-money laundering (AML) and know your customer (KYC) regulations, which can reduce anonymity even further.

Furthermore, anonymity in cryptocurrency is not just a matter of user privacy. It can also be used for malicious purposes, such as money laundering, tax evasion, and the financing of illegal activities. Because of this, many governments and financial institutions are skeptical of the use of cryptocurrency for anonymous transactions and are working to develop regulations that require greater transparency in cryptocurrency transactions. Despite the limitations of anonymity in cryptocurrency, there are still ways to maintain privacy while using cryptocurrency. One such method is the use of a virtual private network (VPN), which can mask a user's internet protocol (IP) address and location, making it more difficult to trace their activity online.

Overview of Top Cryptocurrencies

Currently, there are thousands of cryptocurrencies in existence, but only a handful have gained significant popularity and market capitalization. Here are the top cryptocurrencies by market capitalization:

- Bitcoin (BTC): Created in 2009 by an unknown person or group under the name of Satoshi Nakamoto, Bitcoin is the first and most popular cryptocurrency. It is currently valued at over $1 trillion with a market dominance of over 40%. Bitcoin operates on a decentralized blockchain network and is mined by solving complex mathematical algorithms.
- Ethereum (ETH): Created in 2015 by Vitalik Buterin, Ethereum is the second-largest cryptocurrency by market capitalization and is valued at over $300 billion. Ethereum is a decentralized platform that enables developers to build decentralized applications (DApps) on its blockchain network. It operates on a Proof-of-Stake consensus mechanism and is secured by its native cryptocurrency, Ether.
- Solana (SOL): Solana is a high-speed, low-cost blockchain network that was launched in 2020. It uses a Proof-of-Stake consensus mechanism and can process over 65,000 transactions per second. Solana has a market capitalization of over $50 billion and is used for a variety of purposes, including decentralized finance (DeFi) applications and non-fungible tokens (NFTs).
- Ripple (XRP): Ripple is a blockchain-based payment protocol that aims to provide a more efficient and cost-effective way to transfer value between individuals and institutions. The cryptocurrency used on the Ripple network is called XRP. Ripple is designed to be a faster and cheaper alternative to traditional payment networks like SWIFT, and it also features a unique consensus mechanism called "Ripple Protocol Consensus Algorithm," which is intended to enable greater

scalability and security in the network. Ripple has also partnered with many major financial institutions around the world, which is intended to help drive the adoption of its technology.

- Polkadot (DOT): Polkadot is a blockchain network that was launched in 2020 by Gavin Wood, one of the co-founders of Ethereum. It is a scalable, interoperable platform that allows for the creation of decentralized applications and the transfer of value across different blockchains. Polkadot has a market capitalization of over $15 billion.
- Avalanche (AVAX): Avalanche is a blockchain network that was launched in 2020. It uses a Proof-of-Stake consensus mechanism and is designed to be highly scalable and interoperable. Avalanche has a market capitalization of over $10 billion and is used for a variety of purposes, including decentralized finance and asset tokenization.
- Terra (LUNA): Terra is a blockchain platform that was launched in 2019. It is designed to be a stablecoin platform and uses a stablecoin called UST as its native currency. Terra has a market capitalization of over $5 billion.
- Binance Coin (BNB): Binance Coin is the native cryptocurrency of Binance, which is currently the world's largest cryptocurrency exchange by trading volume. Binance Coin was initially launched on the Ethereum blockchain as an ERC-20 token, but later it migrated to its own blockchain called the Binance Chain. The main use case of Binance Coin is to provide users with discounted trading fees on the Binance exchange. However, it can also be used to pay for other services offered by Binance, such as listing fees, transaction fees, and more.
- Cardano (ADA): Cardano is a blockchain-based platform that aims to provide a more secure and sustainable infrastructure for decentralized applications and smart contracts. The cryptocurrency used on the Cardano platform is called ADA. Cardano is designed to be a more energy-efficient blockchain than its predecessors, and it also features a unique consensus mechanism called Ouroboros, which is based on a Proof-of-Stake algorithm. Cardano is also known for its focus on academic research and peer-review, which is intended to ensure that the platform is built on solid scientific principles.
- Dogecoin (DOGE): Dogecoin is a cryptocurrency that was created in 2013 as a joke. It is based on the popular "Doge" meme, which features a Shiba Inu dog with captions written in broken English.

Despite its origins as a joke, Dogecoin has become one of the most popular cryptocurrencies, thanks in part to support from celebrities like Elon Musk. Dogecoin is designed to be a fast and cheap way to transfer value between individuals, and it also features a unique consensus mechanism called "Proof-of-Work with Scrypt," which is intended to make it more accessible to individual miners.

- Polkadot (DOT): Polkadot is a blockchain-based platform that aims to provide a more scalable and interoperable infrastructure for decentralized applications and smart contracts. The cryptocurrency used on the Polkadot platform is called DOT. Polkadot features a unique architecture that allows different blockchains to connect and communicate with each other, which is intended to enable greater flexibility and innovation in the blockchain space. Polkadot also features a unique consensus mechanism called "Nominated Proof-of-Stake," which is based on a hybrid of Proof-of-Stake and delegated Proof-of-Stake algorithms.

Stablecoins

Stablecoins are a type of cryptocurrency that are designed to maintain a stable value relative to an underlying asset, typically a fiat currency like the US dollar or a commodity like gold. Unlike other cryptocurrencies, such as Bitcoin or Ethereum, which can experience significant price volatility, stablecoins aim to provide stability and reduce the risk associated with price fluctuations. This stability makes stablecoins more suitable for use in everyday transactions, store of value, and as a medium of exchange. This section describes three main types of stablecoins.

Fiat-Collateralized Stablecoins

Fiat-collateralized stablecoins are a type of stablecoin that is backed by reserves of fiat currency, such as the US dollar, euro, or another government-issued currency. These stablecoins are designed to maintain a stable value equivalent to the underlying fiat currency they are pegged to. The main concept behind fiat-collateralized stablecoins is to provide a digital representation of traditional currency, combining the benefits of cryptocurrencies with the stability of fiat.

The stablecoin issuer holds a reserve of fiat currency in a bank account or other custodial arrangement. The reserve is maintained to ensure that each unit of the stablecoin is backed by an equivalent unit of the underlying fiat currency. When someone wants to acquire stablecoins, they deposit the corresponding amount of fiat currency into the reserve. Once the deposit is verified, an equivalent amount of stablecoins is issued to the user's digital wallet. Fiat-collateralized stablecoins often employ regular audits conducted by reputable third-party firms to verify that the reserves match the outstanding supply of stablecoins. This auditing process helps ensure transparency and builds trust among users. The stablecoin's value is maintained by pegging it to the value of the underlying fiat currency on a one-to-one basis. For example, if the stablecoin is pegged to the US dollar, each stablecoin is intended to have a value of $1. Users can redeem their stablecoins by sending them back to the issuer and receiving the equivalent fiat currency from the reserve. The redemption process allows users to convert stablecoins back into traditional currency. Examples of fiat-collateralized stablecoins include Tether (USDT), USD Coin (USDC), and TrueUSD (TUSD).

Crypto-Collateralized Stablecoins

Crypto-collateralized stablecoins are a type of stablecoin that is backed by a reserve of other cryptocurrencies, typically high-liquidity and widely accepted cryptocurrencies. These stablecoins aim to maintain a stable value relative to a pegged fiat currency or another stable asset, leveraging the value and security of the collateralized cryptocurrencies. The stablecoin issuer creates a reserve by holding a pool of cryptocurrencies as collateral. The collateral is usually held in smart contracts on a blockchain platform. To ensure stability and cover potential price fluctuations in the collateral, crypto-collateralized stablecoins often require overcollateralization. For example, if the stablecoin is pegged to the US dollar, the value of the collateral might need to be more than the value of the stablecoins in circulation. The smart contract governing the stablecoin establishes the rules for maintaining the peg. It determines how the collateral is managed, calculates the stablecoin supply, and facilitates mechanisms for stabilizing the value. Various mechanisms are employed to maintain price stability. These can include price feeds from trusted sources, automated rebalancing of the collateral, and algorithms that adjust the stablecoin supply based on market demand. If the value of the collateral falls below a certain threshold, triggering a potential instability, liquidation mechanisms may be implemented. These mechanisms can involve the automatic sale of the collateral to maintain stability or allow users to participate in auctions to purchase the collateral. Users can often redeem their stablecoins by returning them to the smart contract and receiving the collateralized cryptocurrencies in return. This redeemability helps ensure liquidity and provides an exit option for stablecoin holders. DAI, issued on the Ethereum blockchain, is an example of a crypto-collateralized stablecoin.

Algorithmic Stablecoins

Algorithmic stablecoins are a type of stablecoin that aims to maintain a stable value through algorithmic mechanisms, rather than relying on collateral or pegging to external assets. These stablecoins use complex algorithms and smart contracts to dynamically adjust the stablecoin supply and maintain price stability. Algorithmic stablecoins adjust their supply based on market conditions to maintain stability. When the stablecoin price exceeds the target value, the algorithm increases the supply to drive the price down. Conversely, when the price falls below the target value, the algorithm contracts the supply to increase demand and push the price up. Algorithmic stablecoins often introduce incentives for users to maintain the stability of the stablecoin. These incentives can include mechanisms such as yield farming, staking, or governance participation, where users are rewarded for taking actions that support stability. Some algorithmic stablecoins may incorporate a reserve fund or collateral pool to provide an additional layer of stability. These funds can be used to absorb fluctuations in demand or to backstop the stablecoin's value during periods of high volatility. Algorithmic stablecoins rely on oracles or external data feeds to obtain real-time information about market conditions and price movements. These data sources help inform the algorithm's decision-making process and ensure accurate adjustments to the stablecoin supply. Many algorithmic stablecoins are built on decentralized blockchain platforms and employ governance mechanisms that allow token holders to participate in decision-making processes. This ensures community involvement in the stability management and the evolution of the stablecoin's protocol.

References

Angelo, M., & Slazer, G. (2020). Wallet contracts on ethereum. *IEEE Xplore, 20*(3), 23–24.

Antonopoulos, A. M. (2014). *Mastering bitcoin: Unlocking digital cryptocurrencies*. O'Reilly Media. https://books.google.co.uk/books?id=IXmrBQAAQBAJ

Antonopoulos, A. M., & Wood, G. (2018). *Mastering ethereum: Building smart contracts and Dapps*. O'Reilly Media. https://books.google.co.uk/books?id=nJJ5DwAAQBAJ

Bashir, I. (2017). *Mastering blockchain*. Packt Publishing. https://books.google.co.uk/books?id=urkrDwAAQBAJ

Bernhard, M., Bracciali, A., Gudgeon, L., Haines, T., Perez, D., Sala, M., & Werner, S. (2021). *Financial cryptography and data security*. Springer.

Bhuiyan, T., Rahman, M., & Ali, A. (2020). *Cyber security and computer science*. Springer.

Bolliger, C. (2020). *Stablecoins—Classification of stablecoins and their impact on the financial sector* (Issue October).

Bourany, T., & Vandeweyer, Q. (2021). *Are stablecoins stable?* (Banque de France working paper, 02–21).

Burke, J. J. A. (2021). *Financial services in the twenty-first century*. Palgrave Macmillan.

Cai, W. E. I., & Wang, Z. (2018). Decentralized applications: The blockchain-empowered software system. *IEEE Access, 6*, 53019–53033. https://doi.org/10.1109/ACCESS.2018.2870644

Chen, Y., Lu, Y., Bulysheva, L., & Yu, M. (2022). Applications of blockchain in industry 4.0: A Review. *Information Systems Frontiers, January*. https://doi.org/10.1007/s10796-022-10248-7

Christianson, B., Malcolm, J., Matyáš, V., Švenda, P., Stajano, F., Anderson, J., & Hutchison, D. (2014). *Security Protocols XXII*.

Davidson, S., Filippi, P. D., & Potts, J. (2016). Economics of blockchain. In *SSRN* (pp. 1–23).

Eichengreen, B. (2019). From commodity "to fiat" and now to crypto: What does history tell us? In *NBER working paper series*.

Erinle, Y., Kethepalli, Y., Feng, Y., & Xu, J. (2023). SoK: Design, vulnerabilities, and security measures of cryptocurrency wallets. In *arXiv: 2307*, 12874.

Frankenfield, J. (2021). What is cryptocurrency's difficulty? Definition and bitcoin example. *Investopedia*.

Fu, S., Wang, Q., Yu, J., & Chen, S. (2023). Rational Ponzi game in algorithmic stablecoin. *IEEE International Conference on Blockchain and Cryptocurrency (ICBC), 2023*, 1–6.

Gennaro, R., & Robshaw, M. (2015). *Advances in Cryptology–CRYPTO 2015*.

Goldberg, I., Eds, T. M., & Goos, G. (2019). *Financial cryptography and data security*. 23rd International Conference, FC 2019, Frigate Bay, St. Kitts and Nevis.

He, S., Wu, Q., Luo, X., & Liang, Z. H. I. (2018). A social-network-based cryptocurrency wallet-management scheme. *IEEE Access, 6*, 7654–7663. https://doi.org/10.1109/ACCESS.2018.2799385

Hong, E. (2022). *How does bitcoin mining work?* Investopedia.

Houy, S., Schmid, P., & Bartel, A. (2023). Security aspects of cryptocurrency wallets—A systematic literature review. *ACM Computing Surveys, 1*(1), 1–31. https://doi.org/10.1145/3596906

Imine, A., Fernandez, J. M., Marion, E., Logrippo, L., & Garcia-alfaro, J. (2017). Foundations and practice of security. *Springer International Publishing*. https://doi.org/10.1007/978-3-319-75650-9

Jain, S., Rastogi, U., Bansal, N., & Kaur, G. (2019). Blockchain based Cryptocurrency for IOT. *2019 6th International Conference on Signal Processing and Integrated Networks (SPIN)* (pp. 744–749).

Karantias, K. (2020). SoK: A taxonomy of cryptocurrency wallets. In *Cryptology ePrint Archive*.

Kazemian, S., Huan, J., & Shomroni, J. (2022). Frax: A fractional-algorithmic stablecoin protocol. *2022 IEEE International Conference on Blockchain (Blockchain)* (pp. 406–411).

Kh-madhloom, J. (2022). Dynamic cryptography integrated secured decentralized applications with blockchain programming. *Wasit Journal of Computer and Mathematic Science, 1*(2), 21–33.

Kim, H., & Lee, S. (2023). Design and implementation of a private and public key crypto processor and its application to a security system. *IEEE Transactions on Consumer Electronics, 50*(1), 214–224. https://doi.org/10.1109/TCE.2004.1277865

Kim, S., & Deka, G. C. (2020). *Advanced applications of blockchain technology*. Springer.

Kim, S., Member, S., & Hahn, S. (2019). Mining pool manipulation in blockchain network over evolutionary block withholding attack. *IEEE Access, 7*, 144230–144244. https://doi.org/10.1109/ACCESS.2019.2945600

Koblitz, N., & Menezes, A. J. (2016). Cryptocash, cryptocurrencies, and cryptocontracts. *Designs, Codes and Cryptography, 78*(1), 87–102. https://doi.org/10.1007/s10623-015-0148-5

Lakhani, K. R. (2017, February). The truth about blockchain. *Harvard Business Review*.

Leal, F., Chis, A. E., & González, H. (2020). Performance evaluation of private ethereum networks. *SN Computer Science, 1*(5), 1–17. https://doi.org/10.1007/s42979-020-00289-7

Lin, C., He, D., Huang, X., Xie, X., Choo, K. R., & Member, S. (2021). PPChain: A privacy-preserving permissioned blockchain architecture for cryptocurrency and other regulated applications. *IEEE Systems Journal, 15*(3), 4367–4378. https://doi.org/10.1109/JSYST.2020.3019923

Miraz, M. H., & Ali, M. (2018). Applications of blockchain technology beyond cryptocurrency. *Annals of Emerging Technologies in Computing (AETiC), 2*(1), 1–6. https://doi.org/10.33166/AETiC.2018.01.001

Mita, M., Ito, K., Ohsawa, S., & Tanaka, H. (2019). What is stablecoin? A survey on price stabilization mechanisms for decentralized payment systems. *2019 8th International Congress on Advanced Applied Informatics (IIAI-AAI) What* (pp. 60–66).

Nofer, M., Gomber, P., Hinz, O., & Schiereck, D. (2017). Blockchain. *Business & Information Systems Engineering, 59*(3), 183–187. https://doi.org/10.1007/s12599-017-0467-3

Orenes-Lerma, L. (2023). What is a blockchain validator? *Ledger SAS.*

Peiter, K., & Roman, J. (2022). Universal wallets. *Business & Information Systems Engineering, 64*(1), 115–125. https://doi.org/10.1007/s12599-021-00736-6

Pierro, M. D. (2017). What is the blockchain? *Computing in Science & Engineering, 19*(October), 92–95. https://doi.org/10.1109/MCSE.2017.3421554

Rees, K. (2022). *What is crypto mining difficulty? Does it affect you?* MUO.

Rezaeighaleh, H., & Zou, C. C. (2019). New secure approach to backup cryptocurrency wallets. *IEEE Global Communications Conference (GLOBECOM), 2019*, 1–6.

Sai, R. (2019). Privacy and Security analysis of cryptocurrency mobile applications. *2019 Fifth Conference on Mobile and Secure Services (MobiSecServ)* (pp. 1–6).

Salimitari, M., Chatterjee, M., Yuksel, M., & Pasiliao, E. (2017). Profit maximization for Bitcoin pool mining: A prospect theoretic approach. *2017 IEEE 3rd International Conference on Collaboration and Internet Computing 0–7695–6303–1/17/31*, 267–274.

Sergeenkov, A. (2023). *Bitcoin mining difficulty: Everything you need to know.* Coindesk.

Sharma, T. K. (2023). *Types of crypto wallets explained.* Blockchain Council.

Shi, S., He, D., Li, L., Kumar, N., Khurram, M., & Choo, K. R. (2020). Computers & security applications of blockchain in ensuring the security and privacy of electronic health record systems: A survey. *Computers & Security Journal, 97*, 1–20. https://doi.org/10.1016/j.cose.2020.101966

Singh, S. (2016). Blockchain: Future of financial and cyber security. *2016 2nd International Conference on Contemporary Computing and Informatics (IC3I)* (pp. 463–467).

Suratkar, S., Shirole, M., & Bhirud, S. (2020). Cryptocurrency wallet: A review. *2020 4th International Conference on Computer, Communication and Signal Processing (ICCCSP) Cryptocurrency*.

Swan, M. (2015). *Blockchain: Blueprint for a new economy*. O'Reilly Media. https://books.google.co.uk/books?id=RHJmBgAAQBAJ

Tapscott, A., & Tapscott, D. (2017). How blockchain is changing finance. *Harvard Business Review*, 2–6.

Tasatanattakool, P. (2018). Blockchain: Challenges and applications. *2018 International Conference on Information Networking (ICOIN)* (pp. 473–475).

Taylor, S., Kim, S. H., Akram, K., & Arif, Z. (2022). Forensic science international: Digital investigation a comprehensive forensic preservation methodology for crypto wallets. *Forensic Science International: Digital Investigation, 43*, 1–17. https://doi.org/10.1016/j.fsidi.2022.301477

Thota, A. R., Upadhyay, P., Kulkarni, S., Selvam, P., & Viswanathan, B. (2020). Software wallet based secure participation in hyperledger fabric networks. *2020 International Conference on COMmunication Systems & NETworkS (COMSNETS)* (pp. 1–6).

Tran, D. A., Thai, M. T., & Krishnamachari, B. (2022). *Handbook on blockchain*. Springer.

Tuan, T., Dinh, A., Liu, R., Zhang, M., & Chen, G. (2018). Untangling blockchain: A data processing view of blockchain systems. *IEEE Transactions on Knowledge and Data Engineering, 30*(7), 1366–1385. https://doi.org/10.1109/TKDE.2017.2781227

Varghese, H. M. (2021). Cryptocurrency security and privacy issues : A research perspective. *2021 6th International Conference on Communication and Electronics Systems (ICCES)* (pp. 902–907).

Walker, J. (2018). *Cryptocurrency mining types*. Polygant.

Wüst, K., & Gervais, A. (2018). Do you need a blockchain? *2018 Crypto Valley Conference on Blockchain Technology*.

Xu, M., Chen, X., & Kou, G. (2019). A systematic review of blockchain. *Financial Innovation, 5*(27), 1–14.

Xu, X., Pautasso, C., Gramoli, V., Ponomarev, A., & Chen, S. (2016). The blockchain as a software Connector. *2016 13th Working IEEE/IFIP Conference on Software Architecture (WICSA)* (pp. 182–191).

Xu, X., Weber, I., & Staples, M. (2019). *Architecture for Blockchain applications*. Springer.

Yaga, D., & Yaga, D. (2018). Blockchain technology overview Blockchain technology overview. In *NISTIR 8202 Blockchain* (p. 66). NIST.

Zamani, E. D., & Giaglis, G. M. (2018). With a little help from the miners: Distributed ledger technology and market disintermediation. *Industrial Management & Data Systems, 118*(3), 637–652.

CHAPTER 5

Central Bank Digital Currency

Introduction

This chapter provides a broad analytical discussion on how the current advancements in financial technology can force central banks to change their practices and policies to adopt to the new financial ecosystem. This will be highlighted by the fact that these technological disruptions are transforming the financial market and payment systems, which have significant repercussions for the central banks as the regulators of monetary and financial stability. For this purpose, this chapter delves into various issues surrounding central bank digital currency (CBDC) which is an emerging term in banking and finance industry.

The primary goal of this chapter is to offer a detailed discussion on the scope of CBDC mainly from a retail payment perspective, including token-based and value-based currencies. Along with providing global examples of CBDC, this chapter highlights the advantages of transforming physical cash into digital form by central banks, vulnerabilities of digital currency, challenges posed to financial institutions, particularly banks, by facilitating the entry of new institutions and also implications for international payments and currency exchange.

B. Naysary and A. Tarazi, *The Digital Finance Era*,
https://doi.org/10.1007/978-981-97-3970-7_5

What Is CBDC and How It Works?

CBDC is a digital form of fiat currency issued by a central bank that is designed to function as a legal tender and is backed by the full faith and credit of the issuing government. It is a digital representation of a country's physical currency that can be used to make payments and settle financial transactions, which is essentially a digital version of the physical cash that is issued and regulated by the central bank. The concept of CBDC can be traced back to the early days of digital currencies, such as Bitcoin, which emerged in 2009. However, the idea of a central bank issuing its own digital currency did not gain much attention until 2014, when the Bank of England became the first central bank to release a research paper on the topic. Since then, many central banks around the world have been exploring the idea of CBDC and conducting research to determine the potential benefits and risks of such a currency. Among the first attempts, in 2016, the People's Bank of China (PBOC) announced that it had begun researching and developing a digital version of the Chinese yuan, which would be known as Digital Currency Electronic Payment (DCEP). The PBOC conducted several pilot programs of DCEP in different cities across China and started testing it for interbank transactions in 2018. Other central banks, including the Bank of Canada, the Bank of Japan, the European Central Bank (ECB), and the Bank of Thailand, also started researching and exploring the potential of CBDC during this time. In 2018, the ECB created a task force to explore the possibility of issuing a digital euro, and in 2019, the Bank of Japan released a report stating that it was considering the issuance of a CBDC. In 2020, the COVID-19 pandemic caused a surge in the use of digital payments, which further accelerated the development and adoption of CBDC. Many central banks around the world started to increase their research efforts and accelerate their plans for the development of CBDC. In July 2020, the Bank for International Settlements (BIS) released a report stating that 80% of the world's central banks were already engaged in some form of CBDC research. In October 2020, the PBOC became the first major central bank to launch a digital currency, with the pilot project for DCEP expanding to several major cities across China. The digital yuan was designed to be used for everyday transactions, and it was tested in various scenarios, such as transportation, retail, and government payments. In December 2020, the ECB announced that it was launching a public consultation on the digital euro, which received a record-breaking response of over 8,000 submissions from the public and industry participants. The ECB stated that the digital euro would be designed to complement cash, not replace it, and that it would be issued by the central bank, just like cash. In March 2021, the Bank of Japan announced that it would start the first phase of a CBDC proof-of-concept in April 2021, which would focus on the technical feasibility of a CBDC. Other central banks, including the Bank of Canada, the Bank of Thailand, and the Central Bank of Russia, also announced plans to conduct CBDC pilot projects. As of early 2023, several central banks around the world are actively exploring the development of CBDC, and some have already launched pilot projects. While the timeline for the widespread adoption of CBDC remains uncertain, it is clear that digital currencies will play an increasingly important role in the global financial system in the coming years.

Infrastructure

The infrastructure for CBDC is a critical component in the issuance and implementation of a digital currency. It includes the technical, operational, and regulatory frameworks that support the issuance, distribution, and use of CBDC. The infrastructure must be designed to ensure that the CBDC operates efficiently, securely, and transparently, while also providing a seamless user experience. Followings are some of the key components of CBDC infrastructure:

- The blockchain platform is the underlying technology that supports CBDC issuance and maintenance. A blockchain is a distributed ledger technology that provides a decentralized and secure way to record and verify transactions. The choice of blockchain platform will depend on the specific requirements of the CBDC, such as scalability, security, and interoperability. Some of the popular blockchain platforms used for CBDC include Ethereum, Hyperledger Fabric, and Corda.
- Digital wallets are software applications that allow users to store and manage CBDC. They provide a secure and convenient way to access and use CBDC, and can be accessed through various devices, such as smartphones, tablets, or computers. Digital wallets may also offer additional features, such as payment processing and value-added services, such as loyalty programs.

- CBDC payment systems facilitate the transfer of CBDC between users and merchants. They provide a secure and efficient way to process transactions in real time, ensuring that users can send and receive CBDC quickly and securely. CBDC payment systems can also support various types of transactions, such as peer-to-peer transfers, merchant payments, and cross-border transactions. CBDC also requires a robust regulatory framework that ensures compliance with local laws and regulations.
- The regulatory framework should provide clear guidance on the issuance, distribution, and use of CBDC, and address issues such as privacy, security, and consumer protection. Regulatory frameworks should also provide a clear legal framework for CBDC transactions, ensuring that users have legal recourse in case of disputes or fraud.
- Identity verification and e-KYC systems are a critical component of CBDC infrastructure, as they help prevent fraud and money laundering. Identity verification systems can use various forms of biometric authentication, such as facial recognition or fingerprint scanning, to verify the identity of CBDC users. They may also require additional documentation, such as a passport or driver's license, to ensure that users are who they claim to be.
- CBDC back-end systems support the operational and administrative functions of CBDC, such as managing user accounts, tracking transactions, and monitoring compliance. They are typically integrated with other payment systems, such as central bank settlement systems, to ensure seamless operation of the CBDC network. Back-end systems must also be designed to ensure the security and integrity of CBDC data, including encryption, access controls, and audit trails.
- Interoperability refers to the ability of CBDC to work seamlessly with other payment systems and digital currencies. Interoperability is critical for ensuring that CBDC can be used across borders and with different currencies, and can support a wide range of use cases. Interoperability can be achieved through the use of common standards and protocols, such as ISO 20022 or SWIFT.
- CBDC governance frameworks ensure that the CBDC network is operated in a transparent and accountable manner. Governance frameworks may include various stakeholders, such as central banks, commercial banks, payment service providers, and end users and may include mechanisms for decision-making, dispute resolution,

and oversight. Governance frameworks can also ensure that CBDC is developed and operated in accordance with best practices, such as those developed by international standard-setting organizations.

Issuance

CBDC is issued by a central bank and is backed by the full faith and credit of the issuing government. The central bank is responsible for creating the digital currency and distributing it to authorized participants, such as commercial banks or payment service providers. The issuance process of CBDC involves several key steps that ensure the digital currency is created, distributed, and maintained in a secure and efficient manner. The exact process of CBDC issuance can vary depending on the design of the specific currency, but there are some key features that are common to most CBDCs. The first step in the issuance of CBDC is the initial planning and design phase. This involves the central bank determining the goals and objectives for the CBDC, such as its intended use cases and the features it will offer. The central bank will also consider the technical and regulatory requirements for CBDC issuance, such as the choice of blockchain platform and the legal framework for the digital currency. Once the initial planning and design phase is complete, the central bank will select the blockchain platform that will be used to issue and maintain the CBDC. The central bank will consider factors such as the platform's scalability, security, and interoperability, as well as any technical requirements for integrating the CBDC into existing payment systems. The next step in the issuance process is the creation of the CBDC. The central bank will create the digital currency and define the parameters that govern its use, such as the maximum supply and the rules for issuance and redemption. The CBDC may be issued as either an account-based or token-based currency, depending on the design of the specific currency.

Account-Based CBDC

Account-based CBDC is a type of CBDC that operates through a centralized ledger system. It is designed to provide a digital representation of traditional bank accounts, allowing users to hold and transfer digital funds in a manner similar to traditional bank accounts. Account-based CBDC is characterized by several key features that differentiate it from other types of CBDC. Account-based CBDC operates through a centralized ledger system that is maintained by the central bank. The ledger records all transactions, balances, and other relevant data and is accessible only to authorized parties. It provides users with digital representations of their traditional bank accounts. Users can hold and transfer digital funds in a manner similar to traditional bank accounts, with balances being recorded and updated in real time on the centralized ledger. Account-based CBDC is backed by the central bank, providing users with a high degree of confidence in the safety and security of their funds. It is also subject to regulatory and supervisory frameworks established by the central bank. These frameworks are designed to ensure compliance with applicable laws and regulations, and to provide users with legal recourse in case of disputes or fraud.

Account-based CBDC can provide individuals and businesses with access to digital payment systems, even if they do not have a traditional bank account to improve financial inclusion, especially in regions where access to traditional banking services is limited. It can reduce transaction costs associated with traditional payment systems, such as processing fees and currency conversion costs, which benefit both consumers and businesses, making transactions more affordable and efficient. Account-based CBDC can provide users with enhanced payment security, as transactions are processed through a centralized and regulated system which can help prevent fraud, reduce the risk of cyber-attacks, and increase trust in digital payment systems. Account-based CBDC can provide central banks with increased control over the monetary system. This can enable central banks to implement more effective monetary policies, monitor financial stability, and respond more quickly to economic shocks.

Despite its potential benefits, account-based CBDC also faces several challenges. It requires the development and maintenance of complex technological and operational infrastructure, which can be expensive and time-consuming. Account-based CBDC may raise privacy concerns, as transactions are recorded and monitored by the central bank. This may lead to concerns about government surveillance and invasion of privacy. It may also disintermediate traditional financial intermediaries, such as commercial banks, which could have a significant impact on the financial system. Account-based CBDC may face challenges in terms of adoption, as consumers and businesses may be reluctant to switch from traditional payment systems to a new and unfamiliar technology.

Token-Based CBDC

Token-based CBDC is another approach to creating digital currency, and it is different from account-based CBDC. Token-based CBDC is a form of digital currency that is stored on a digital ledger, such as a blockchain, and is represented by a digital token that can be transferred between parties without the need for a central intermediary. It is possible for anyone with a digital wallet to hold and transfer token-based CBDC, making it a potentially powerful tool for financial inclusion. Token-based CBDC also offers a high degree of security and transparency. Because the tokens are recorded on a digital ledger, it is possible to track their movements and verify their authenticity. This means that token-based CBDC can be used to reduce the risk of fraud and money laundering, and to enhance the security of digital payments.

There are several potential benefits to using token-based CBDC. One is that it can reduce the need for cash, making transactions faster, more efficient, and more secure. Another is that it can provide greater financial inclusion by making it easier for people who do not have bank accounts to participate in the digital economy. Token-based CBDC can also improve cross-border payments, making it easier and less expensive to transfer money across borders.

However, token-based CBDC also has several challenges that must be addressed. One of the most significant is scalability. Because transactions on a blockchain can be slower and more expensive than traditional payment systems, it may be difficult to scale token-based CBDC to a level that can support widespread adoption. Another challenge is interoperability. Token-based CBDC must be able to work with existing payment systems and be accepted by merchants and other financial institutions. Additionally, there are concerns about privacy and security, as token-based CBDC transactions can be traced and recorded on a public ledger.

The process of issuing token-based CBDC is different from account-based CBDC. Instead of creating digital accounts for users, central banks would create digital tokens that represent the value of the CBDC. These tokens would be stored on a digital ledger, and users would be able to hold them in digital wallets. To use token-based CBDC, users would need to download a digital wallet that is compatible with the CBDC. They would then be able to purchase CBDC from a central bank or an authorized dealer, using traditional payment methods such as credit cards, bank transfers, or cash. Once the CBDC is purchased, it would be transferred to the user's digital wallet, where it could be used to make payments, transfer funds, or store value. To transfer CBDC to another user, the sender would need to initiate a transaction on the digital ledger. The transaction would be validated by the network of nodes that maintain the ledger, and once it is confirmed, the CBDC would be transferred to the recipient's digital wallet. The transaction would be recorded on the digital ledger, providing a record of the transfer that can be used for auditing and accounting purposes.

Distribution and Redemption

Once authorized, participants (such as commercial banks and other payment service providers) can distribute the CBDC to end users through digital wallets or other authorized platforms. End users can then use the CBDC to make purchases or transfer funds to other users on the network. The central bank will also provide a mechanism for the redemption of CBDC back into traditional currency, ensuring that the CBDC remains fully backed by the issuing government. Distribution and redemption are key aspects of any digital currency system, and the same is true for CBDC. The distribution of CBDCs can be achieved through a variety of mechanisms, depending on the design and implementation of the system.

Single-Tiered

The single-tiered or direct issuance model is one of the operating models of CBDC in which the central bank issues CBDC directly to the public or to the banks, which then distributes it to their customers. This model can be further divided into two sub-models of the account-based model, where CBDC is held in accounts with the central bank or commercial banks, and the token-based model, where CBDC is issued in the form of digital tokens that are stored on digital wallets.

One of the primary advantages of the direct issuance model of CBDC is that it allows the central bank to have direct control over the issuance and distribution of the currency. This means that the central bank can ensure the safety and stability of the CBDC, and prevent fraud and money laundering. It also enables the central bank to monitor the use of the CBDC and to implement monetary policy more effectively. Another advantage of the direct issuance model is that it can promote financial inclusion by providing access to banking services to people who are unbanked or under-banked. The direct issuance model can also improve the efficiency of payment systems by reducing the need for intermediaries, such as payment processors and clearing houses, which can reduce transaction costs and processing times.

Implementing the direct issuance model of CBDC requires a number of technical and operational challenges to be addressed. One of the key challenges is to ensure the security and resilience of the CBDC infrastructure. This includes ensuring the security of digital wallets, preventing fraud and counterfeiting, and protecting against cyber-attacks. Another challenge is to ensure interoperability between different CBDC systems, as well as with traditional payment systems. This would require the development of standards and protocols for CBDC, as well as the integration of CBDC with existing payment systems. This is necessary to ensure that CBDC can be used for a wide range of transactions, and that it can be used across different jurisdictions and currencies. Another challenge is to ensure that the CBDC system is scalable and can handle a large volume of transactions. This would require the development of a robust and scalable infrastructure that can support the demand for CBDC, as well as the development of efficient and effective payment systems.

Two-Tiered Model

A two-tiered CBDC model is an operating model in which the central bank issues CBDC to commercial banks, who in turn offer the CBDC services to the public. The commercial banks are intermediaries between the central bank and the public and are responsible for distributing and managing the CBDC. The two-tiered model is different from the direct issuance model, where the central bank issues CBDC directly to the public without the involvement of commercial banks. The main difference between the two-tiered CBDC model and the Hybrid CBDC model is the role of the central bank in issuing and distributing CBDC. In the two-tiered CBDC model, the central bank relies on commercial banks to distribute CBDC to the public, while in the Hybrid CBDC model, the central bank issues CBDC directly to the public and also provides CBDC services to commercial banks. This gives the central bank a more direct role in the payment system and allows for greater control over the issuance and distribution of CBDC.

In the two-tiered model, the central bank is responsible for issuing and regulating the CBDC. The central bank creates the CBDC, sets the rules and regulations for its use, and manages the overall supply of the CBDC in the economy. Commercial banks are intermediaries between the central bank and the public, and they provide the CBDC services to their customers. Commercial banks are responsible for distributing and managing the CBDC, maintaining customer accounts, and providing payment services. In the two-tiered model, commercial banks hold CBDC in reserve, which they can use to settle payments between themselves or with the central bank. The CBDC held in reserve is backed by collateral, such as government bonds or other assets, that can be used to guarantee the value of the CBDC. CBDC is accessible to the public through commercial banks, which are responsible for ensuring that the CBDC is widely available and can be easily used by customers.

The two-tiered model maintains the existing relationships between commercial banks and their customers, allowing commercial banks to continue to provide value-added services to their customers. The two-tiered model can lower the costs of CBDC distribution, as commercial banks are responsible for distributing and managing the CBDC. This can reduce the operational costs of the central bank. The two-tiered model reduces the risk of financial disintermediation, as commercial banks continue to play a key role in the payment system.

The two-tiered model requires close coordination between the central bank and commercial banks, as commercial banks are responsible for distributing and managing the CBDC. This requires the development of clear rules and regulations governing the issuance and distribution of CBDC. The two-tiered model is more complex than other CBDC operating models, as it involves multiple actors and institutions. This can increase the risk of operational failures and increase the difficulty of implementing effective risk management measures. The two-tiered model presents privacy and security concerns, as users may be required to disclose personal information when using CBDC. This could increase the risk of identity theft and fraud, and require the development of robust security measures.

Security

Security is perhaps the most critical aspect of any CBDC system. Given the high value of CBDC units and the potential for fraud and theft, it is essential that the system be designed with robust security features and protocols. One of the key security challenges in a CBDC system is ensuring that users are who they say they are. This can be achieved through a variety of identity verification mechanisms, such as biometric authentication, digital signatures, and multi-factor authentication. Another important aspect of CBDC security is protecting the system from hacking and other types of attacks. This can be achieved through a variety of measures, including encryption, firewalls, and intrusion detection systems. CBDC systems may also include mechanisms for detecting and preventing fraudulent transactions. For example, the system may monitor user activity and transaction patterns to identify suspicious behavior, or may require users to provide additional verification of high-value transactions. In addition to these technical security measures, CBDC systems may also be subject to regulatory and legal requirements aimed at preventing money laundering and terrorist financing. These requirements may include e-KYC and Anti-Money Laundering (AML) regulations, which may require the collection of personal information from users and the monitoring of transactions for suspicious activity. Finally, it is important to note that security is an ongoing concern for CBDC systems, and that new threats and vulnerabilities may emerge over time.

CBDC Project Objectives

CBDC projects are being developed and implemented by central banks around the world for a variety of policy goals. These goals vary depending on the country, but they generally fall into several broad categories, including monetary policy, financial stability, payment system efficiency, and financial inclusion.

Monetary Policy

The introduction of CBDC has the potential to significantly impact monetary policy, as it provides central banks with new tools to manage the economy. Central banks use a variety of tools to manage monetary policy, including interest rates, reserve requirements, and open market operations. CBDC can be used as an additional tool to achieve these goals.

Managing Interest Rates

CBDC can be used by central banks to manage interest rates in several ways. CBDC is a digital version of a central bank's fiat currency, and it can be used to facilitate transactions between individuals, businesses, and financial institutions. By leveraging CBDC, central banks can potentially increase the efficiency and effectiveness of their monetary policy tools, including interest rate management. One way that CBDC can be used to manage interest rates is by providing a new channel for conducting open market operations (OMOs). OMOs are the primary tool that central banks utilize to influence the short-term interest rates in the economy. Through OMOs, central banks buy or sell government securities in the open market, which affects the supply of money and the cost of borrowing. By using CBDC in OMOs, central banks can potentially achieve a more precise and targeted impact on interest rates.

Managing Reserve Requirements
CBDC can also be used by central banks to manage reserve requirements. Reserve requirements refer to the amount of reserves that banks are required to hold on their balance sheets, typically in the form of deposits with the central bank. Reserve requirements are an important tool for central banks to regulate the money supply and maintain financial stability. CBDC can potentially facilitate the management of reserve requirements in several ways. One way is through the direct issuance of CBDC to banks. Instead of requiring banks to hold physical cash or deposits with the central bank, CBDC can be used as a digital reserve asset that banks can hold on their balance sheets. This could potentially increase the efficiency and effectiveness of reserve requirements by reducing the costs associated with physical cash handling and storage. CBDC could also potentially enable more granular and targeted reserve requirements. With CBDC, central banks could potentially set reserve requirements on a more specific basis, such as by industry, geography, or the type of deposit. This could enable central banks to tailor reserve requirements to the specific needs and risks of different segments of the banking system. In addition, CBDC could potentially enable more dynamic and flexible reserve requirements. With CBDC, central banks could potentially adjust reserve requirements in real time based on changing market conditions or macroeconomic factors. This could enable central banks to respond more quickly and effectively to changes in the economy, potentially reducing the risk of financial instability.

Managing Direct Cash Transfers
CBDC can be used by central banks to manage direct cash transfers in a more efficient and effective way. Direct cash transfers refer to payments

made by the government to individuals or households for social welfare programs, disaster relief, or other purposes. Traditionally, direct cash transfers have been made through physical cash or bank transfers, which can be costly, time-consuming, and prone to errors and fraud. With CBDC, direct cash transfers can be made more securely, transparently, and instantaneously, potentially improving the efficiency and effectiveness of social welfare programs and other government initiatives. One potential use case for CBDC in direct cash transfers is through the use of digital wallets. With CBDC, digital wallets could be used to distribute direct cash transfers directly to individuals or households, eliminating the need for physical cash or bank transfers. Digital wallets can also potentially provide additional benefits for direct cash transfer recipients. For example, digital wallets can enable recipients to access their funds more easily and securely, potentially reducing the risk of theft or loss.

Financial Stability

CBDC has the potential to impact financial stability in a number of ways. The introduction of CBDC could potentially impact bank deposits. If individuals and firms begin to shift their deposits to CBDC accounts, this could reduce the amount of funding available to banks, potentially impacting their ability to lend and finance economic activity. This could have broader implications for financial stability if it leads to a credit crunch or other systemic issues. CBDC could impact the transmission of monetary policy. For example, if CBDC enables individuals and firms to more easily and directly access central bank reserves, this could impact the effectiveness of traditional monetary policy tools, such as interest rate adjustments. Central banks will need to carefully consider how CBDC fits into their overall monetary policy framework and whether adjustments may be necessary. CBDC could potentially impact the functioning of payment systems. For example, if CBDC leads to a significant reduction in the use of traditional payment systems, such as cash and commercial bank deposits, this could impact the infrastructure and stability of those systems. Central banks will need to consider how to ensure the resilience and efficiency of payment systems in a CBDC world. CBDC could also impact the role of financial intermediaries, such as banks and other financial institutions. If CBDC enables individuals and firms to directly access central bank reserves, this could reduce the need for intermediaries to provide liquidity and other services. This could have broader implications for financial stability if it leads to a concentration of financial activity in a smaller number of institutions or if it reduces the diversity of financial intermediaries in the system. CBDC could have implications on the financial inclusion by providing a new and more accessible means of payment and financial access for individuals and firms who are currently underserved by traditional financial institutions. On the other hand, the introduction of CBDC may require individuals and firms to have access to digital infrastructure and financial literacy skills, which could exacerbate existing inequalities in access to financial services. Overall, the impact of CBDC on financial stability will depend on a range of factors, including the design of the CBDC system, the regulatory environment, and broader economic and financial conditions.

Bank Runs Risk

CBDC has the potential to impact the risk of bank runs or bank failures in several ways. If CBDC is widely adopted, it could lead to a reduction in bank deposits as individuals and firms shift their deposits to CBDC accounts. This could potentially impact the funding available to banks and increase their liquidity risk. If banks are unable to meet deposit withdrawals, this could lead to bank runs and even bank failures. To mitigate this risk, central banks may need to introduce new liquidity management tools or other measures to ensure that banks have sufficient funding to meet deposit withdrawals. If banks experience a reduction in deposits, this could impact their ability to lend and finance economic activity. This could have broader implications for financial stability if it leads to a credit crunch or other systemic issues. CBDC could potentially impact the business models of banks and other financial institutions. If CBDC enables individuals and firms to more easily and directly access central bank reserves, this could reduce the need for banks to provide liquidity and other services which potentially leads to a concentration of financial activity in a smaller number of institutions, and increase systemic risk if those institutions become too big to fail. In case CBDC leads to a reduction in bank deposits, this could impact the effectiveness of deposit insurance schemes. If a large number of banks fail at the same time, the deposit insurance scheme may not have sufficient resources to cover all depositors. To mitigate this risk, central banks may need to consider adjusting deposit insurance schemes to ensure that they remain effective in a CBDC environment.

Payment System Efficiency

Another key policy goal of CBDC projects is to improve the efficiency of the payment system. First, CBDC can potentially have a significant impact on faster and cheaper transactions by allowing users to transfer funds directly from one person to another without needing to go through an intermediary, such as a bank. This could potentially reduce transaction times and costs, as well as increase accessibility for individuals who may not have access to traditional banking services by settling transactions in real time, meaning that funds would be immediately available to the recipient. This would eliminate the need for intermediaries to verify and settle transactions, reducing transaction times and costs. It can also lead to charging lower fees for transactions, which can be costly for both consumers and merchants.

Second, CBDC has the potential to increase competition in the payment system, lowering the barriers to entry for new payment system providers, as they would no longer need to rely on the existing financial infrastructure. This could create more competition in the payment system, which could lead to more innovation and lower costs for consumers and increased interoperability with other payment systems, making it easier for different payment systems to work together.

And third, CBDCs have the potential to significantly impact cross-border transactions and increase their volume by reducing transaction costs, increasing speed, improving accessibility, enhancing security, and promoting the development of more efficient cross-border payment infrastructure. However, the adoption of CBDCs for cross-border transactions would require significant coordination and collaboration between central banks, regulatory bodies, and financial institutions, as well as the development of new international payment infrastructure.

Financial Inclusion

CBDC has the potential to significantly impact financial inclusion by increasing access to financial services for individuals and businesses, particularly those who are currently excluded from traditional financial systems. Financial inclusion is defined as the process of ensuring access to appropriate financial products and services, such as savings accounts, loans, and insurance, for all individuals and businesses, regardless of their income, location, or social status. Financial inclusion is essential for promoting economic growth and reducing poverty by providing individuals and businesses with the means to save, invest, and access credit.

Currently, millions of people around the world do not have access to basic financial services, which limits their ability to participate in the formal economy and hinders economic growth. According to a 2018 report by the World Bank,[1] around 1.7 billion adults worldwide do not have access to a bank account. CBDC has the potential to address some of the challenges that limit access to financial services and promote financial inclusion. CBDC can improve the accessibility of financial services for individuals and businesses that are currently excluded from traditional financial systems. CBDC can be accessed through mobile phones, which are widely used even in underdeveloped regions, allowing for a more inclusive financial system. It can potentially lower the transaction costs associated with financial transactions, making it more affordable for individuals and businesses to access financial services. This can be particularly beneficial for those who live in rural areas or remote regions where traditional banking infrastructure is limited. CBDC can be settled in real time, which can significantly reduce the time it takes to complete financial transactions. This can make financial services more attractive to individuals and businesses that need to send and receive funds quickly. It can improve the security of financial transactions by providing greater transparency and traceability. This can reduce the risk of fraud and other illicit activities, making financial services safer and more secure. Using CBDC leads to reducing the reliance on cash, which can improve financial inclusion by providing individuals and businesses with an alternative means of payment.

Illicit Activities

CBDC has the potential to impact illicit activities in both positive and negative ways. Illicit activities, such as money laundering, terrorism financing, and tax evasion, pose significant threats to the stability and integrity of the financial system. CBDC is different from traditional digital currencies, such as Bitcoin, as it is issued and backed by a central bank and is considered legal tender. CBDC can be used for peer-to-peer transactions, payments at merchants, and cross-border transactions. CBDC can

[1] https://www.worldbank.org/en/topic/financialinclusion/overview.

increase the traceability of financial transactions, making it easier to identify and track illicit activities. This is because all CBDC transactions are recorded on a central ledger, allowing regulators and law enforcement agencies to monitor and analyze transactions in real time. CBDC can enhance due diligence by enabling regulators and financial institutions to verify the identity of individuals and businesses that use CBDC. This can help to prevent money laundering and terrorism financing by ensuring that CBDC is only used for legitimate purposes. It can reduce anonymity by requiring users to provide personal information, such as their name and address, when they use CBDC. This can help to prevent the use of CBDC for illicit activities by making it more difficult for individuals and businesses to remain anonymous. CBDC can improve transparency by providing greater visibility into the flow of funds. This can help regulators and law enforcement agencies to identify and track illicit activities and improve their understanding of the financial system.

However, the adoption of CBDC for illicit activities also poses some challenges and risks. The adoption of CBDC also poses significant cybersecurity risks, particularly regarding the risk of cyber-attacks and the theft of personal data. Regulators and central banks would need to develop strong security measures and protocols to protect CBDC transactions and prevent the use of CBDC for illicit activities. The adoption of CBDC also poses privacy concerns, particularly regarding the collection and use of personal data. Regulators and central banks would need to develop privacy regulations and policies that balance the need for transparency and traceability with the right to privacy. The adoption of CBDC also poses technological challenges, particularly regarding the scalability and interoperability of CBDC with other payment systems.

CBDC Types

Retail CBDC

Retail CBDC is a digital version of physical cash that is issued by the central bank and is available to the public. It can be used for day-to-day transactions, such as buying goods and services, and can be held in digital wallets or other digital payment apps. Retail CBDC can be further classified into two categories: account-based and token-based.

Wholesale CBDC

Wholesale CBDC is a digital currency that is used for interbank transactions, such as settling payments between commercial banks or financial institutions. It is not available to the public and is only used by banks and financial institutions.

CBDC Projects Around the World

CBDC projects are currently being explored and developed by central banks around the world. Here are some examples of CBDC projects:

China—Digital Currency Electronic Payment (DCEP)

The Digital Currency Electronic Payment (DCEP) system is a CBDC being developed by the People's Bank of China (PBOC). The DCEP is a digital version of China's fiat currency, the yuan (also known as the renminbi), and aims to provide a secure and efficient means of payment for the Chinese public. The development of the DCEP began in 2014, and in April 2020, the PBOC conducted a pilot test of the digital currency in four cities: Shenzhen, Suzhou, Xiong'an, and Chengdu. The pilot involved distributing digital yuan to a select group of residents and allowing them to use the currency for daily transactions, such as shopping and paying bills. One of the key features of the DCEP is that it uses a two-tier system. The PBOC is the sole issuer of the digital currency, and it distributes the currency to commercial banks and other financial institutions, which then distribute the currency to the public. This two-tier system is similar to the traditional banking system, with the PBOC acting as the central bank and the commercial banks acting as the intermediaries. Another important aspect of the DCEP is that it uses a blockchain-based system to manage transactions. The blockchain system ensures that transactions are secure and transparent, and it also allows the PBOC to track the movement of the digital currency.

The DCEP is also designed to work offline, allowing users to make transactions even when they are not connected to the internet. This is achieved through a "touch and go" feature, which enables users to transfer digital yuan simply by tapping their mobile phone against another user's phone. One of the main objectives of the DCEP is to reduce the dependence on cash in the Chinese economy. The use of digital currency is expected to improve the efficiency of transactions, reduce the costs of cash handling, and increase financial inclusion for those who are not able to access traditional banking services.

Sweden—E-krona

The e-krona is a CBDC being developed by Sweden's central bank, the Riksbank. Sweden has been a pioneer in the shift toward a cashless society, with cash accounting for just 1% of the country's total transactions in 2020. The Riksbank has been exploring the potential benefits and risks of a CBDC since 2017, and in 2020 it launched a pilot project to test the feasibility of an e-krona. The e-krona would be a digital version of Sweden's national currency, the krona. It would be issued and backed by the Riksbank, and would be designed to complement the existing payment infrastructure, rather than replacing it. The e-krona would be accessible to all individuals and businesses, and would be stored in digital wallets or accounts, rather than physical wallets or bank accounts. The e-krona is intended to provide a secure and efficient means of payment, particularly in situations where cash is not available or not practical. It is also designed to support financial inclusion, as it would provide access to payment services for those who may not have access to traditional banking services.

The Riksbank is exploring several technological solutions for the e-krona, including blockchain technology, distributed ledger technology, and centralized databases. The e-krona would be designed to be resilient to cyber-attacks and other forms of disruption, and would be subject to the same level of security and regulatory oversight as traditional banking services. The e-krona project is still in the testing phase, and there is currently no timeline for its launch. The Riksbank is continuing to evaluate the potential benefits and risks of the e-krona, and is working closely with stakeholders to ensure that the digital currency is designed to meet the needs of users. One of the key challenges facing the e-krona project is the potential impact on the existing financial infrastructure. The Riksbank is working to ensure that the e-krona complements the existing payment infrastructure, rather than replacing it, and that it is designed to work seamlessly with other payment systems.

Bahamas—Sand Dollar

The Sand Dollar is a CBDC being developed by the Central Bank of the Bahamas. The project was launched in December 2019, and the Sand Dollar became the world's first CBDC to be launched nationwide in October 2020. The Sand Dollar is designed to be a digital version of the Bahamian dollar, the country's national currency. It is intended to provide a secure and efficient means of payment, particularly in situations where cash is not available or not practical, such as in remote or underserved areas. The Sand Dollar is also designed to support financial inclusion, as it would provide access to payment services for those who may not have access to traditional banking services. The Sand Dollar is accessible to all individuals and businesses in the Bahamas and is stored in digital wallets or accounts, rather than physical wallets or bank accounts. Users can access the Sand Dollar through a mobile app, which is available on both Android and iOS devices. The Sand Dollar is designed to be easy to use and understand, even for those who may not be familiar with digital currencies or technology. It is also designed to be resilient to cyber-attacks and other forms of disruption, and is subject to the same level of security and regulatory oversight as traditional banking services.

The Sand Dollar project has been well received in the Bahamas, where it has been embraced as a means of promoting financial inclusion and supporting economic growth. The Central Bank of the Bahamas has also been working to ensure that the Sand Dollar complements the existing payment infrastructure, rather than replacing it, and that it is designed to work seamlessly with other payment systems. The launch of the Sand Dollar has generated significant interest from other countries and central banks, who are closely monitoring the project as a potential model for their own CBDC initiatives. The Sand Dollar represents a significant development in the global trend toward the adoption of CBDCs and could have significant implications for the future of digital currencies and the global financial system.

European Union—Digital Euro

The Digital Euro is a proposed CBDC being developed by the European Central Bank (ECB), the central bank of the European Union (EU). The Digital Euro is intended to complement existing forms of payment, such as cash and bank deposits, and to provide a secure and efficient means of payment for consumers and businesses across the EU. The Digital Euro would be issued and backed by the ECB, and would be available to all individuals and businesses in the EU. It would be stored in digital wallets or accounts, and could be used to make payments and transfers instantly and securely, without the need for intermediaries such as banks or payment processors.

The ECB has identified several key objectives for the Digital Euro, including promoting financial stability, ensuring financial inclusion, and safeguarding the privacy and security of users. The ECB has also emphasized the need for the Digital Euro to be interoperable with existing payment systems and to comply with existing regulations and standards, including those related to anti-money laundering and data protection. The ECB has launched a public consultation on the Digital Euro, which is open to all interested parties, including individuals, businesses, and financial institutions. The consultation is intended to gather feedback and insights on the design, features, and potential impact of the Digital Euro, and to inform the ECB's decision-making process as it moves forward with the development of the Digital Euro.

The ECB has indicated that the development of the Digital Euro is still in its early stages, and that it may take several years before a Digital Euro is launched. The ECB has also emphasized the need for careful consideration and analysis of the potential benefits and risks of the Digital Euro, and for close collaboration with other central banks and regulatory authorities. The Digital Euro represents a significant development in the global trend toward the adoption of CBDCs and could have significant implications for the future of digital currencies and the global financial system. The development of the Digital Euro will be closely watched by other countries and central banks, who are also exploring the potential of CBDCs, and could have a significant impact on the future of payments and financial services in the EU and beyond.

United States—Digital Dollar

The Digital Dollar is a proposed CBDC being considered by the United States government and various stakeholders in the financial industry. The idea of a Digital Dollar has gained traction in recent years as interest in digital currencies has grown and as other countries have begun exploring the development of their own CBDCs. The potential benefits of a Digital Dollar include increased financial inclusion, greater efficiency and security in payment systems, and reduced reliance on intermediaries such as banks and payment processors. A Digital Dollar could also have geopolitical implications, as it could potentially compete with other global currencies and provide the US with greater control over the international financial system.

Several initiatives have been launched to explore the feasibility of a Digital Dollar, including proposals from the Digital Dollar Foundation, a non-profit organization dedicated to advancing the adoption of a Digital Dollar in the United States. The Foundation has proposed the creation of a US Digital Dollar wallet that would allow individuals and businesses to hold and transact with Digital Dollars, as well as a framework for regulating the use of Digital Dollars and ensuring their interoperability with existing payment systems. In addition to the Digital Dollar Foundation, various government agencies and committees have expressed interest in exploring the development of a Digital Dollar, including the Federal Reserve, the US Treasury Department, and the Senate Banking Committee. These entities have emphasized the need for careful consideration and analysis of the potential benefits and risks of a Digital Dollar, as well as the need to ensure that any Digital Dollar initiative is compliant with existing laws and regulations.

The development of a Digital Dollar is still in its early stages, and it remains unclear if and when a Digital Dollar will be launched in the United States. However, the increasing interest in CBDCs and the potential benefits of a Digital Dollar suggest that it is a possibility worth exploring further in the coming years.

Thailand—Project Inthanon

Project Inthanon is a CBDC initiative launched by the Bank of Thailand (BOT) in collaboration with several private sector partners. The project is named after Mount Inthanon, the highest peak in Thailand, and is aimed at exploring the potential use cases and implications of CBDCs for the Thai financial system.

The main objectives of Project Inthanon include developing a proof-of-concept prototype for a CBDC platform that can be used for interbank settlements and wholesale payments, examining the technical, legal, and regulatory issues related to the development and implementation of CBDC and enhancing the efficiency, security, and resiliency of Thailand's financial infrastructure.

Project Inthanon is a multi-phase initiative that has been ongoing since 2018. The first phase of the project involved the development of a proof-of-concept prototype for a wholesale CBDC platform that could be used for interbank settlements and other large-value transactions. The prototype was developed in collaboration with several private sector partners, including commercial banks, payment service providers, and technology firms. In 2019, the BOT announced that it was expanding Project Inthanon to include a retail CBDC platform that could be used by consumers for everyday transactions. The retail CBDC platform is still in the development phase, and the BOT has not yet announced a timeline for its launch. The BOT has emphasized that Project Inthanon is a research and development initiative aimed at exploring the potential benefits and risks of CBDCs, rather than a commitment to launch a CBDC in the near future. The development of Project Inthanon has also led to closer collaboration between the BOT and the private sector, with several banks and technology firms involved in the project. This collaboration is expected to continue as the BOT explores the potential uses of CBDCs in the Thai financial system.

These are just a few examples of the CBDC projects that are currently underway around the world. Each project has its own unique features and objectives, and the development and implementation of CBDCs will vary depending on the needs and circumstances of each country.

Demand for CBDC

The concept of CBDC has gained significant attention in recent years, as technological advancements have created new opportunities and challenges for the global financial system. While the demand for CBDC varies depending on the region and specific economic context, there are several broad drivers that are contributing to the growing interest in CBDCs. One of the key drivers of demand for CBDC is the increasing shift toward digital payments and the rise of FinTech. The growth of digital payment systems, such as mobile payments and e-wallets, has created new opportunities for financial inclusion and economic growth, particularly in emerging markets. However, it has also raised concerns about financial stability, consumer protection, and the role of central banks in ensuring the safety and efficiency of payment systems. CBDC is seen as a potential solution to these challenges, as they would allow central banks to provide a safe and efficient digital payment system that is fully backed by the central bank's balance sheet. CBDC could also help to reduce the reliance on commercial banks and other intermediaries in the payment system, potentially lowering costs and increasing competition.

Another driver of demand for CBDC is the increasing use of cashless payments and the potential risks associated with a cashless society. While cashless payments offer many benefits, such as convenience and security, they also raise concerns about financial privacy, cybersecurity, and the potential for exclusion of certain groups from the financial system. CBDC could help to address some of these concerns by providing a secure and anonymous form of digital currency that is backed by the central bank. This would provide a level of trust and confidence in digital payments that is currently lacking, and could help to ensure that all members of society have access to a safe and efficient payment system. Another driver of demand for CBDC is the growing interest in blockchain and distributed ledger technology (DLT). CBDC could leverage DLT to create a more efficient and transparent payment system, while also reducing the risks associated with centralization and intermediation.

CBDC could also provide new opportunities for financial innovation and experimentation, such as the integration of smart contracts and other programmable features into the payment system. This could create new opportunities for financial inclusion and economic growth, particularly in emerging markets where traditional financial infrastructure is lacking. Finally, the growing interest in CBDC is also being driven by geopolitical and economic considerations. Some countries are exploring CBDC as a way to increase their financial autonomy and reduce their dependence on the US dollar and other foreign currencies. CBDC could also provide a way to mitigate the risks associated with cross-border transactions and global financial instability.

CBDC and Cryptocurrency

CBDC and cryptocurrency are two distinct forms of digital currencies, and they have some fundamental differences in terms of their nature, control, underlying technology, and purpose.

Control and Issuance

CBDCs are issued and regulated by central banks, which are typically government-controlled entities. They have full control over the issuance, distribution, and maintenance of the currency. CBDCs are considered legal tender and are backed by the central bank's reserves.

Cryptocurrencies are decentralized digital currencies that operate on blockchain technology. They are not controlled by any central authority or government. Cryptocurrencies are typically created through a process called mining or distributed through initial coin offerings (ICOs).

Regulatory Framework

CBDCs operate within existing regulatory frameworks and comply with the laws and regulations of the respective countries. Central banks have the authority to establish rules and oversight for CBDCs, ensuring compliance with AML and KYC requirements.

Cryptocurrencies operate in a relatively unregulated environment, with regulations varying across different jurisdictions. While some countries have introduced regulations to govern cryptocurrencies, the regulatory landscape is still evolving and lacks global uniformity.

Technology

CBDCs can be built on different technologies, including centralized databases or distributed ledger technologies (DLTs) like blockchain. The choice of technology depends on the specific objectives and requirements of the central bank.

Cryptocurrencies are predominantly built on blockchain technology, which is a decentralized and transparent ledger that records all transactions. Blockchain ensures the immutability and security of cryptocurrency transactions, allowing for peer-to-peer transfers without the need for intermediaries.

Stability and Value

CBDCs are designed to maintain stability and reflect the value of the national currency. They are typically pegged to a fiat currency, ensuring that their value remains stable and predictable.

Cryptocurrencies are known for their volatility, as their value is determined by market demand and supply dynamics. Cryptocurrency prices can fluctuate significantly, leading to potential risks and speculative behavior.

Purpose and Use Cases

CBDCs are primarily intended for use as a digital form of fiat currency. They aim to enhance the efficiency of financial transactions, promote financial inclusion, and provide a secure and accessible means of payment. CBDCs can also facilitate the implementation of monetary policies and improve financial system resilience.

Cryptocurrencies have broader use cases beyond traditional payments. They can enable peer-to-peer transactions, smart contracts, and decentralized finance (DeFi) and provide an alternative store of value. Cryptocurrencies also offer potential solutions for cross-border transactions.

Privacy and Anonymity

CBDCs can be designed with varying degrees of privacy and anonymity. Central banks can implement privacy features while complying with regulations related to AML and KYC requirements.

Cryptocurrencies offer varying degrees of privacy and anonymity, depending on the specific cryptocurrency and associated technologies. Some cryptocurrencies, like Bitcoin, provide pseudonymous transactions, while others offer enhanced privacy features like zero-knowledge proofs.

References

Abdelli, M. E. A., & Shahbaz, M. (2023). *Digital economy, energy and sustainability: Opportunities and challenges*.

Ahnert, T., Hoffmann, P., Leonello, A., & Porcellacchia, D. (2023). *CBDC and financial stability*. SSRN 4361136.

Armas, A., Ruiz, L., & Luis Vásquez, J. (2022). *Assessing CBDC potential for developing payment systems and promoting financial inclusion in Peru*. Bank for International Settlements, Issue 123, pp. 131–151.

Armelius, H., Guibourg, G., Levin, A. T., & Söderberg, G. (2018). The rationale for issuing e-krona in the digital era. Sveriges Riksbank Economic Review, 6–18.

Arromdee, V., & Koonprasert, T. (2022). Hands-on CBDC experiments and considerations—A view from the Bank of Thailand. *Bank for International Settlements, 123*, 189–192.

Ashmarina, S. I., Horák, J., Vrbka, J., & Šuleř, P. (2021). *Economic systems in the new E: Stable systems in an unstable world*, 1–901.

Auer, R., & Böhme, R. (2020, March). The technology of retail central bank digital. *Bank for International Settlements*, 85–100.

Auer, R., & Raphael, B. (2020). *CBDC architectures, the financial system, and the central bank of the future*. The Centre for Economic Policy Research (CEPR).

Banerjee, S., & Sinha, M. (2023). Promoting financial inclusion through central bank digital currency: An evaluation of payment system viability in India. *Australasian Accounting, Business and Finance Journal, 17*(1), 176–204.

Bhowmik, D. (2021). Monetary policy implications of central bank digital currency with special reference to India. *Asia-Pacific Journal of Management and Technology Online, 2*(3), 1–8.

Bindseil, U. (2020a). Central Bank digital currency: Financial system implications and control. *International Journal of Political Economy, 48*(4), 303–335. https://doi.org/10.1080/08911916.2019.1693160

Bindseil, U. (2020b). *Tiered CBDC and the financial system*. European Central Bank, Issue 2351.

Bitter, L. (2020). *Banking crises under a CBDC*. ZBW—Leibniz Information Centre for Economics, Kiel, Hamburg.

Blustein, P. (n.d.). *Can a central bank digital currency work? The Bahamas offers lessons*. Centre for International Governance Innovation.

Boonstra, W. (2022). *CBDC and the international position of the euro*. The European money and finance forum, pp. 1–11.

Bordo, M., & Levin, A. (2017). *Central bank digital currency and the future of monetary policy* (NBER Working Paper No. 23711, pp. 1–32).

Botta, A., Bruno, P., & Galvin, J. (2021). *The 2021 McKinsey global payments report*. McKinsey and Company, Issue October.

Calle, G., & Eidan, D. (2020). Central Bank digital currency: An innovation in payments. R3 White Paper, Issue April.

Chaum, D., Grothoff, C., & Moser, T. (2021). *How to issue a central bank digital currency* (SNB Working Papers).

Chen, H., & Siklos, P. L. (2022). Central bank digital currency: A review and some. *Journal of Financial Stability, 60*(February), 100985. https://doi.org/10.1016/j.jfs.2022.100985

Cœuré, B., & Loh, J. (2018, March). *Committee on payments and market infrastructures markets committee: Central bank digital currencies*. Bank for International Settlements.

Colebrook, C. R. (2022). The digitalization of money in the Bahamas. Central Bank of the Bahamas.

Crawford, J., Hastings, U. C., Menand, L., & Ricks, M. (2021). Fed accounts: Digital Dollars. *Columbia Law School, 951*.

Davoodalhosseini, M., Rivadeneyra, F., & Zhu, Y. (2020). *CBDC and Monetary Policy*. Bank of Canada.

Davoodalhosseini, S. M. (2022). Central bank digital currency and monetary policy. *Journal of Economic Dynamics and Control, 142*, 104150. https://doi.org/10.1016/j.jedc.2021.104150

Denecker, O., D'Estienne, A., Gompertz, P.-M., & Sasia, E. (2022). *Central bank digital currencies : An active role for commercial banks*. McKinsey and Company, Issue October.

Duffie, D. (2019). *Digital currencies and fast payment systems: Disruption is coming*. Asian Monetary Policy Forum.

Duffie, D. (2020). *Interoperable payment systems and the role of Central Bank digital currencies*. Finance and Insurance Reloaded. Institut Louis Bachelier Annual Report.

Empowered, D. L. T., & Currencies, D. (2022). *The (r)evolution of money III: CBDC is here, careful design needed now*. Accenture.

Fáykiss, P., Nyikes, A., & Szombati, A. (2022). CBDC—An opportunity to support digital financial inclusion: Digital student safe in hungary. *Bank for International Settlements, 123*, 79–87.

Garratt, R., Lee, M., Malone, B., & Martin, A. (2020). *Token- or Account-Based? A Digital Currency Can Be Both*. Federal Reserve Bank of New York Liberty Street Economics.

Gross, M., & Letizia, E. (2023). *To demand or not to demand: On quantifying the future appetite for CBDC*. International Monetary Fund: Vol. WP/23/9.

Hall, I. (2022). *Bahamas central bank shares CBDC lessons from Sand Dollar' first two years*. Global Government FinTech.

Himes, J. (2022). *Winning the future of money: A proposal for a US central bank digital currency*.

Kaili, E., & Psarrakis, D. (2021). *Disintermediation economics: The impact of blockchain on markets and policies* (pp. 1–336).

Khiaonarong, T., & Humphrey, D. (2022). *Falling use of cash and demand for retail Central Bank digital currency*.

Kiffmeister, & Sonjadav. (2021). *FinTech's perspectives from a bunch of policy wonks. The views expressed herein are those of the authors and should not be attributed to the Bank for International Settlements or the International Monetary Fund*. The Global FinTech Intelligencer.

Kim, Y., & Kwon, O. (2023). Central Bank digital currency, credit supply, and financial stability. *Journal of Money, Credit and Banking*, *55*(1). https://doi.org/10.1111/jmcb.12913

Kim, Y. S., & Kwon, O. (2019). *Central Bank digital currency and financial stability*.

Kumhof, M., & Noone, C. (2018). *Central bank digital currencies—Design principles and balance sheet implications*. Bank of England, 725.

Kumhof, M., & Noone, C. (2021). Central bank digital currencies—Design principles for financial stability ☆. *Economic Analysis and Policy, 71*, 553–572. https://doi.org/10.1016/j.eap.2021.06.012

Kuo, D., Lee, C., Yan, L., & Wang, Y. (2021). A global perspective on central bank digital currency. *China Economic Journal, 14*(1), 52–66. https://doi.org/10.1080/17538963.2020.1870279

Lan, S., & Kashani, S. V. (2021). *Influence of e-krona & e-CNY on individual privacy: A comparative study between Sweden and China.*

Li, J. (2023). Predicting the demand for central bank digital currency: A structural analysis with survey data R. *Journal of Monetary Economics, 134*, 73–85. https://doi.org/10.1016/j.jmoneco.2022.11.007

Li, S., & Huang, Y. (2021). The genesis, design and implications of China's central bank digital currency. *China Economic Journal, 14*(1), 67–77. https://doi.org/10.1080/17538963.2020.1870273

Lukonga, I. (2023). *Monetary policy implications central bank digital currencies: Perspectives on jurisdictions with conventional and Islamic banking systems.* International Monetary Fund: Vol. WP/23/60.

Mancini-griffoli, T., Martinez, M. S., Agur, I., Ari, A., Kiff, J., Popescu, A., Rochon, C., Khan, A., & Poh, K. (n.d.). *Casting light on central bank digital currency.* International Monetary Fund.

Meaning, J., Dyson, B., Barker, J., & Clayton, E. (2018). *Broadening narrow money: monetary policy with a central bank digital currency.* Bank of England, 724.

Minh, V., Nguyen, P. V., Huu, H., Xuan, H., & Tram, T. (2023). Research in international business and finance governance and monetary policy impacts on public acceptance of CBDC adoption. *Research in International Business and Finance, 64*(December 2022), 101865. https://doi.org/10.1016/j.ribaf.2022.101865

Minwalla, C. (2020). *Security of a CBDC.* Bank of Canada.

Mooij, A. A. M. (2021). *European Central Bank digital currency: The digital euro what design of the digital euro is a possible legal framework?* (Bridge Working paper, Vol. 14).

Mooij, A. M. (2023). A digital euro for everyone: Can the European system of Central Banks introduce general purpose CBDC as part of its economic mandate? *Journal of Banking Regulation, 24*(1), 89–104. https://doi.org/10.1057/s41261-021-00186-w

Morales-resendiz, R., Ponce, J., Picardo, P., Velasco, A., Chen, B., Sanz, L., Guiborg, G., Segendorff, B., Luis, J., Arroyo, J., Aguirre, I., Haynes, N., Panton, N., Griffiths, M., Pieterz, C., & Hodge, A. (2021). Latin American Journal of Central Banking Implementing a retail CBDC: Lessons learned and key insights. *Latin American Journal of Central Banking, 2*(1), 100022. https://doi.org/10.1016/j.latcb.2021.100022

Morgan, P. J. (2022). FinTech and financial inclusion in Southeast Asia and India. *Asian Economic Review, 17*, 183–208. https://doi.org/10.1111/aepr.12379

Niepelt, D. (2021). *Central bank digital currency considerations, projects, outlook.* Centre for economic policy research.

Oordt, M. R. C. V. (2022). Journal of economic dynamics & control discussion of "central bank digital currency: Stability and information." *Journal of Economic Dynamics and Control, 142*, 104503. https://doi.org/10.1016/j.jedc.2022.104503

Opare, E. A., & Kim, K. (2020). A compendium of practices for central bank digital currencies for multinational financial infrastructures. *IEEE ACCESS, 8*, 110810–110847. https://doi.org/10.1109/ACCESS.2020.3001970

Ozili, P. K. (2022). Circular economy and central bank digital currency. *Circular Economy and Sustainability*, 1501–1516.https://doi.org/10.1007/s43615-022-00170-0

Panetta, B. F. (2018). *21st century cash: Central banking, technological innovation and digital currencies*. The European money and finance forum, pp. 1–9.

Pardalos, P., & Kotsireas, I. (2022). *Mathematical research for blockchain economy*. 3rd International Conference MARBLE.

Peterson, K. (2022). *Can central bank digital currency increase financial inclusion? Arguments for and against Can central bank digital currency increase financial inclusion? Arguments for and against*. Munich Personal RePEc Archive, Issue 110786.

Peterson, K. (2023). *CBDC, FinTech and cryptocurrency for financial inclusion and financial stability*. Munich Personal RePEc Archive, Issue 115768.

Piazzesi, M., & Schneider, M. (2022). *Credit lines, bank deposits or CBDC? Competition & efficiency in modern payment systems* (Unpublished). Stanford University, pp. 1–40.

Popescu, A. (2022). *Cross-border Central Bank digital currencies, bank runs and capital flows volatility*.

Redaelli, S. (2021). *CBDC and Bank Runs in an open economy context*.

Ricks, M., Crawford, J., & Menand, L. (2020). *FedAccounts: Digital dollar*, Issue April.

Samudrala, R. S. (2021). Central bank digital currency: Risks, challenges and design considerations for India. *CSI Transactions on ICT, 9*(4), 245–249. https://doi.org/10.1007/s40012-021-00344-5

Supadulya, C., Tansanguan, K., Sethaput, V., Wattanasiriwiroj, W., & Areechitranusorn, K. (2019). *Project Inthanon and the project DLT scripless bond*. Asian Development Bank Institute, Issue 1030.

Teplý, P., Roshwalb, Y., & Polena, M. (2021). Financial disintermediation: The case of peer-to-peer lending. In *The Palgrave handbook of FinTech* (pp. 375–401). Springer International Publishing. https://doi.org/10.1007/978-3-030-66433-6_17

Terracciano, T., & Somoza, L. (2020). *Central bank digital currency: The devil is in the details*. London School of Economics.

Vallet, G., Rochon, L.-P., & Kappes, S. (2022). *Central banking, monetary policy and the future of money.*

Ward, O., & Rochemont, S. (2019). *An addendum to "A Cashless Society-Benefits, Risks and Issues.* Institute and Faculty of Actuaries.

Xia, H., Gao, Y., & Zhang, J. Z. (2023). Understanding the adoption context of China's digital currency electronic payment. *Financial Innovation.* https://doi.org/10.1186/s40854-023-00467-5

Xiaochuan, Z. (2020). *Understanding China's Central Bank digital currency.* CF40 Group.

Yao, Q. (2018). A systematic framework to understand central bank. *Information Sciences March, 61*(March), 1–8.

Zhang, T., & Huang, Z. (2022). Blockchain and central bank digital currency. *ICT Express, 8*(8), 264–270.

CHAPTER 6

Neobanks

Introduction

In light of the systemic shift in financial access that would render traditional banks' business models inefficient in near future, and the fact that retrofitting the traditional products and processes for digital transformations has proven to be ineffective, this chapter attempts to highlight the urge in the banking industry to rethink their customer relationships and methods of delivering value to satisfy the needs of modern customers in the new financial ecosystem.

For this purpose, the rise of neobanks in the past few years in response to the above-mentioned challenges is expounded in this chapter by focusing on cases from Europe, US, and Asia. The main argument in this chapter revolves around characteristics of neobanks and numerous ways by which they generate value for the customers such as digital payments (domestic and foreign as well as enabling P2P interactions), digital wallets, artificial intelligence (AI) assisted customer interaction through various channels including social media, AI-based financial planning and advisory services, utilizing big data to provide more customized services to clients and new credit scoring and risk assessment models based on big data which facilitates credit provision to Small and Medium-sized Enterprises (SMEs). Finally, challenges faced by neobanks such as security concerns, customer awareness and IT infrastructure are highlighted.

B. Naysary and A. Tarazi, *The Digital Finance Era*,
https://doi.org/10.1007/978-981-97-3970-7_6

What Is Neobank?

A neobank (or challenger bank) is a type of financial institution that offers banking services primarily through digital channels, such as mobile apps, websites, and other online platforms. Unlike traditional banks, neobanks often do not have physical branch locations and rely on technology to interact with customers and manage their accounts. Neobanks are typically designed to be more user-friendly and offer a more seamless banking experience compared to traditional banks. They often provide faster and more convenient services, such as opening an account, applying for a loan, or making a payment, and may also offer unique features, such as budgeting tools, investment options, and rewards programs. Neobanks also tend to have lower fees and offer higher interest rates on savings accounts than traditional banks, as they have lower overhead costs and can pass on those savings to their customers. There are several alternative terms used for neobanks such as Digital banks, Online banks, Challenger banks, FinTech banks, App-based banks, Virtual banks, Digital-only banks, Branchless banks, and Non-traditional banks.

Neobanks aim to differentiate themselves from traditional banks by offering competitive interest rates on savings accounts, lower fees, and more flexible and personalized financial services. They may also leverage advanced technologies, such as artificial intelligence and machine learning, to provide more personalized and efficient services to their customers. Many neobanks are FinTech companies that have obtained banking licenses, allowing them to offer banking services. However, some neobanks partner with traditional banks to provide their services.

Neobanks vs. Traditional Banks

Traditional banks and neobanks are two different types of financial institutions with unique characteristics and business models. This section explains some of the main differences between the two.

Physical Presence

One of the most significant differences between traditional banks and neobanks is their physical location. Traditional banks have an extensive network of branches and ATMs, whereas neobanks do not have physical branches and operate solely through digital channels. Traditional banks have been around for centuries, and their business model has primarily relied on building physical branches in various locations to serve their customers. These branches are staffed with employees who provide customer service, handle transactions, and offer financial advice. They also have a network of ATMs that customers can use to withdraw cash, deposit checks, and perform other transactions. In contrast, neobanks do not have physical branches and operate primarily through digital channels, such as mobile apps and websites. They do not have any physical locations that customers can visit, and all their services are offered online. Instead of visiting a branch, customers can perform most banking tasks, such as opening an account, transferring money, or paying bills, through their mobile app or website. Some neobanks may partner with other financial institutions to provide access to ATMs, but they do not have their own ATM network. The lack of physical branches is one of the reasons why neobanks can offer lower fees. Traditional banks have significant expenses related to building and maintaining physical branches, which can be passed on to customers in the form of higher fees and lower interest rates. In contrast, neobanks can operate at lower costs as they do not have to bear these expenses, which allows them to offer more competitive pricing. However, the lack of physical branches can be a disadvantage for some customers who prefer to do their banking in person or need assistance with complex financial products. Traditional banks offer personalized customer service through their branch employees, who can provide financial advice, resolve issues, and help customers with their banking needs. In contrast, neobanks offer customer service through digital channels such as chatbots and messaging services, which may not be as personalized as traditional bank customer service.

Fee Structures

Traditional banks charge a variety of fees, including monthly maintenance fees, ATM fees, overdraft fees, wire transfer fees, and foreign transaction fees. These fees can add up quickly and can be a significant burden for customers. For example, a customer may have to pay a monthly maintenance fee, an ATM fee, and an overdraft fee, which can add up to a few hundred dollars in fees annually. Neobanks, on the other hand, often have lower or no fees. Many challenger banks offer fee-free checking accounts and do not charge monthly maintenance fees or ATM fees. They may also offer other fee-free services, such as free wire transfers or free foreign transactions. This can result in significant cost savings for customers, especially those who frequently use their bank accounts for transactions. In addition to lower fees, neobanks may also offer higher interest rates on savings and checking accounts. They may also offer cashback rewards and other incentives for using their services, which can further benefit customers. However, it is important to note that, while neobanks may offer lower fees, they may have limited services compared to traditional banks. For example, they may not offer as many financial products, such as loans or mortgages, or have a limited network of ATMs. They may also have stricter eligibility criteria for opening an account or may not offer joint accounts or overdraft protection.

Financial Products

Traditional banks offer a wide range of financial products, such as checking accounts, savings accounts, certificates of deposit, credit cards, loans, mortgages, investment products, and insurance. They also offer financial advice and planning services, and many have a team of financial advisors who work with customers to develop personalized investment plans. In contrast, neobanks typically offer a more limited range of products and services, with a focus on basic banking services such as checking and savings accounts, and some offer credit cards and personal loans. Some neobanks may also offer investment products, but generally do not offer as wide a range of investment products as traditional banks. However, neobanks may offer some advantages in terms of the ease and convenience of opening and managing accounts. Many neobanks offer instant account opening, and customers can manage their accounts entirely through digital channels, such as mobile apps and websites. They also often have more intuitive and user-friendly interfaces, making it easier for customers to manage their finances. Ultimately, the choice between traditional banks and neobanks depends on the individual's needs and preferences. If a customer is looking for a wide range of financial products and personalized financial advice, a traditional bank may be a better fit. On the other hand, if a customer is looking for low fees and the convenience of digital banking, a neobank may be a better option.

Customer Service

Traditional banks and neobanks differ in their approach to customer service. Traditional banks typically have more extensive customer service offerings, with physical branch locations, telephone customer service, and online chat support. They also often have a team of financial advisors who can offer personalized advice and support to customers. However, traditional banks may also have longer wait times for customer service and may be less responsive to customer feedback. Neobanks, on the other hand, often offer more convenient and efficient customer service through digital channels, such as in-app chat support or 24/7 customer service hotlines. They may also have shorter wait times for customer service inquiries and may be more responsive to customer feedback. However, neobanks may have limitations in their customer service offerings. They may not have physical branch locations or in-person support, which can be a disadvantage for customers who prefer face-to-face interactions.

Size

Traditional banks are typically much larger in terms of assets and market capitalization compared to neobanks. Many traditional banks have been in business for decades, if not centuries, and have grown to become some of the largest financial institutions in the world. For example, JPMorgan Chase, one of the largest banks in the US, has over $3.7 trillion in assets and a market capitalization of over $400 billion. Similarly, HSBC, one of the largest banks in the world, has over $2.5 trillion in assets and a market capitalization of over $100 billion. In contrast, neobanks are relatively new and smaller in size compared to traditional banks. While some neobanks have achieved significant growth in recent years, they are still relatively small compared to the largest traditional banks. For example, Chime, a popular US-based challenger bank, has over 12 million customers and a valuation of $14.5 billion, but has only around $1 billion in deposits. Similarly, Revolut, a UK-based challenger bank, has over 16 million customers worldwide but has total assets of around $2 billion. It's worth noting, however, that the size of a bank does not necessarily reflect its ability to provide high-quality financial services or offer competitive pricing.

Technology

Traditional banks and neobanks differ significantly in terms of the technology they employ to provide financial services. Traditional banks often rely on legacy IT systems that have been developed over many years, making them difficult to update or replace. As a result, traditional banks can struggle to keep up with rapidly evolving technological advances and provide modern, user-friendly digital banking experiences. Neobanks, on the other hand, are typically built on modern technology stacks that enable them to provide more innovative and user-friendly digital banking experiences. They often offer mobile-first or mobile-only platforms, allowing customers to manage their finances entirely from their smartphones. This approach enables challenger banks to offer streamlined and personalized user experiences, such as real-time spending insights, instant money transfers, and other features that are difficult for traditional banks to replicate. Additionally, neobanks often leverage data and artificial intelligence (AI) to improve their services. For example, they may use AI-powered algorithms to analyze customer data and provide personalized recommendations or investment advice.

Reputation

Traditional banks and neobanks differ in terms of their reputation, largely due to differences in their histories, size, and public perceptions. Traditional banks, especially those that have been around for decades or centuries, often have established reputations that are built on a long history of providing financial services to customers. These banks are generally considered to be stable, reliable, and trustworthy. However, traditional banks have also been involved in a number of high-profile scandals, such as the 2008 financial crisis and various cases of misconduct, which have damaged their reputations. In contrast, neobanks are relatively new and do not have the same established reputations as traditional banks. However, they are often viewed as more innovative and customer-focused, which has helped to build a positive reputation in the market. Neobanks are generally seen as more agile and able to respond quickly to changing customer needs, as well as being more transparent in their operations. That being said, some customers may have concerns about the safety and security of their funds with neobanks, especially if they are not familiar with the brand or are used to traditional banking models. Additionally, neobanks are often viewed as riskier due to their smaller size and lack of established track record.

Digital Banking vs. Neobanks

Digital banking could include traditional banks that have adopted digital technologies to provide banking services to their customers. Digital banking services may include online account management, mobile banking apps, online bill payment, and digital wallets. Digital banking has been around for decades, but they have become increasingly important in recent years due to the rise of mobile devices and the internet. Many traditional banks have invested heavily in digital technologies to improve their services and compete with other banks that operate primarily through digital channels. It is worth noting that for digital banking, physical branch locations where customers can go to open accounts, deposit cash, and speak with bank representatives in person still exist. Additionally, it offers traditional banking services such as checking and savings accounts, loans, credit cards, and other financial products. It also offers online and mobile banking services that allow customers to manage their accounts, transfer money, pay bills, and perform other banking functions. On the other hand, neobanks, also known as challenger banks, are a newer type of financial institution that operates primarily through digital channels. They are often startups or FinTech companies that have obtained banking licenses to offer financial services. They aim to disrupt the traditional banking industry by offering innovative and user-friendly digital banking services that are more accessible and affordable than those offered by traditional banks.

Neobanks Products

This section explores some of the innovative products and services offered by neobanks that are transforming the financial industry.

Digital-Only Bank Accounts

One of the most fundamental products offered by neobanks is digital-only bank accounts. These accounts can be opened and managed entirely through a mobile app or website, without the need to visit a physical branch. Neobanks typically offer a range of account types, including checking, savings, and credit accounts, each with its own set of features and benefits. Digital-only bank accounts provide a number of advantages over traditional bank accounts. They are typically easier and more convenient to use, with features like instant account activation and easy online transfers. They also tend to have lower fees and better interest rates, making them an attractive option for customers looking to save money.

Instant Money Transfers

Another key product offered by neobanks is instant money transfers. These transfers allow customers to send and receive money quickly and easily, often within seconds. Neobanks typically offer both domestic and international money transfers, with lower fees and faster processing times than traditional banks. Instant money transfers are particularly useful for customers who need to make urgent payments or send money to family and friends in other countries. They are also ideal for freelancers and small businesses that need to receive payments quickly and efficiently.

Savings Goals and Automatic Savings

Many neobanks offer features that allow customers to set savings goals and automatically transfer money to reach those goals. These features make it easier for customers to save money and achieve their financial goals. For example, some neobanks allow customers to set specific savings goals, such as saving for a vacation or a down payment on a house. The bank will then automatically transfer a set amount of money from the customer's checking account to their savings account each month, helping them to reach their goal without even thinking about it.

Budgeting Tools

Another innovative product offered by neobanks is budgeting tools. These tools help customers track their spending and manage their finances more effectively. For example, some neobanks provide real-time alerts when a customer exceeds their budget for a particular category, such as groceries or entertainment. Other neobanks provide insights into a customer's spending habits, such as how much they spend on dining out each month or how much they spend on online shopping. These insights can help customers make more informed financial decisions and identify areas where they can cut back on spending.

Personalized Financial Advice

Some neobanks use artificial intelligence (AI) algorithms to provide personalized financial advice and investment recommendations to customers. These algorithms analyze a customer's financial data, including their spending habits and income, and provide tailored advice to help them achieve their financial goals. For example, a neobank might recommend a particular investment strategy based on a customer's risk tolerance and financial objectives. Alternatively, the bank might suggest ways to reduce debt or increase savings based on the customer's spending habits and income.

Cryptocurrency Integration

Several neobanks offer cryptocurrency integration, allowing customers to buy, hold, and sell cryptocurrencies through their bank account (for example N26, the German neobank headquartered in Berlin). This is an increasingly popular feature, as more and more people become interested in cryptocurrencies as a form of investment or as a way to make purchases. By offering cryptocurrency integration, neobanks are able to provide a convenient and secure way for customers to buy and sell cryptocurrencies without having to use a separate exchange. They can also offer competitive fees and more user-friendly interfaces than traditional cryptocurrency exchanges.

Foreign Currency Accounts

Some neobanks offer multi-currency accounts that allow customers to hold and manage multiple currencies within a single account, making it easier and more affordable to make international transactions.

Round-Up Savings

Round-up savings are a feature that allows you to automatically save small amounts of money from your daily transactions. Whenever you make a purchase with your debit card, the transaction is rounded up to the nearest dollar, and the extra change is transferred to your savings account. Some neobanks like Monzo, Starling Bank, and Revolut offer this feature to help users save money without even noticing it.

International Money Transfers

One of the biggest advantages of using a neobank is the ability to make international money transfers at a fraction of the cost of traditional banks. Traditional banks typically charge high fees and offer unfavorable exchange rates, which can be a hassle for those who frequently transfer money overseas. However, neobanks like TransferWise and Revolut offer low-cost international transfers and competitive exchange rates, making it easier for users to send money abroad.

Technological Infrastructure

Neobanks, or challenger banks, rely heavily on technology to provide their services to customers. Therefore, a robust technological infrastructure is essential for neobanks to operate effectively. This section explains some of the key technological infrastructure crucial to the operations of neobanks.

Cloud Computing

Cloud computing can be incredibly important for neobanks, for several reasons. First, neobanks are often small, agile organizations that need to move quickly to compete with larger, more established banks. Cloud computing can provide them with the flexibility and scalability they need to grow their business without the high upfront costs associated with traditional IT infrastructure. This can help them to bring new products and services to the market faster, which can be critical in a highly competitive market. Second, cloud computing can provide neobanks with access to powerful tools and resources that might otherwise be out of reach. For example, they can use cloud-based analytics platforms to gain insights into customer behavior and preferences, which can help them to tailor their offerings and improve customer satisfaction. They can also use cloud-based security tools to protect against cyber threats and comply with regulations, which is critical in a highly regulated industry. Third, cloud computing can help neobanks to lower their costs by reducing the need for on-premise infrastructure and IT staff. This can be particularly important for smaller banks that may not have the resources to invest in expensive IT systems. By leveraging cloud services, they can access enterprise-level infrastructure and support without the high costs typically associated with these services.

Application Programming Interfaces (APIs)

APIs enable different software systems to communicate and share data with each other. APIs allow neobanks to easily integrate with other financial services providers and third-party applications. This can help them to offer a wider range of products and services to their customers without having to build everything in-house. For example, they could partner with a payments provider to offer their customers a seamless payment experience or integrate with a personal finance management tool to provide customers with insights into their spending habits. APIs can help neobanks to improve the customer experience by providing a more seamless, integrated experience across different channels and devices. By exposing their services through APIs, they can enable customers to access their accounts and perform transactions through a variety of channels, such as mobile apps, websites, and chatbots. APIs can also help challenger banks to improve their internal operations by enabling better data sharing and collaboration across different systems and departments. For example, they could use APIs to connect their customer relationship management (CRM) system with their transaction processing system to provide more personalized customer service. Finally, APIs can help challenger banks to stay competitive and innovative by enabling them to rapidly experiment with new products and services. By exposing their services through APIs, they can quickly iterate on new features and test them with a small group of customers before rolling them out more broadly.

Mobile Apps

Neobanks are mobile-first, which means that their mobile apps are the primary interface through which customers interact with the bank. Therefore, the mobile app must be user-friendly, intuitive, and offer all the necessary features and functionalities. Mobile apps enable neobanks to provide customers with a convenient, on-the-go banking experience. With more people using their mobile devices to manage their finances, having a well-designed mobile app is essential for any bank, including neobanks. Mobile apps can provide customers with access to their accounts, the ability to perform transactions, and a variety of other features that can enhance the banking experience. Mobile apps can help neobanks to differentiate themselves from more traditional banks by offering innovative features and services. For example, they could offer mobile-only accounts or allow customers to easily split bills with their friends through the app. These types of features can help neobanks to attract a younger, tech-savvy demographic that is looking for a more modern banking experience. Mobile apps can help neobanks to reduce their costs by enabling them to provide customer support through self-service channels. With a well-designed mobile app, customers can perform many tasks on their own, such as checking their balance, transferring funds, and paying bills. This can reduce the need for customer service representatives, which can help to lower operating costs. Finally, mobile apps can provide neobanks with valuable insights into customer behavior and preferences. By tracking how customers use the app and which features they use most frequently, neobanks can gain insights that can help them to improve the app and better serve their customers.

Artificial Intelligence (AI) and Machine Learning (ML)

AI and ML can help neobanks to better understand their customers and personalize their offerings. By analyzing customer data, such as transaction history and spending habits, AI and ML algorithms can identify patterns and make predictions about what products and services customers might be interested in. This can enable neobanks to offer more targeted and relevant products, which can improve customer satisfaction and loyalty. AI and ML can help neobanks to improve fraud detection and prevention. By analyzing patterns in customer behavior and transaction data, AI and ML algorithms can quickly identify suspicious activity and alert bank staff. This can help to prevent fraud before it occurs and reduce the risk of financial losses. AI and ML can help neobanks to automate routine tasks and improve operational efficiency. For example, they could use AI-powered chatbots to handle customer inquiries and support requests, freeing up staff to focus on more complex tasks. They could also use ML algorithms to optimize their lending decisions, identifying the most creditworthy borrowers and reducing the risk of default. Finally, AI and ML can help neobanks to stay competitive and innovative by enabling them to rapidly experiment with new products and services. By analyzing customer data and testing new features with a small group of customers, neobanks can quickly iterate on new ideas and bring them to market faster than more traditional banks.

Cybersecurity

Neobanks are operating on a digital-only basis, which means that they are entirely reliant on online platforms and technology to provide their services. This makes them particularly vulnerable to cyber-attacks, as any disruption to their systems can quickly lead to a loss of customer trust and business. Neobanks often lack the resources and expertise of more established banks, which can make them an attractive target for cyber criminals. Without robust cybersecurity measures in place, they may be more vulnerable to attacks, which can result in the theft of sensitive customer data or financial losses. Neobanks are subject to the same regulatory requirements as more established banks when it comes to data protection and cybersecurity. Failure to comply with these regulations can result in significant fines and damage to the bank's reputation. To address these risks, neobanks must invest in robust cybersecurity measures that can protect their systems, data, and customers from cyber-attacks. This includes implementing strong encryption protocols, using multi-factor authentication, and regularly testing their systems for vulnerabilities. Neobanks should also ensure that their staff are trained in cybersecurity best practices and that they have a robust incident response plan in place to respond quickly and effectively in the event of a cyber-attack.

Personnel Expertise Composition

The employee expertise needed for traditional banks and neobanks differs significantly due to the distinct business models and operational priorities of each type of financial institution. This section describes some of the key differences in the employee expertise needed for traditional banks vs. neobanks.

Digital Banking Expertise

Neobanks rely heavily on digital platforms and technologies to provide their services, so it's essential to have employees with expertise in mobile app development, UX (user experience)/UI (user interface) design, digital marketing, and analytics. In contrast, traditional banks may have a less emphasis on digital banking expertise since they have already established their digital presence and may have a large customer base that prefers in-person banking.

Regulatory and Compliance Experts

Both traditional and neobanks are subject to regulatory requirements, but neobanks may require employees with more expertise in regulatory compliance due to their newer operating models and disruptive technologies. Additionally, challenger banks may need employees who can navigate regulatory environments in different countries or regions, as they may be expanding their operations globally.

Risk Management Experts

Risk management is essential for both traditional and neobanks. However, neobanks may require employees with more expertise in managing cybersecurity risks due to their reliance on digital platforms and technologies. They may also need employees with expertise in managing operational risk due to their less-established operating models.

Financial Experts

Both traditional and neobanks require employees with expertise in finance. However, traditional banks may require more employees with experience in managing complex financial products and services, such as investment banking or wealth management. In contrast, neobanks may require employees with experience in developing innovative financial products and services that cater to the needs of their customers.

Customer Service Experts

Both traditional and neobanks require employees with expertise in customer service. However, neobanks may require more employees with expertise in customer experience design, as they differentiate themselves from traditional banks by offering customer-centric services and may need to be more responsive to customer feedback.

Data Scientists and Analysts

Neobanks collect vast amounts of data on their customers and their transactions, so it's crucial to have employees with expertise in data analysis. Traditional banks may also require employees with expertise in data analysis, but may have more established data management and analysis processes.

Product Management Experts

Neobanks are constantly innovating and developing new products and services, so it's essential to have employees with expertise in product management. Traditional banks may also require employees with expertise in product management, but they may have more established processes for product development and launch.

Human Resources Experts

Both traditional and neobanks require employees with expertise in human resources. However, neobanks may require employees with more expertise in managing a fast-growing, entrepreneurial culture, as they are typically smaller and more agile than traditional banks.

Neobanks and e-KYC

One of the key features of neobanks is their use of technology to provide seamless and convenient services to customers. Electronic Know Your Customer (e-KYC) is one such technology that has been instrumental in the growth and success of neobanks. This section explores the role of e-KYC in neobanks.

What Is e-KYC?

KYC is a process that banks, and other financial institutions used to verify the identity of their customers. KYC requirements are in place to prevent money laundering, fraud, and other illegal activities. Traditional KYC involves physical document verification, which can be time-consuming and inconvenient for customers. E-KYC, on the other hand, is a digital process that allows customers to verify their identity using electronic means. E-KYC works by using various technologies, including biometrics, Artificial Intelligence (AI), and Machine Learning (ML), to verify the customer's identity. This process involves the collection of personal information from the customer, such as name, address, and identification documents, which are then verified against government databases or other sources. The customer's biometric information, such as fingerprints or facial recognition, is also collected and verified to ensure that the person is who they claim to be.

Benefits of e-KYC for Neobanks

Here are some of the potential uses and benefits that e-KYC offers for neobanks:

- Enhanced Customer Experience: e-KYC is a faster and more convenient process than traditional KYC, which can take days or even weeks to complete. By using e-KYC, challenger banks can offer a seamless and hassle-free onboarding process for their customers.
- Cost Savings: e-KYC eliminates the need for physical document verification, which can be a costly and time-consuming process for banks. By using e-KYC, challenger banks can reduce their operational costs and pass on the savings to their customers.
- Improved Security: e-KYC uses advanced technologies, such as biometrics and AI, to verify the customer's identity. This process is more secure than traditional KYC, which is susceptible to fraud and identity theft.
- Compliance: e-KYC is compliant with regulatory requirements, such as AML regulations. This ensures that challenger banks are operating within the legal framework and are not at risk of regulatory penalties.

Challenges of e-KYC for Challenger Banks

While e-KYC has several benefits, it also presents some challenges for challenger banks, including:

- Technical Challenges: e-KYC requires the use of advanced technologies, such as biometrics and AI, which can be expensive and complex to implement. Challenger banks may need to invest in new technologies and expertise to implement e-KYC effectively.
- Data Privacy: e-KYC involves the collection and storage of sensitive customer information, such as biometric data. Challenger banks must ensure that they comply with data privacy regulations and protect their customers' data from unauthorized access and misuse.

- Accessibility: e-KYC may not be accessible to all customers, particularly those who do not have access to smartphones or the internet. Challenger banks must provide alternative methods of KYC verification for these customers.
- Security Risks: e-KYC involves the use of sensitive customer information, which makes it a target for cybercriminals. Challenger banks must implement robust security measures to protect against data breaches and cyber-attacks.

Global Cases of Neobanks

This section is dedicated to introduce some of the global cases of neobanks with a brief description of each.

Revolut

Revolut is a UK-based challenger bank that was founded in 2015. It offers a range of financial services, including currency exchange, debit cards, and money transfers. Revolut has gained popularity for its low fees and user-friendly app, which allows customers to manage their finances easily. Revolut has raised over $900 million in funding and has a valuation of $33 billion, making it one of the most valuable FinTech startups in Europe. It has over 15 million customers worldwide and has expanded its services to the US, Australia, and Singapore. Revolut has disrupted the traditional banking industry by offering lower fees and more transparency. Its user-friendly app has also made it popular among millennials and tech-savvy customers.

Chime

Chime is a US-based challenger bank that was founded in 2013. It offers a variety of financial services, including checking and savings accounts, debit cards, and personal loans. Chime has gained popularity for its no-fee banking and early access to paychecks. Chime has raised over $1.5 billion in funding and has a valuation of $14.5 billion, making it one of the most valuable FinTech startups in the US. It has over 12 million customers and has partnered with several US retailers to offer cashback rewards to its customers. Its early access to paychecks has also helped customers avoid overdraft fees and other penalties.

N26

N26 is a German-based challenger bank that was founded in 2013. It provides a range of financial services, including checking and savings accounts, debit cards, and insurance. N26 has gained popularity for its user-friendly app and transparent fees. N26 has raised over $800 million in funding and has a valuation of $3.5 billion. It has over 7 million customers worldwide and has expanded its services to several European countries and the US. N26 has disrupted the traditional banking industry by offering lower fees and more flexibility in banking services.

Monzo

Monzo is a UK-based challenger bank that was founded in 2015. It provides a number of different financial services, including checking and savings accounts, debit cards, and loans. Monzo has gained popularity for its user-friendly app and transparent fees. Monzo has raised over $600 million in funding and has a valuation of $2 billion. It has over 5 million customers and has expanded its services to the US. Monzo has disrupted the traditional banking industry by offering lower fees and more flexibility in banking services.

Ally Bank

Ally Bank is a US-based neobank that was founded in 2004. It offers a range of financial services, including checking and savings accounts, debit cards, and loans. Ally Bank has over 2 million customers and has consistently been recognized for its customer service and low fees. Ally Bank has also been innovative in its use of technology, such as its virtual assistant, Ally Assist, which can help customers with their banking needs through voice or chat commands.

Neobanks and SMEs

Small and Medium Enterprises (SMEs) play a vital role in the economy, and their success is crucial for economic growth and job creation. However, SMEs often struggle with access to financing and banking services, as they may not meet the requirements of traditional banks or may not have the collateral to secure loans. This is where challenger or neobanks can help. These banks offer innovative products and services that cater to the specific needs of SMEs, making banking more accessible and convenient for them. For example, some challenger banks offer invoice financing, which allows SMEs to access cash by selling their outstanding invoices to the bank. This provides immediate liquidity, which is especially important for SMEs with tight cash flow. Other banks offer loans based on business performance data, rather than collateral or credit scores. Traditional banks often charge high fees for banking services, which can be a significant burden for SMEs. Neobanks, however, typically have lower fees or no fees at all, making banking more affordable for SMEs.

Neobanks also offer streamlined processes that make banking more convenient and accessible for SMEs. They typically have user-friendly apps and online platforms that allow SMEs to manage their finances and banking needs from anywhere, at any time. They also often have dedicated customer service teams that can provide guidance and assistance on a range of financial topics.

While challenger neobanks offer many benefits to SMEs, they also face some challenges in supporting them. Neobanks often have limited resources compared to traditional banks. This can make it challenging for them to provide the same level of services and support to SMEs. They are subject to the same regulatory requirements as traditional banks. However, they may have less experience and resources to navigate complex regulatory frameworks. This can be particularly challenging for SMEs that may require more support and guidance.

Following are a few examples of neobanks supporting SMEs:

- OakNorth is a UK-based neobank that provides financing to SMEs through its lending platform. The bank uses data analytics and machine learning to assess credit risk and offer flexible financing options to SMEs. OakNorth also provides a range of business advisory services to help SMEs grow and expand.

- Kabbage is a US-based digital lender that provides small business loans to SMEs. The company uses a range of data sources to assess creditworthiness and offer loans based on business performance data, rather than collateral or credit scores. Kabbage also offers a range of financial tools and services to help SMEs manage their finances and grow their businesses.
- Revolut Business is a UK-based neobank that offers business accounts to SMEs with no monthly fees, no minimum balances, and no transaction fees. The bank also offers a range of features and services designed specifically for SMEs, including invoice management, expense tracking, and integrated accounting software.
- Novo is a US-based neobank that offers banking services to SMEs. The bank provides free business checking accounts with no hidden fees and a range of features designed to help SMEs manage their finances more efficiently. Novo also offers integrations with popular business tools and platforms, such as Stripe and Shopify.

Neobanks: Disruptive or Sustaining Innovation

Neobanks, have been disrupting the traditional banking industry in recent years. However, there has been some debate about whether these banks are truly disruptive or merely sustaining innovation. In this section, we argue that challenger banks are primarily sustaining innovation rather than disruptive innovation.

First, it is important to define what is meant by disruptive innovation. Disruptive innovation refers to the introduction of a new product or service that fundamentally changes the existing market, often by creating a new market or disrupting an existing one. Disruptive innovation typically involves a low-end disruption, where a new entrant targets a less demanding segment of the market and gradually moves upmarket as it gains traction. On the other hand, sustaining innovation refers to the improvement of existing products or services to better meet the needs of existing customers. Sustaining innovation may lead to incremental improvements in performance, quality, or functionality, but it does not fundamentally change the existing market or create a new one.

Challenger banks have been disrupting the traditional banking industry by offering alternative banking services that are more convenient, affordable, and accessible than those offered by traditional banks. However, these alternative banking services are primarily sustaining innovation rather than disruptive innovation. First, challenger banks are not fundamentally changing the existing banking market or creating a new one. Instead, they are offering alternative banking services that are more convenient, affordable, and accessible than those offered by traditional banks. For example, challenger banks offer mobile banking apps that allow customers to access their accounts and make transactions from anywhere, at any time. They also offer lower fees, no minimum balance requirements, and faster loan approvals than traditional banks. However, these alternative banking services are not fundamentally changing the existing banking market or creating a new one. Instead, they are improving the existing banking market by providing better customer experiences and more innovative products and services. Traditional banks are also able to adopt these alternative banking services and offer them to their customers, which suggests that challenger banks are not fundamentally disrupting the banking industry. Second, challenger banks are primarily targeting less demanding segments of the market and gradually moving upmarket as they gain traction. This is consistent with a low-end disruption strategy, which is a type of disruptive innovation. However, the fact that challenger banks are primarily targeting fewer demanding segments of the market suggests that they are not fundamentally disrupting the existing banking market. For example, many challenger banks have started by offering basic banking services, such as checking accounts and debit cards, to consumers who are underserved or overlooked by traditional banks. As they gain traction and build their customer base, they may gradually expand their product offerings to include more sophisticated banking services, such as loans, mortgages, and investment products. While this low-end disruption strategy is consistent with a type of disruptive innovation, it does not fundamentally change the existing banking market or create a new one. Instead, it is a sustaining innovation that improves the existing banking market by providing better customer experiences and more innovative products and services. Finally, traditional banks are able to adopt many of the alternative banking services offered by challenger banks, which suggests that challenger banks are not fundamentally disrupting the banking industry. Traditional banks are able to offer mobile banking apps, lower fees, and faster loan approvals, among other services, in response to the competition from challenger banks.

In conclusion, while challenger banks have been disrupting the traditional banking industry by offering alternative banking services that are more convenient, affordable, and accessible than those offered by traditional banks, these alternative banking services are primarily sustaining innovation rather than disruptive innovation. Challenger banks are not fundamentally changing the existing banking market or creating a new one, and their low-end disruption strategy is consistent with a type of disruptive innovation, but not one that fundamentally changes the existing market. Therefore, it is important to understand the limitations of the challenger bank model and not overestimate their disruptive nature.

References

Ady. (2023). *NeoBanks vs traditional banks–What's the difference?* Diro.

Antosz, D. (2023). *What is a neobank? How FinTech is transforming banking*. Plaid.

Arun, T., Markos, S., Murinde, V., Kostov, P., Khan, A., & Ari, N. (2023). Impact of Neo-banks (digital banks): India-UK comparison. In *Policy paper 1-UK India Fintrade* (pp. 1–34).

Banerjee, R., Majumdar, S., & Albastaki, M. (2022). Ideal self-congruence: Neobanking by traditional banks and the impact on market share: A case of UAE Banks. *International Journal of Professional Business Review, 7*(4), 1–21. https://doi.org/10.26668/businessreview/2022.v7i4.e779

Banga, C., Beena, F., Manchandani, P., & Shukla, V. (2023). Growth and future of neo banks-a survey. *Proceedings of 3rd IEEE International Conference on Computational Intelligence and Knowledge Economy, ICCIKE 2023*, 467–472. https://doi.org/10.1109/ICCIKE58312.2023.10131692

Barbarawi, N. (2022). *Altering overdraft fee policies to promote consumer financial health*. The University of Arkansas.

Barodawala, Y. A. (2022). Neo banking: An innovative window of banking arena. *Global Journal of Interdisciplinary Studies, V*(III), 27–33.

Beyer, F. J. G. (2022). *Optimizing the business model of neobanks in Germany*. Nova School of Business and Economics.

Bhattacharjee, A., Chung, V., Singh, S., & Thomas, R. (2022). *Building a winning AI neobank*. McKinsey & Company.

Bradford, T. (2020). Neobanks: Banks by any other name? *Federal Reserve Bank of Kansas City, 12*.

Cat, H. (2022). *Adopting new ways of working to meet evolving banking customer expectations*. Linkedin.

Chong, T. (2023). *Unpacking neobanks for SMEs*. Medium.

Dzulhidayat. (2022). *Optimizing the business model of neobanks in Germany: Increasing the monetization of clients by product portfolio expansion* (pp. 1–125). Nova School of Business and Economics.

Elinzano, G. B. O., & Ching, M. R. D. (2022). Factors that leads to adoption and use of online bank account opening through e-KYC using UTAUT and its extensions. *RSF Conference Series: Engineering and Technology, 2*(1), 85–94. https://doi.org/10.31098/cset.v2i1.508

Fugkeaw, S. (2022). Enabling trust and privacy-preserving e-KYC system using blockchain. *IEEE Access, 10*, 49028–49039. https://doi.org/10.1109/ACCESS.2022.3172973

Goel, V. (2021). *Deconstructing technology stack of a neobank*. Twimbit.

Gorodianska, L. V., Nosenko, T., & Vember, V. (2019). Neobanks operations and security features. *2019 IEEE International Scientific-Practical Conference: Problems of Infocommunications Science and Technology, PIC S and T 2019—Proceedings*, 839–842. https://doi.org/10.1109/PICST47496.2019.9061268

Haefliger, R. (2020). *In the banking sector, what skill set will be required for human advisors to succeed in a more digitalized industry?* (pp. 1–102). Haute école de gestion de Genève (HEG-GE).

Hannan, M. A., Shahriar, M. A., Ferdous, M. S., Chowdhury, M. J. M., & Rahman, M. S. (2023). A systematic literature review of blockchain-based e-KYC systems. *Computing, 105*(10), 2089–2118. https://doi.org/10.1007/s00607-023-01176-8

Huebner, J., Vuckovac, D., Fleisch, E., & Ilic, A. (2019). FinTechs and the new wave of financial intermediaries. *Proceedings of the 23rd Pacific Asia Conference on Information Systems: Secure ICT Platform for the 4th Industrial Revolution, PACIS 2019*.

Jagrič, T., & Amon, A. (2023). Key factors of neobanking's occurrence. *Journal of Innovative Business and Management, 15*(1). https://doi.org/10.32015/JIBM.2023.15.1.1

Kümpers, J.-L. (2022). *Optimizing the business model of neobanks in Germany: Ways to reduce dependencies on BaaS providers* (pp. 1–132). Nova School of Business and Economics.

Langjahr, T. (2023). *Customer Experience (CX) for FinTechs & Neobanks*. Majorel.

Leonhardt, M. (2021). *Considering a 'neobank' or FinTech? The lowdown on the fees, perks, and long-term prospects of challenger banks*. Fortune.

Lin, C. (2022). *Financial products marketing in neobanks*. SimTrade Blog.

Lindström, V., & Nilsson, O. (2023). *The sudden rise of neobanks and the threat it poses upon the traditional banking system*. Jonkoping University.

Louis, J. E., & Jang, B. (2022). A comparative legal study on neobank between South Korea and Indonesia. *Journal of Law and Policy Transformation, 7*(1), 109. https://doi.org/10.37253/jlpt.v7i1.6753

Maiti, M., Vuković, D., Mukherjee, A., Paikarao, P. D., & Yadav, J. K. (2022). Advanced data integration in banking, financial, and insurance software in the age of COVID-19. *Software—Practice and Experience, 52*(4), 887–903.https://doi.org/10.1002/spe.3018

Malyshev, A. (2023). *Neobanking: Stats, future & top software solutions in 2023. SDK. Finance.*

Meijer, K. (2021). *Customer acceptance of Neobanks: What role does national culture play?* (p. 69). University of Twente. http://essay.utwente.nl/87910/

Melethil, A. (2023). *Customer experience—Game changer for neobanks in retail.* Finextra.

Monis, E., & Pai, R. (2023). Neo Banks: A paradigm shift in banking. *International Journal of Case Studies in Business, IT, and Education, 7*(2), 318–332. https://doi.org/10.47992/ijcsbe.2581.6942.0275

Morozko, Y. (2023). *Neobank technology: Architecture, integrations, and tools for building a banking app.* Jatapp.

MSME. (2022). Neobank for SMEs open joins Razorpay, Mswipe, others to get RBI approval for payment aggregator license. *Financial Express.*

Nwosu, C. P., Evbuomwan, O. O., & Bosha, E. O. (2022). FinTech and financial stability in Nigeria: A case study of Neobanks. *Central Bank of Nigeria, Abuja, 234*, 1–18.

Pajila, P. J. B., & Julie, E. G. (2020). Intelligent communication technologies and virtual mobile networks. *Proceedings of ICICV 2023, 33*, 438–452. http://link.springer.com/10.1007/978-3-030-28364-3

Pearson, S. (2020). *Technology and the rise of neobanks.* Medium.

Precious, E. (2022). *Neobanks vs Traditional Banks.* AskWallet.Io.

Prove. (2021). *The rise of neo/digital banks that cater only to SMEs.* Prove.

Rajasekhar, Y., Sekhar, K. C., Ranil, G., Maneesh, L. V. N., & Venu, K. (2023). Enabling trust and privacy preserving e-KYC. *International Journal of Research in Engineering, IT and Social Sciences, 13*(5), 250–261.

Riemann, J. C. (2021). *An examination of critical factors influencing the future usage intention of innovative digital financial solutions for investment activities* (pp. 1–86). Nova School of Business and Economics.

Schweinbacher, L. (2021). *Strategic business models in European banking industry: business model optimization for neobanks* (pp. 1–83). Nova School of Business and Economics.

Shanmugam, S., & Supervisor, D. (2022). Digital transformation through FinTech: An analytical study. *Shodhsamhita: Journal of Fundamental & Comparative Research, VIII*(1), 2022.

Sowjanya, T. (2023). Neo banking—A new era of financial services. *International Research Journal of Humanities and Interdisciplinary Studies, 4*(2), 137–140.
Temelkov, Z. (2020a). Differences between traditional bank model and FinTech based digital bank and neobanks models. *SocioBrains, 5721*(74), 8–15.
Temelkov, Z. (2020b). Overview of neobanks model and its implications for traditional banking. *Third International Scientific Conference*, 156–165.
Thakkar, J. (2023). Impact of rapidly changing supply chain management methods, ethics and digital marketing strategies on the fast fashion industry. *Annual Research Journal of SCMS, February*.
Théaud, B. (2023). *What is a Neobank? How it works, examples, pros & cons*. Statrys.
Tierney, S., Burnette, M., Bessette, C., & Sarreal, R. (2023). *16 Neobanks or banking FinTech firms and what they offer*. Nerdwallet.
Tyzack, T. (2023). *A new genre of talent for the neobank*. Tyzackpartners.
Why are SMEs turning towards Neobanking? (2023). *ZikZuk*.

CHAPTER 7

Digital Currencies' Implications for the Monetary System and Financial Stability

Introduction

Inspired by recent initiatives taken by various central banks to issue their own version of digital currencies, along with rapid developments in the cryptocurrency market, this chapter aims at identifying and discussing the implications of such transformations on the monetary system and financial stability. Thus, the discussions in this chapter distinguish between privately issued virtual currencies and digital currencies issued by central banks in terms of their potential risk and opportunities.

Although it is acknowledged that major risks by cryptocurrencies to the conduct of monetary policy appear to be less likely, considering the relatively small scale of this market and characteristics which limit their function as a stable medium of exchange such as volatility; however, the risks can materialize in case of increasing demand for cryptocurrencies and the development of underlying technologies which correct their current deficiencies and increase their popularity and strengthen their role as a suitable substitute and alternative to official currencies. Consequently, the autonomous decisions of private issuers can disrupt money supply and diminish the ability of central banks to effectively implement their monetary policies.

This possibility of weakened transmission of monetary policy and reduced control of central banks over a portion of economy due to widespread adoption of privately issued virtual currencies has forced

B. Naysary and A. Tarazi, *The Digital Finance Era*,
https://doi.org/10.1007/978-981-97-3970-7_7

central banks to respond, and CBDC has been in the forefront of their policies to counter these adverse impacts. To this end, CBDC has the potential to maintain the effectiveness of monetary policy by reducing the incentives to adopt cryptocurrencies; however, there are still uncertainties and questions surrounding the feasibility and consequences of replacing cash with CBDC, which are equally covered in this chapter.

Cryptocurrency and Monetary Policy

Cryptocurrencies have emerged as a new form of digital currency that operates independently of traditional financial institutions and government regulations. They have significant implications for monetary policy, as they challenge the traditional role of central banks in regulating the money supply and managing the economy. This section explains some of the potential implications of cryptocurrency on monetary policy.

Reduced Control of Central Banks

The emergence of cryptocurrencies has significant implications for the role of central banks in the global financial system. Cryptocurrencies, such as Bitcoin, are decentralized and operate independently of traditional financial institutions, which reduces the control that central banks have over the money supply and the economy. Central banks are responsible for regulating the money supply and managing the economy. They do this by adjusting interest rates, influencing lending, and controlling the amount of money in circulation. These tools are designed to ensure price stability and promote economic growth. However, cryptocurrencies operate outside of the traditional financial system, which limits the ability of central banks to regulate the money supply and implement monetary policy.

One of the principal ways in which cryptocurrencies reduce the control of central banks is by decentralizing the money supply. Cryptocurrencies are created through a process called mining, which involves solving complex mathematical equations to verify transactions and generate new units of currency. Unlike traditional currencies, which are controlled by central banks, the supply of cryptocurrencies cannot be adjusted by any single entity. This decentralized nature of cryptocurrencies challenges the traditional role of central banks as the sole regulators of the money supply. Central banks have traditionally used their control over the money supply to influence interest rates and regulate the economy. However, cryptocurrencies operate outside of this system and are not subject to the same regulatory controls. This reduces the ability of central banks to influence the money supply and implement monetary policy.

Regulatory uncertainty is another potential implication of the reduced control of central banks because of cryptocurrencies. Cryptocurrencies operate in a largely unregulated environment, which can create uncertainty and increase the risk of market manipulation, fraud, and other illegal activities. This can undermine the stability of the financial system and erode confidence in cryptocurrencies as a viable alternative to traditional currencies. The rise of cryptocurrencies has also led to concerns about financial system fragmentation. As cryptocurrencies gain in popularity, they may create a separate financial system that operates independently of the traditional financial system. This could lead to a situation where some users are excluded from the traditional financial system, which could exacerbate financial inequality and increase the risk of financial instability. Moreover, the reduced control of central banks because of cryptocurrencies also has implications for cross-border payments and exchange rates. Cryptocurrencies are not subject to the same exchange rate mechanisms as traditional currencies, which can lead to greater volatility in exchange rates. This can create challenges for businesses that operate across borders and rely on stable exchange rates to manage their operations.

Impact on Inflation

The emergence of cryptocurrencies has brought about significant changes to the global financial landscape, challenging the traditional role of central banks and the conventional financial system. One of the most significant impacts of cryptocurrencies is on inflation, which has been a key focus of monetary policy for central banks around the world. Inflation is defined as the rate at which the general level of prices for goods and services is rising, and subsequently, the purchasing power of money is falling. Central banks aim to maintain stable inflation rates by using monetary policy tools such as adjusting interest rates and the money supply. Historically, central banks have primarily used traditional currencies to control inflation. However, with the emergence of cryptocurrencies, this approach may no longer be sufficient.

One of the primary ways in which cryptocurrencies are affecting inflation is by their supply mechanism. Cryptocurrencies are produced through the process of mining. This stands in contrast to traditional currencies, where central banks can adjust the money supply by printing more money. The supply of cryptocurrencies may lead to pressures, which could affect inflation rates. The supply pattern of cryptocurrencies dictates that they are not subject to the same inflationary pressures as traditional currencies. This has led some to argue that cryptocurrencies could be a hedge against inflation. In times of inflation, where the value of traditional currencies is decreasing, the value of cryptocurrencies may hold steady or even increase, making them a potentially attractive investment for those seeking to preserve their wealth. However, it is important to note that cryptocurrencies are still subject to market forces and can experience significant volatility. This can lead to large price swings that can affect their value as a store of value or hedge against inflation.

Another way in which cryptocurrencies are affecting inflation is by creating new forms of demand for goods and services. As cryptocurrencies become more widely adopted, they are creating new markets for goods and services that were previously difficult to monetize. This could lead to increased demand for these goods and services, which could affect inflation rates. Moreover, cryptocurrencies are also making it easier for people to engage in cross-border transactions. This is particularly important for people living in countries with weak or unstable currencies, where it can be difficult to engage in international trade. The ability to use cryptocurrencies to engage in cross-border transactions could lead to increased demand for goods and services, which could also impact inflation rates.

One potential approach for central banks is to regulate cryptocurrencies to ensure that they do not cause instability in the financial system. This could include implementing regulations around cryptocurrency exchanges and requiring cryptocurrencies to adhere to the same anti-money laundering and counter-terrorism financing regulations as traditional financial institutions. By regulating cryptocurrencies, central banks could potentially reduce the impact of cryptocurrencies on inflation and maintain stability in the financial system. Another potential approach for central banks is to develop their own digital currencies. Central banks in several countries are currently exploring the possibility of creating their own digital currencies. These digital currencies would be controlled by central banks and would function similarly to traditional currencies. By creating their own digital currencies, central banks could maintain control over the money supply and potentially reduce the impact of cryptocurrencies on inflation.

Difficulty in Implementing Monetary Policy

The rise of cryptocurrencies has created significant challenges for central banks in implementing monetary policy. Central banks are responsible for maintaining price stability, controlling inflation, and managing economic growth. However, the emergence of cryptocurrencies has disrupted the traditional methods by which central banks implement monetary policy. One of the primary difficulties that cryptocurrencies present for central banks is their decentralized nature. Cryptocurrencies operate on a distributed ledger technology known as blockchain, which is a decentralized network of computers that verifies and records transactions. This means that cryptocurrencies are not controlled by any central authority, such as a central bank. As a result, central banks are unable to directly influence the supply of cryptocurrencies, which makes it difficult for them to implement their monetary policies. In traditional monetary policy, central banks use interest rates to control inflation. If inflation is too high, central banks can increase interest rates to reduce demand for goods and services, which in turn reduces inflation. Conversely, if inflation is too low, central banks can decrease interest rates to stimulate demand and increase inflation. However, this approach does not work with cryptocurrencies because central banks have no control over the supply of cryptocurrencies.

Another difficulty that cryptocurrencies present for central banks is their anonymity. Cryptocurrencies are often used for illegal activities such as money laundering and terrorism financing because they allow users to remain anonymous. This anonymity makes it difficult for central banks to monitor and regulate cryptocurrency transactions. Additionally, cryptocurrencies are known for their volatility, which can make it difficult for central banks to predict how changes in the market will impact the economy. For example, if the price of Bitcoin were to suddenly plummet, this could cause a significant decrease in consumer spending, which would impact inflation. However, because central banks have no control over the supply or price of cryptocurrencies, they cannot predict or prevent such events.

Moreover, cryptocurrencies pose a challenge to central banks' ability to control capital flows. In traditional monetary policy, central banks can influence capital flows by adjusting interest rates and exchange rates.

However, cryptocurrencies are not subject to the same regulations as traditional financial institutions, which means that capital flows can be difficult to control. For example, if a country experiences a sudden influx of capital through cryptocurrencies, this could cause an appreciation in the currency, which could negatively impact the country's exports. Furthermore, cryptocurrencies create challenges for central banks in terms of their ability to monitor and track economic activity. This makes it difficult for central banks to gather accurate information about economic activity, which in turn makes it difficult to implement monetary policy.

Cryptocurrency and Financial Stability

The emergence of cryptocurrencies has significant implications for financial stability, as they present both opportunities and challenges for the traditional financial system. This section explains some key implications of cryptocurrency for financial stability.

Volatility

The high volatility of cryptocurrencies has significant implications for financial stability. One of the most significant risks associated with cryptocurrency volatility is the potential for systemic risk. Systemic risk refers to the risk that a disruption in one part of the financial system could spread to other parts of the system, leading to a broader financial crisis. Cryptocurrency markets are highly interconnected with other financial markets, and a sudden collapse in the value of cryptocurrencies could potentially lead to a wider financial crisis.

Moreover, the high volatility of cryptocurrencies can make it difficult for financial institutions to manage risk. Financial institutions such as banks, hedge funds, and other investors often hold cryptocurrencies as part of their portfolio. However, the high volatility of cryptocurrencies can make it difficult for these institutions to accurately assess the value of their holdings or manage risk effectively. This can lead to financial instability and potential losses for these institutions. Additionally, the high volatility of cryptocurrencies can also impact consumer and investor confidence. If consumers and investors perceive cryptocurrencies as being highly risky, they may be less likely to invest in or use them. This can lead to a decline in demand for cryptocurrencies, which can further exacerbate volatility and potentially lead to a wider financial crisis.

Furthermore, the high volatility of cryptocurrencies can also impact the broader economy. For example, a sudden decline in the value of cryptocurrencies can lead to a decline in wealth for individuals and businesses that hold cryptocurrencies. This can lead to a decline in consumer spending and investment, which can impact economic growth and stability. Additionally, the high volatility of cryptocurrencies can also make it more difficult for governments to regulate financial markets effectively. The high volatility of cryptocurrencies can particularly impact the stability of the financial system in developing countries. Developing countries often have weaker financial systems and less regulation, which can make them more vulnerable to financial instability. It can exacerbate these vulnerabilities, potentially leading to financial crises and economic instability.

Cybersecurity

The rise of cryptocurrencies has brought about numerous benefits such as decentralization, increased efficiency, and lower transaction costs. However, it has also created new vulnerabilities, specifically with regard to cybersecurity. One of the most significant risks associated with cryptocurrencies is the potential for cyber-attacks. Cyber attackers can exploit weaknesses in the cryptocurrency system to gain unauthorized access, steal digital currencies, and disrupt the functioning of the system. For example, in January 2018, the Japanese cryptocurrency exchange Coincheck lost $534 million worth of digital currencies due to a cyber-attack.[1] Such attacks can have severe consequences for the individuals and businesses who hold cryptocurrencies, as well as the broader financial system.

Furthermore, the impact of cyber-attacks on financial institutions can be amplified by the interconnectivity of the financial system. Cyber-attacks on financial institutions can spread quickly, potentially leading to a wider financial crisis. As cryptocurrencies become increasingly integrated into the financial system, the potential impact of cyber-attacks on digital currencies can become more significant. The lack of regulation in the cryptocurrency market can make it more difficult for policymakers to address cybersecurity risks effectively.

[1] https://www.cnbc.com/2018/01/26/japanese-cryptocurrency-exchange-loses-more-than-500-million-to-hackers.html.

Regulatory Uncertainty

Cryptocurrencies have been around for over a decade, and their use has expanded exponentially in recent years. Despite their growth, the regulatory framework for cryptocurrencies remains uncertain, particularly in many developing countries. This lack of regulatory clarity can impact the stability of the financial system in various ways. For example, regulatory uncertainty surrounding cryptocurrencies can impact the ability of financial institutions to provide services related to digital currencies. Financial institutions, such as banks, are subject to regulatory requirements, including anti-money laundering (AML) and Know Your Customer (KYC) regulations, to prevent illegal activities such as money laundering and terrorism financing. The lack of regulatory clarity can make it challenging for financial institutions to determine how to comply with these regulations when dealing with cryptocurrencies. As a result, many financial institutions may avoid providing services related to cryptocurrencies altogether, which can limit the accessibility of digital currencies and impede the growth of the cryptocurrency market. Furthermore, the lack of regulatory clarity can create an environment in which bad actors can thrive. For example, without clear regulations on cryptocurrency exchanges, unscrupulous individuals can take advantage of loopholes to engage in fraudulent activities, such as market manipulation, insider trading, and pump-and-dump schemes. These activities can destabilize the cryptocurrency market, causing harm to innocent investors and disrupting the broader financial system.

Regulatory uncertainty can make it challenging for law enforcement agencies to investigate and prosecute illegal activities related to cryptocurrencies. Without clear regulations, it can be difficult to determine the legal status of cryptocurrencies, making it more challenging to track their flow and prevent their use in illegal activities. This lack of clarity can lead to a perception that cryptocurrencies are a haven for illicit activities, which can further harm investor confidence in the market and impede the growth of the cryptocurrency market.

Additionally, regulatory uncertainty can also impact the development of innovative technologies and services related to cryptocurrencies. Many FinTech startups have emerged to offer services, such as cryptocurrency wallets, trading platforms, and payment systems. However, these companies may be hesitant to invest in new technologies and services due to regulatory uncertainty. This can slow down innovation in the cryptocurrency market, potentially stifling its growth and limiting its impact on the broader financial system.

Disintermediation

Cryptocurrencies have disrupted traditional financial systems, primarily through their ability to disintermediate financial transactions. Disintermediation refers to the process of removing intermediaries or middlemen from a transaction, making it more direct and efficient. The use of cryptocurrencies has enabled individuals and businesses to conduct financial transactions without the need for traditional financial intermediaries, such as banks or payment processors. While disintermediation can lead to increased efficiency and lower transaction costs, it can also impact financial stability.

One significant impact of disintermediation is the reduced role of traditional financial intermediaries. With the rise of cryptocurrencies, individuals and businesses can now transact directly with one another, reducing the need for traditional financial intermediaries. This has led to concerns among financial regulators that traditional financial institutions may become less relevant, leading to a loss of financial stability. Moreover, disintermediation can lead to a shift in the balance of power in the financial system. With the ability to transact directly, individuals and businesses may have more control over their financial transactions, reducing the power of traditional financial intermediaries. This shift in power can create uncertainty in the financial system, particularly if traditional intermediaries fail to adapt to the changing landscape. Additionally, it may lead to a lack of accountability for bad actors, who may use cryptocurrencies to engage in illegal activities such as money laundering and terrorist financing.

CBDC and Monetary Policy

CBDC is a centralized digital currency that is fully regulated and controlled by the central bank. One of the primary impacts of CBDC on monetary policy is that it provides central banks with greater control over the money supply. With the issuance of CBDC, central banks can monitor and manage the money supply more efficiently, enabling them to implement monetary policy more effectively. CBDC can provide central banks with greater transparency and visibility into financial transactions, enabling them to better manage the money supply and control inflation.

CBDC can provide central banks with greater flexibility in implementing monetary policy. CBDC can be programmed to have specific features, such as expiry dates, transaction limits, and restrictions on the use of funds. This flexibility can enable central banks to implement more targeted and nuanced monetary policy, enabling them to respond more effectively to economic conditions. Furthermore, CBDC can enable central banks to reduce the cost of issuing and managing currency. With the introduction of CBDC, central banks can reduce the cost of printing and distributing physical currency, enabling them to allocate resources to other areas. This cost reduction can lead to increased efficiency and lower costs for the central bank, potentially enabling them to pass on these savings to consumers in the form of lower fees and charges.

Additionally, CBDC can enable central banks to improve financial inclusion. CBDC can provide individuals and businesses with access to digital financial services, enabling them to participate in the financial system more easily. This increased access to financial services can promote financial inclusion, enabling individuals and businesses to access credit and savings products more easily, potentially leading to increased economic growth. CBDC can enable central banks to improve the speed and efficiency of cross-border payments. Cross-border payments are currently slow and expensive, with high fees and long settlement times. However, there are potential risks and challenges associated with the introduction of CBDC. For instance, the increased availability of CBDC may lead to bank runs during periods of financial stress, as individuals and businesses may prefer to hold their funds in the digital currency rather than depositing them in a bank. Additionally, CBDC may reduce the demand for traditional banking services, leading to financial disintermediation and potentially destabilizing the financial system.

CBDC and Financial Stability

The development of CBDC has been driven by the increasing use of digital payments, the growth of cryptocurrencies, and the desire for central banks to maintain control over their monetary systems. The implications of CBDC for financial stability are complex and multifaceted. On the one hand, CBDC has the potential to enhance financial stability by providing a more secure and reliable means of payment, reducing transaction costs, and increasing the efficiency of the payments system. CBDC could also reduce the need for cash, which is often associated with illicit activities such as money laundering and tax evasion. On the other hand, the introduction of CBDC could also pose risks to financial stability. For example, if CBDC were to replace physical cash, it could increase the likelihood of bank runs and other forms of financial instability. CBDC could also lead to the concentration of payment systems in the hands of a few large players, potentially reducing competition and increasing systemic risk. Another potential risk of CBDC is that it could lead to disintermediation of the financial system, whereby individuals and businesses bypass banks and other intermediaries to access central bank money directly. This could reduce the role and profitability of banks, leading to a consolidation of the banking sector and potentially reducing the availability of credit. CBDC could also have an impact on cross-border payments and foreign exchange markets. If CBDC were to be widely adopted, it could reduce the role of traditional currencies in international transactions, potentially leading to a reduction in demand for foreign exchange and increasing exchange rate volatility.

Stablecoins and Monetary System

Stablecoins

Stablecoins are digital currencies that are designed to maintain a stable value against a certain asset or basket of assets. They achieve this stability by either holding the underlying asset in reserve, or by using algorithms to adjust the supply of the stablecoin in response to changes in demand, thereby maintaining a stable price.

Impact on Monetary Policy

Stablecoins can have an impact on monetary policy in a number of ways. One of the main ways is by providing an alternative store of value and means of payment to traditional fiat currencies. If stablecoins were to become widely adopted as a means of payment, this could reduce the demand for central bank money, which would have implications for monetary policy. Central banks typically implement monetary policy by adjusting the supply of money in the economy. By controlling the supply of money, central banks can influence interest rates and inflation. However, if stablecoins were to become widely used as a means of payment, this could reduce the demand for central bank money, which would make it more difficult for central banks to control the supply of money in the economy. For example, if a stablecoin pegged to the US dollar became widely adopted as a means of payment, this could reduce the demand for US dollars and US dollar-denominated assets, which could make it more difficult for the Federal Reserve to control the supply of US dollars in the economy. In this scenario, the Federal Reserve may need to adjust its monetary policy tools to take into account the impact of stablecoins on the demand for central bank money.

Another way stablecoins can impact monetary policy is by influencing the velocity of money. The velocity of money is the rate at which money is exchanged in the economy. If stablecoins were to become widely used as a means of payment, this could increase the velocity of money, as transactions can be processed faster and more efficiently than with traditional fiat currencies. This could make it more difficult for central banks to control inflation, as an increase in the velocity of money could lead to an increase in prices. Additionally, stablecoins can also affect the transmission mechanism of monetary policy. The transmission mechanism is the process by which changes in the supply of money are transmitted to the real economy, such as through changes in interest rates or credit availability. If stablecoins were to become widely used, this could change the transmission mechanism of monetary policy, as changes in the supply of central bank money may have a different impact on the real economy compared to changes in the supply of stablecoins.

Impact on Financial Stability

Stablecoins are designed to address the volatility that is inherent in cryptocurrencies and offer the potential benefits of blockchain technology while also providing the stability of traditional currencies. However, stablecoins also raise concerns regarding their impact on financial stability, particularly as they become more widely adopted and integrated into the financial system.

One potential impact of stablecoins on financial stability is the risk of a run on the stablecoin. If there is a sudden loss of confidence in the stablecoin issuer or the stability of the reference asset, users may rush to redeem their stablecoins for the reference asset, potentially causing the stablecoin to lose its peg and creating a systemic risk. This risk is heightened if the stablecoin issuer operates with limited reserves, meaning that it may not have sufficient assets to honor all redemption requests. Another potential risk is the impact of stablecoins on the traditional banking system. Stablecoins could potentially compete with traditional bank deposits, as they offer similar functionalities, such as a stable store of value and a means of payment. This could lead to a shift in demand away from bank deposits, reducing the amount of deposits that banks hold and potentially leading to a reduction in their ability to lend. This could have a negative impact on the overall stability of the banking system.

Furthermore, stablecoins could also raise concerns about money laundering and terrorism financing, as they provide a means of anonymous, cross-border transactions. Finally, stablecoins could also raise concerns about financial fragmentation and instability, particularly if different stablecoins begin to emerge, each with their own reference asset and exchange rate. This could lead to a complex and fragmented financial system, with potential cross-border payment issues and exchange rate risks.

References

Adachi, M., Cominetta, M., Kaufmann, C., & van der Kraaij, A. (2020). *A regulatory and financial stability perspective on global stablecoins*. European Central Bank.

Afzal, A. (2019). Cryptocurrencies, blockchain and regulation: A review. *The Lahore Journal of Economics*, *24*(1), 103–130. https://doi.org/10.35536/lje.2019.v24.i1.a5

Ahnert, T., Hoffmann, P., & Leonello, A. (2023). *CBDC and financial stability*. European Central Bank.

Akdag, M., & Bozma, G. (2022, April). Central bank digital currency and monetary policy. *Ardahan Üniversitesi İktisadi ve İdari Bilimler Fakültesi Dergisi*, *4*, 75–80.

Al Ayub Ahmed, A., Paruchuri, H., Vadlamudi, S., & Ganapathy, A. (2021). Cryptography in financial markets: Potential channels for future financial stability. *Academy of Accounting and Financial Studies Journal*, *25*(4), 1–9.

Assenmacher, K. (2020). Monetary policy implications of digital currencies. *SUERF Policy Note*, *165*, 1–9.

Azar, P. D., Baughman, G., Carapella, F., Gerszten, J., Lubis, A., Perez-Sangimino, J. P., Scotti, C., Swem, N., Vardoulakis, A., & Rappoport Wurgaft,

D. E. (2022). The financial stability implications of digital assets. *SSRN Electronic Journal, 1034*. https://doi.org/10.2139/ssrn.4234695
Beniak, P. (2019). Central bank digital currency and monetary policy: A literature review. *Munich Personal RePEc Archive, 96663*, 1–11.
Benigno, P. (2022). Monetary policy in a world of cryptocurrencies. *Journal of the European Economic Association, 21*(2002), 1363–1396. https://doi.org/10.1093/jeea/jvac066
Bordo, M., & Levin, A. (2017). *Central bank digital currency and the future of monetary policy* (NBER Working Paper No. 23711, pp. 1–32).
Chen, H., & Siklos, P. L. (2022). Central bank digital currency: A review and some macro-financial implications. *Journal of Financial Stability, 60* (January 2021), 100985. https://doi.org/10.1016/j.jfs.2022.100985
Dabrowski, M., & Janikowski, L. (2018, July). Virtual currencies and central banks monetary policy: Challenges ahead. *Policy Department for Economic, Scientific and Quality of Life Policies*, 33.
Davoodalhosseini, M., Rivadeneyra, F., & Zhu, Y. (2020). *CBDC and Monetary Policy*. Bank of Canada.
Davoodalhosseini, S. M. (2022). Central bank digital currency and monetary policy. *Journal of Economic Dynamics and Control, 142*, 104150. https://doi.org/10.1016/j.jedc.2021.104150
Dirk, K. A. P., & Bullmann, J. (2011). Crypto-Assets: Implications for financial stability, monetary policy, and payments and market infrastructures. *European Central Bank, 22*.
ECB Crypto-Assets Task Force. (2020). *Stablecoins: Implications for monetary policy, financial stability, market infrastructure and payments, and banking supervision in the Euro area*. European Central Bank.
Echelpoel, F. van E., Chimienti, M. T., Adachi, M. M., Athanassiou, P., Balteanu, I., Barkias, T., Ganoulis, I., Kedan, D., Neuhaus, H., Pawlikowski, A., Philipp, G., Poignet, R., Sauer, S., Schneeberger, D., Tapking, J., & Toolin, C. (2021). Stablecoins: Implications for monetary policy, financial stability, market infrastructure and payments, and banking supervision in the Euro area. *SSRN Electronic Journal*.
Elsayed, A. H., & Sousa, R. M. (2022). International monetary policy and cryptocurrency markets: Dynamic and spillover effects. *European Journal of Finance*. https://doi.org/10.1080/1351847X.2022.2068375
Fama, M., Fumagalli, A., & Lucarelli, S. (2019). Cryptocurrencies, monetary policy, and new forms of monetary Sovereignty. *International Journal of Political Economy, 48*(2), 174–194. https://doi.org/10.1080/08911916.2019.1624318
Fry, J., & Cheah, E. T. (2016). Negative bubbles and shocks in cryptocurrency markets. *International Review of Financial Analysis, 47*, 343–352. https://doi.org/10.1016/j.irfa.2016.02.008

Garratt, R., Yu, J., & Zhu, H. (2022). The case for convenience: How CBDC design choices impact monetary policy pass-through. *Bank for International Settlements, 1046.*

Giudici, G., Milne, A., & Vinogradov, D. (2020). Cryptocurrencies: Market analysis and perspectives. *Journal of Industrial and Business Economics, 47*(1), 1–18. https://doi.org/10.1007/s40812-019-00138-6

Grobys, K., Junttila, J., Kolari, J. W., & Sapkota, N. (2021, September). On the stability of stablecoins. *Journal of Empirical Finance, 64*, 207–223. https://doi.org/10.1016/j.jempfin.2021.09.002

Halal Cryptocurrency Management. (2019).

He, D. (2018). Monetary policy in the digital age: Crypto assets may one day reduce demand for central bank money. *IMF Finance & Development, 55*(2), 13–16.

Hellwig, M. (2022). Monetary policy and sustainability. *Wirtschaftsdienst, 102*(5), 341–343. https://doi.org/10.1007/s10273-022-3185-5

Huber, J. (2023). *The monetary turning point: From bank money to central bank digital currency (CBDC)* (pp. 1–198). Springer Nature Switzerland.

Jacobs, G. (2018). Cryptocurrencies & the challenge of global governance. *Cadmus, 3*(4), 109–123.

Jagtiani, J., Papaioannou, M., Tsetsekos, G., Dolson, E., & Milo, D. (2021). Cryptocurrencies: Regulatory perspectives and implications for investors. In *The Palgrave handbook of technological finance* (pp. 161–186). Springer International Publishing.

Jonas Gross, J. S. (2021). A Model for central bank digital currencies: Implications for bank funding and monetary policy. *SSRN Electronic Journal*, 1–46.

Kaili, E., & Psarrakis, D. (2021). *Disintermediation economics: The impact of blockchain on markets and policies*. Palgrave Macmillan.

Kang, K.-Y., & Lee, S. (2019). Money, cryptocurrency, and monetary policy. *SSRN Electronic Journal*.

Kim, Y. S., & Kwon, O. (2023). Central bank digital currency, credit supply, and financial stability. *Journal of Money, Credit and Banking, 55*(1), 297–321. https://doi.org/10.1111/jmcb.12913

Kumhof, M., & Noone, C. (2021). Central bank digital currencies—Design principles for financial stability. *Economic Analysis and Policy, 71*, 553–572. https://doi.org/10.1016/j.eap.2021.06.012

Lucey, B. M., Vigne, S. A., Yarovaya, L., & Wang, Y. (2022). The cryptocurrency uncertainty index. *Finance Research Letters, 45*(May 2021), 102147. https://doi.org/10.1016/j.frl.2021.102147

Lyons, R. K., & Viswanath-Natraj, G. (2023). What keeps stablecoins stable? *Journal of International Money and Finance, 131*, 102777. https://doi.org/10.1016/j.jimonfin.2022.102777

MacDonald, C., & Zhao, L. (2023). Stablecoins and their risks to financial stability. *SSRN Electronic Journal*. https://doi.org/10.2139/ssrn.4466522

Malloy, M., Martinez, F., Styczynski, M.-F., & Thorp, A. (2022). *Retail CBDC and US monetary policy implementation: A stylized balance sheet analysis* (Finance and Economics Discussion Series 032, pp. 1–17). https://doi.org/10.17016/feds.2022.032

Meaning, J., Dyson, B., Barker, J., & Clayton, E. (2018). Broadening narrow money: Monetary policy with a central bank digital currency. *Bank of England, 724*.

Mikhaylov, A., Danish, M. S. S., & Senjyu, T. (2021, February). A new stage in the evolution of cryptocurrency markets: Analysis by Hurst method. *Strategic Outlook in Business and Finance Innovation: Multidimensional Policies for Emerging Economies*, 35–45. https://doi.org/10.1108/978-1-80043-444-820211004

Nelson, B. (2018, June). Financial stability and monetary policy issues associated with digital currencies. *Journal of Economics and Business, 100*, 76–78. https://doi.org/10.1016/j.jeconbus.2018.06.002

Ngo, V. M., Van Nguyen, P., Nguyen, H. H., Thi Tram, H. X., & Hoang, L. C. (2023). Governance and monetary policy impacts on public acceptance of CBDC adoption. *Research in International Business and Finance, 64*(May 2022), 101865. https://doi.org/10.1016/j.ribaf.2022.101865

Nguyen, T. V. H., Nguyen, B. T., Nguyen, K. S., & Pham, H. (2019). Asymmetric monetary policy effects on cryptocurrency markets. *Research in International Business and Finance, 48*(December 2018), 335–339. https://doi.org/10.1016/j.ribaf.2019.01.011

Nguyen Thanh, B., Perera, D., Nguyen Thanh, P., Nguyen, T. V. H., Pham Thi Thu, T., Nguyen Thi My, L., Chu, T. T., & Kiong Kok, S. (2023). Monetary policy in the age of cryptocurrencies. *SSRN Electronic Journal*. https://doi.org/10.2139/ssrn.4407460

Niepelt, D. (2021, November). Monetary policy with reserves and CBDC: Optimality, equivalence, and politics. *SSRN Electronic Journal*. https://doi.org/10.2139/ssrn.3740324

Noam, E. M. (2019). The macro-economics of crypto-currencies: Balancing entrepreneurialism and monetary policy. *SSRN Electronic Journal*. https://doi.org/10.2139/ssrn.3493333

Ozili, P. K. (2023a). Assessing global and local interest in eNaira CBDC and cryptocurrency information: Implications for financial stability. *Journal of Internet and Digital Economics*. https://doi.org/10.1108/jide-10-2022-0019

Ozili, P. K. (2023b). CBDC, FinTech and cryptocurrency for financial inclusion and financial stability. *Digital Policy, Regulation and Governance, 25*(1), 40–57. https://doi.org/10.1108/DPRG-04-2022-0033

Perkins, D. W. (2020). Cryptocurrency: The economics of money and selected policy issues. *Congressional Research Service*, 1–32.

Pernice, I. G. A., Henningsen, S., Proskalovich, R., Florian, M., Elendner, H., & Scheuermann, B. (2019). Monetary stabilization in cryptocurrencies—Design approaches and open questions. *Proceedings—2019 Crypto Valley Conference on Blockchain Technology, CVCBT 2019*, 47–59. https://doi.org/10.1109/CVCBT.2019.00011

Pfister, C. (2017, September). Monetary policy and digital currencies: Much ado about nothing? *SSRN Electronic Journal*. https://doi.org/10.2139/ssrn.3038906

Pravdiuk, M. (2021). International experience of cryptocurrency regulation. *Norwegian Journal of Development of the International Science, 53*(6), 31–36.

Saadah, S., & Ahmad Whafa, A. A. (2020). Monitoring financial stability based on prediction of cryptocurrencies price using intelligent algorithm. *2020 International Conference on Data Science and Its Applications, ICoDSA 2020*. https://doi.org/10.1109/ICoDSA50139.2020.9212968

Sauer, B. (2016). Virtual currencies, the money market, and monetary policy. *International Advances in Economic Research, 22*(2), 117–130. https://doi.org/10.1007/s11294-016-9576-x

Saving, T. R. (2018). *Cryptocurrencies and monetary policy* (Bruegel Policy Contribution, No. 2018/10, pp. 263–278). https://doi.org/10.1142/9789811201783_0022

Shen, W., & Hou, L. (2021). China's central bank digital currency and its impacts on monetary policy and payment competition: Game changer or regulatory toolkit? *Computer Law and Security Review, 41*, 105577. https://doi.org/10.1016/j.clsr.2021.105577

Taskinsoy, J. (2019). This time is different: Facebook's Libra can improve both financial inclusion and global financial stability as a viable alternative currency to the US dollar. *Journal of Accounting, Finance and Auditing Studies (JAFAS), 5*(4), 67–86. https://doi.org/10.32602/jafas.2019.38

Yang, J., & Zhou, G. (2022, July). A study on the influence mechanism of CBDC on monetary policy: An analysis based on e-CNY. *PLoS ONE, 17*(7), 1–27. https://doi.org/10.1371/journal.pone.0268471

Yousaf, I., Riaz, Y., & Goodell, J. W. (2023, January). What do responses of financial markets to the collapse of FTX say about investor interest in cryptocurrencies? Event-study evidence. *Finance Research Letters, 53*, 103661. https://doi.org/10.1016/j.frl.2023.103661

CHAPTER 8

FinTech and Financial Inclusion

Introduction

Financial inclusion has become a global priority, aiming to provide individuals and communities with access to affordable and appropriate financial services. However, despite ongoing efforts, a significant portion of the world's population remains financially excluded. One of the main socioeconomic challenges of the past decade, particularly for low- and middle-income economies, is the financial exclusion caused mainly due to high credit and transaction cost and distance barriers. This chapter introduces FinTech services as one of the significant players in promoting financial inclusion by providing access to faster and cheaper financial services to individuals and SMEs.

Discussions in this chapter highlight that, as a complement or substitute to traditional finance, the socioeconomic implications of FinTech go beyond financial inclusion to be positively associated with GDP growth which in turn is linked with income creation, employment, and reducing inequalities such as gender gap and exclusion of women from economic and financial circles. To depict a more thorough picture of FinTech's impact on financial inclusion, barriers to digital inclusion, including access to resources (such as smart phones and the internet), financial literacy and cultural and social determinants, are also highlighted at the end of this chapter.

B. Naysary and A. Tarazi, *The Digital Finance Era*,
https://doi.org/10.1007/978-981-97-3970-7_8

What Is Financial Exclusion?

Financial exclusion refers to the lack of access to formal financial services, including banking, credit, insurance, and savings accounts. It affects individuals and communities across the globe, hindering economic development and perpetuating social inequalities. It encompasses the barriers that prevent individuals from accessing and utilizing financial services effectively, such as lack of access to formal financial institutions, inadequate financial literacy, and exclusion from the broader financial system.

Financial exclusion can have various adverse societal and economic impacts. Limited access to banking services restricts individuals' ability to securely save, borrow, and manage their finances. Without access to formal banking channels, individuals often resort to informal or unregulated financial services, which may be unreliable, predatory, and expensive. This leads to heightened financial insecurity, as individuals lack the necessary tools and resources to build a safety net, handle emergencies, or invest in income-generating opportunities. Additionally, access to credit is crucial for entrepreneurial activities, business expansion, and investment in productive assets. Without access to formal credit, individuals and small businesses are often unable to secure capital to start or grow their ventures. This constrains economic opportunities, inhibits job creation, and hampers economic growth and development in underserved communities.

Financial exclusion could also perpetuate cycles of poverty and exacerbate existing socioeconomic disparities. Without access to affordable savings accounts, individuals find it challenging to accumulate assets and build wealth over time. This lack of financial inclusion further marginalizes disadvantaged communities, deepening income inequality and impeding social mobility. Individuals without access to banking services are more vulnerable to financial shocks and crises. They lack appropriate insurance coverage, making them susceptible to the adverse effects of emergencies, such as natural disasters, health issues, or job loss. The absence of formal financial services also limits their ability to manage and mitigate risks, leading to increased financial instability and hardship.

Without access to banking services, individuals may be excluded from participating fully in the formal economy. They may face challenges in receiving salaries, accessing government benefits, or conducting transactions with formal entities. This exclusion reinforces informality and impedes efforts to promote transparency, accountability, and economic development. Another adverse effect of financial exclusion includes hindering individuals' ability to invest in education and human capital development. Without access to affordable loans or savings products, families struggle to finance education expenses, limiting educational opportunities for themselves and their children. This perpetuates the cycle of limited access to economic opportunities and lower social mobility.

Causes of Financial Exclusion

Geographical Factors

Geographical location is a significant barrier to financial inclusion, particularly for individuals residing in rural and remote areas. In these regions, access to formal financial services is often limited or non-existent. The distance between individuals and financial institutions can be substantial, making it challenging for them to physically visit a bank branch or ATM. The cost and time required to travel to the nearest financial service provider can be prohibitive, especially for those with limited means of transportation. As a result, individuals in rural and remote areas may resort to informal financial services or cash-based transactions, which further perpetuates financial exclusion.

Financial exclusion is not limited to rural areas, but can also be observed in urban settings. Urban deserts refer to areas within cities where there is limited access to banking services. These areas are often characterized by a concentration of low-income neighborhoods and a lack of bank branches or financial service providers. The absence of accessible banking infrastructure in these communities makes it difficult for residents to access basic financial services, such as opening bank accounts, obtaining credit, or conducting financial transactions conveniently. This results in a reliance on alternative financial service providers that may charge exorbitant fees and offer limited consumer protections.

The lack of banking infrastructure in certain regions is a significant geographical barrier to financial inclusion. In some cases, financial institutions may deem certain areas unprofitable and choose not to establish branches or ATMs there. This is particularly true in underserved or economically disadvantaged regions. As a consequence, residents in these areas face limited options for accessing formal financial services. The absence of banking infrastructure not only hinders individuals' ability to save, borrow, or transact securely, but also affects businesses that require banking services to grow and thrive.

In today's increasingly digital world, connectivity and the digital divide pose additional challenges to financial inclusion. Reliable internet access is essential for individuals to utilize digital banking services and access online financial resources. However, many rural and remote areas lack adequate internet infrastructure, leading to limited internet connectivity. This lack of connectivity, commonly referred to as the digital divide, prevents individuals from accessing digital financial services and participating in the formal financial system. Additionally, disparities in digital literacy and access to digital devices further exacerbate the digital divide and hinder financial inclusion efforts in geographically disadvantaged areas.

Socioeconomic Factors

Income inequality and poverty are significant contributors to financial exclusion. In societies where a significant portion of the population lives in poverty or experiences high levels of income inequality, access to financial services becomes challenging. Low-income individuals often lack the necessary funds to meet minimum balance requirements for bank accounts or collateral for loans. Financial institutions may perceive them as risky borrowers, leading to limited access to credit.

High levels of unemployment and reliance on the informal economy also contribute to financial exclusion. Individuals without formal employment may lack the necessary documentation or stable income streams required by financial institutions. In the absence of steady jobs or regular paychecks, accessing financial services becomes difficult. Additionally, those engaged in informal economic activities, such as street vending or small-scale entrepreneurship, may face challenges in accessing financial products tailored to their needs. Financial institutions often have limited understanding of the informal sector, resulting in a lack of appropriate financial solutions for this segment of the population.

Financial education and literacy play a crucial role in enabling individuals to make informed financial decisions and navigate the formal financial system. Limited financial literacy, particularly among marginalized communities, can contribute to financial exclusion. Without an understanding of basic financial concepts, individuals may struggle to access and effectively utilize financial services. They may be unaware of the benefits and risks associated with banking products, making them vulnerable to predatory lending practices or inadequate financial planning. Lack of financial education also hinders individuals' ability to build creditworthiness, manage debt, and make sound investment decisions.

Socioeconomic discrimination and marginalization further exacerbate financial exclusion. Certain segments of society, such as racial or ethnic minorities, immigrants, and people with disabilities, may face systemic barriers that limit their access to financial services. Discriminatory practices within financial institutions can lead to biased lending decisions, restricted access to credit, and unequal treatment based on socioeconomic factors. Marginalized individuals may also experience social exclusion, limited networks, and reduced opportunities for financial inclusion. Overcoming socioeconomic discrimination and promoting inclusive practices within financial institutions are crucial steps toward addressing financial exclusion.

Cultural and Gender-Based Factors

Gender inequality is a significant barrier to financial inclusion, particularly for women. In many societies, women face discriminatory practices and cultural norms that limit their access to financial services. Gender wage gaps, limited employment opportunities, and unequal access to education can result in women having lower incomes and financial resources. Moreover, traditional gender roles often assign women the primary responsibility for household finances, yet they may have limited control over financial decision-making or access to formal financial services. Discrimination in inheritance laws and property rights further compound women's financial exclusion. Addressing gender disparities and promoting women's economic empowerment are crucial for overcoming these barriers.

Cultural norms and stigmas associated with finance and banking can also contribute to financial exclusion. In some communities, there may be a general distrust or lack of understanding of formal financial institutions. Traditional practices, beliefs, and taboos surrounding money and banking may discourage individuals from seeking out and using formal financial services. This can lead to a preference for informal financial arrangements, such as savings groups or community-based lending, which may lack transparency, security, and consumer protections. Overcoming cultural barriers requires targeted efforts to increase financial literacy, raise awareness of the benefits of formal financial services, and promote inclusive financial practices that respect cultural diversity.

The trust and perception of financial institutions can significantly impact individuals' willingness to engage with formal financial services. In some communities, historical experiences of financial exploitation, predatory lending, or unethical behavior by financial institutions have eroded trust. This mistrust can lead individuals to opt for informal financial arrangements or cash-based transactions, even when formal financial services are available. Building trust through transparent and responsible practices, ensuring fair and ethical treatment, and fostering community engagement are essential to address cultural barriers and increase financial inclusion.

Migration and transnational factors can create additional challenges for individuals in accessing financial services. Migrants often face unique financial exclusion issues, including limited access to banking services due to documentation requirements, language barriers, and cultural differences. Sending money across borders may be costly and inefficient, with limited access to affordable remittance services. Furthermore, individuals may encounter difficulties in establishing a credit history or accessing financial products and services in their new host countries. Addressing transnational financial exclusion requires collaboration between countries, regulatory frameworks that facilitate cross-border financial transactions, and initiatives to ensure the inclusion of migrants within the formal financial system.

Technological Factors

Technological factors play a significant role in financial exclusion. Limited access to technology and inadequate digital infrastructure can prevent individuals from accessing and utilizing formal financial services. In many regions, particularly in rural and remote areas, there is a lack of reliable internet connectivity, smartphones, or other digital devices necessary to engage with digital financial services. Without access to these technologies, individuals are unable to benefit from online banking, mobile payments, or other digital financial tools, thus limiting their financial inclusion.

Digital literacy is crucial for individuals to effectively navigate and utilize digital financial services. However, a significant portion of the population, particularly in low-income and marginalized communities, may lack the necessary digital skills and knowledge. Limited understanding of digital platforms, security risks, or how to use financial apps and tools can create barriers to entry and hinder the adoption of digital financial services. Addressing the digital skills gap through targeted education and training programs is essential to ensure that individuals can leverage technology for financial inclusion.

Concerns about privacy and security can also contribute to financial exclusion. Many individuals, especially those with limited experience or understanding of digital platforms, may be hesitant to share their personal and financial information online. Fear of identity theft, fraud, or misuse of personal data can discourage individuals from utilizing digital financial services. Addressing these concerns requires robust data protection regulations, secure and user-friendly digital platforms, and comprehensive consumer protection mechanisms to build trust and confidence in digital financial transactions.

While technology has the potential to promote financial inclusion, it can also inadvertently contribute to exclusion. The rapid pace of technological advancements and the digitization of financial services may leave behind individuals who are unable to keep up with these changes. Older adults, persons with disabilities, or those with limited technological proficiency may face challenges in adapting to new technologies and accessing digital financial services. Designing inclusive technologies that consider diverse user needs, ensuring user-friendly interfaces, and providing support and assistance to individuals with limited technological abilities are crucial to prevent technology-driven exclusion.

FinTech: Enabling Financial Inclusion

Increased Access to Financial Services

FinTech has significantly increased access to financial services by leveraging digital platforms and mobile technology. Individuals who were previously excluded from the formal financial system can now open digital wallets, access basic banking services, make digital payments, and even access loans and insurance products. FinTech has extended financial services to underserved populations, including those in remote areas without physical bank branches.

Cost Reduction and Efficiency Gains

Traditional financial services often involve high transaction costs and fees, making them unaffordable for low-income individuals. FinTech solutions have introduced cost-effective alternatives by minimizing the need for physical infrastructure, paperwork, and intermediaries. Mobile money platforms, for example, enable individuals to perform financial transactions at lower costs compared to traditional banking methods. The efficiency gains achieved through automation and digitization further contribute to cost reduction and affordability.

Empowerment of Underserved Communities

FinTech empowers underserved communities by providing them with the tools and resources to take control of their financial lives. By accessing digital financial services, individuals can save money securely, access credit for entrepreneurial endeavors, and make payments conveniently. FinTech solutions enable individuals to participate in the formal economy, expanding economic opportunities and improving livelihoods.

Enhanced Financial Literacy and Education

FinTech platforms often incorporate financial education and literacy components to empower users with knowledge and skills. Through user-friendly interfaces, personalized recommendations, and educational resources, individuals can develop a better understanding of financial concepts, budgeting, and savings. This enhanced financial literacy equips individuals with the necessary skills to make informed financial decisions and improve their financial well-being.

Job Creation and Economic Growth

FinTech startups have emerged as innovative disruptors in the financial industry. These startups introduce new technologies, business models, and services that create job opportunities. As FinTech companies grow, they require a skilled workforce to develop, operate, and maintain their platforms and services. This leads to the creation of jobs in areas such as software development, data analysis, cybersecurity, customer support, and digital marketing. FinTech solutions enhance efficiency and productivity within the financial sector, leading to economic growth. Automation and digitization of financial processes streamline operations, reduce manual errors, and eliminates inefficiencies. By leveraging technologies like artificial intelligence, machine learning, and big data analytics, FinTech improves decision-making processes and enhances the speed and accuracy of transactions. This increased efficiency and productivity contribute to overall economic growth.

FinTech plays a crucial role in promoting financial inclusion, bringing underserved populations into the formal financial system. By leveraging mobile devices and digital platforms, FinTech enables individuals to access banking services, make digital payments, and access credit. This inclusion leads to increased economic participation and stimulates economic growth. Individuals who were previously excluded from financial services can now save, transact, and invest, contributing to economic activity and job creation. FinTech platforms, such as peer-to-peer lending and crowdfunding, provide alternative sources of capital for individuals and small businesses. These platforms connect borrowers with lenders and investors directly, bypassing traditional financial intermediaries. By democratizing access to capital, FinTech facilitates entrepreneurship, innovation, and job creation. Small businesses can secure funding more easily, enabling them to expand their operations, invest in technology, and hire additional employees.

FinTech has also facilitated the growth of e-commerce and digital marketplaces. Online platforms enable businesses to reach a broader customer base, expand their operations, and create employment opportunities. FinTech solutions, such as secure online payment gateways and fraud prevention systems, have made online transactions safer and more convenient, further fueling the growth of e-commerce. The expansion of e-commerce and digital marketplaces stimulates economic growth and job creation across sectors. FinTech fosters a culture of innovation and entrepreneurship, leading to job creation and economic growth. The dynamic nature of the FinTech industry encourages entrepreneurs to develop new solutions, products, and services. This entrepreneurial activity drives technological advancements and generates employment opportunities. FinTech innovation also attracts investment, spurring economic growth and creating a positive ecosystem for job creation.

FinTech companies often provide services globally, generating export revenues and contributing to economic growth. FinTech solutions can be easily scaled and deployed in multiple markets, allowing companies to expand their operations internationally. This export-oriented approach creates job opportunities in areas such as sales, marketing, customer support, and localization, supporting economic growth and fostering international trade. FinTech is transforming the traditional financial sector, leading to the emergence of new roles and job opportunities. Traditional financial institutions are embracing digital transformation and integrating FinTech solutions into their operations. This transformation requires the upskilling and reskilling of the existing workforce, creating employment opportunities in areas such as data analysis, cybersecurity, compliance, and technology implementation.

FinTech Segments and Financial Inclusion

FinTech encompasses a broad range of technological innovations that disrupt and enhance the delivery of financial services. It leverages digital platforms, mobile connectivity, data analytics, artificial intelligence, and distributed ledger technology to create new financial solutions and improve existing ones. FinTech has the potential to overcome the barriers to financial inclusion by providing cost-effective, accessible, and user-friendly services. FinTech offers a variety of solutions that enable financial inclusion by addressing specific challenges and barriers. This section discusses various FinTech segments and their potential contribution to the financial inclusion.

Mobile Money and Digital Wallets

Mobile money and digital wallets play a significant role in promoting financial inclusion by providing individuals with convenient, accessible, and affordable financial services. Firstly, mobile money and digital wallets leverage mobile phone technology, which has extensive reach even in remote areas where traditional banking services are limited. Individuals can access financial services through their mobile phones, enabling them to perform transactions, such as sending and receiving money, making payments, and accessing other financial services. This accessibility ensures that individuals, including those in underserved areas, can participate in the formal financial system.

Mobile money and digital wallets also offer cost-effective alternatives to traditional banking services. These services reduce the need for physical infrastructure, such as bank branches, which can be expensive to establish and maintain. By leveraging existing mobile networks, individuals can conduct financial transactions at lower costs compared to traditional banking methods. This cost-effectiveness makes financial services more affordable for individuals with limited financial resources, contributing to their financial inclusion. They provide users with convenient and efficient ways to manage their financial transactions. Users can perform transactions at any time and from anywhere, eliminating the need for physical visits to banks or payment centers. This convenience is particularly valuable for individuals who live in remote areas or have limited mobility. Digital wallets also offer features like transaction history tracking, bill payments, and automated payments, further enhancing the efficiency of financial management.

Mobile money and digital wallets provide individuals who have limited or no access to traditional banking services an opportunity to access basic financial services. These services allow individuals to store and transfer money, make payments, and access savings and credit products. For the unbanked population, who may lack formal identification or live in areas without physical bank branches, mobile money and digital wallets offer a viable alternative for financial inclusion. Additionally, they facilitate cross-border remittances, which are vital for individuals who rely on financial support from family members working in other countries. These services enable individuals to receive remittances directly into their mobile wallets, eliminating the need for expensive and time-consuming traditional remittance channels. By simplifying and reducing the cost of remittance transactions, mobile money and digital wallets enhance financial connectivity and contribute to the economic well-being of individuals and families. And finally, mobile money and digital wallet providers often incorporate financial education and literacy components into their platforms. Through user-friendly interfaces, educational resources, and personalized recommendations, users can enhance their financial literacy and develop better financial management skills. This empowerment through education enables individuals to make informed financial decisions, utilize financial services effectively, and improve their financial well-being.

Peer-to-Peer Lending Platforms

Peer-to-peer (P2P) lending platforms have emerged as a disruptive force in the financial industry and play a significant role in promoting financial inclusion. These platforms connect borrowers directly with lenders, bypassing traditional financial intermediaries like banks. P2P lending platforms provide access to credit for individuals and businesses that may have difficulty obtaining loans through traditional channels. These platforms utilize alternative credit assessment methods, considering factors beyond traditional credit scores, such as income, employment history, and social data. This enables borrowers with limited credit history or unconventional profiles to access loans and meet their financial needs. They often have lower eligibility requirements compared to traditional financial institutions. They may offer loans to individuals who would otherwise be deemed too risky by traditional lenders. By reducing the barriers to entry, P2P lending platforms enable individuals with limited collateral, insufficient credit history, or lower income levels to access credit and meet their financial goals.

P2P lending platforms allow individuals to become lenders and invest their money directly in loans. This opens up investment opportunities to a wider range of individuals, including those who may not have access to traditional investment options. By diversifying the pool of lenders, P2P lending platforms increase the availability of funds for borrowers and create a more inclusive lending environment. Compared to the conventional financial institutions, they offer more flexibility in loan terms compared to traditional financial institutions. Borrowers can negotiate loan amounts, interest rates, repayment schedules, and other terms directly with lenders. This flexibility allows borrowers to obtain loans that align with their specific needs and financial situations, promoting financial inclusion by catering to diverse borrower requirements.

P2P lending platforms leverage technology to streamline loan application processes and reduce administrative overheads. Borrowers can apply for loans online, submit necessary documentation digitally, and receive loan approvals or rejections quickly. This efficiency reduces the time and effort required for loan processing, making the lending process more accessible and convenient for borrowers. They also transcend geographic limitations and can reach borrowers in remote or underserved areas. By operating online, these platforms can connect borrowers and lenders across different regions, eliminating the need for physical branch networks. This geographic reach expands access to credit for individuals in areas with limited banking infrastructure, promoting financial inclusion for underserved populations.

P2P lending platforms provide an alternative to informal lending sources, such as loan sharks or unregulated moneylenders. These informal lending channels often exploit borrowers with exorbitant interest rates and unfavorable terms. By offering a transparent and regulated lending platform, P2P lending provides borrowers with a safer and more affordable option, reducing their reliance on predatory lending practices.

Crowdfunding

Crowdfunding contributes to promoting financial inclusion by harnessing the collective power of individuals to fund and support projects, ventures, and social causes. Crowdfunding provides individuals, entrepreneurs, and small businesses with an alternative funding source outside of traditional financial institutions. It allows them to raise funds directly from a large number of individuals, often through online platforms. This opens up opportunities for individuals who may have limited access to capital through conventional channels, such as marginalized communities, aspiring entrepreneurs with unconventional ideas, or projects that may not fit the criteria of traditional investors or lenders.

Crowdfunding platforms enable individuals to tap into a diverse range of funding sources. Contributors can come from various backgrounds, including friends, family, local communities, or individuals interested in supporting specific causes. This diversity of funding sources reduces reliance on a single entity and allows for a broader network of support, creating opportunities for financial inclusion for individuals who may not have connections or access to traditional funding networks. Equity crowdfunding, a subset of crowdfunding, allows individuals to invest in startups, small businesses, and projects in exchange for equity or returns on their investments. This democratizes the investment landscape by enabling a wider pool of individuals, including non-accredited investors, to participate in early-stage investments that were previously limited to venture capitalists or high-net-worth individuals. This inclusivity broadens access to investment opportunities and allows individuals with varying financial means to support innovative ideas and potentially benefit from their success.

Crowdfunding platforms serve as more than just fundraising tools. They provide a platform for creators, entrepreneurs, and innovators to showcase their ideas, products, or social initiatives to a wider audience. Through the support and contributions received, these individuals can validate their concepts, gather market feedback, and refine their offerings. This iterative process enables individuals to fine-tune their projects and increase their chances of success, benefiting from the collective wisdom of the crowd. Crowdfunding is often used for social causes and community-driven initiatives. It empowers individuals and communities to support projects that align with their values and address local needs. Crowdfunding allows communities to rally around causes they care about, providing financial support to projects that aim to make a positive impact on society. This community-driven approach fosters a sense of ownership, solidarity, and empowerment, promoting financial inclusion by giving individuals a voice in supporting initiatives that matter to them.

Crowdfunding and crowdsourcing can spur entrepreneurial development and contribute to economic growth. By providing access to funding and support for innovative ideas, these platforms encourage entrepreneurship and empower individuals to turn their ideas into reality. This entrepreneurial activity can generate employment opportunities, foster innovation, and stimulate economic growth, particularly in underserved communities or regions where traditional funding sources may be limited.

Blockchain and Distributed Ledger Technology

Blockchain and distributed ledger technology (DLT) has the potential to significantly promote financial inclusion by addressing key challenges in the existing financial system. Blockchain and DLT can enable individuals to access financial services, even in underserved areas lacking traditional banking infrastructure. With a smartphone and internet connection, individuals can create digital identities on a blockchain, granting them access to a range of financial services such as digital wallets, payments, remittances, and lending. This technology reduces the need for physical bank branches and provides financial services directly to individuals, bridging the gap in financial access.

Blockchain technology provides a decentralized and transparent ledger that records and verifies transactions. This transparency reduces the risk of fraud and corruption, instilling trust in the financial system. By leveraging cryptographic algorithms, blockchain ensures the integrity and security of transactions, protecting the financial data and identities of users. This secure and transparent environment fosters confidence among individuals who may have been previously excluded from the financial system due to concerns about security and trustworthiness. Blockchain and DLT have the potential to significantly reduce transaction costs and fees associated with traditional financial services. By eliminating intermediaries and automating processes, blockchain-based transactions can be executed more efficiently, leading to cost savings that can be passed on to users. This cost reduction is particularly beneficial for individuals with limited financial resources, as it makes financial services more affordable and accessible. Blockchain and DLT can provide financial services to the unbanked population who lack formal identification or access to traditional banking services. With blockchain-based digital identities, individuals can establish their financial reputation, access credit, and participate in the formal financial system. Smart contracts on the blockchain can enable secure and transparent lending, allowing individuals without a credit history to access loans based on their verifiable transactions and reputation on the blockchain.

Blockchain technology can revolutionize cross-border payments and remittances, particularly for individuals in underserved regions who rely on remittances from family members abroad. Traditional remittance channels are often slow, expensive, and subject to high fees. Blockchain-based solutions enable faster and more cost-effective cross-border transactions, reducing fees and improving the efficiency of remittance services. This empowers individuals to send and receive money internationally, fostering financial inclusion and economic well-being. DLT provides an immutable and auditable record of transactions, promoting financial transparency and accountability. This transparency reduces the risk of corruption and helps combat illicit activities such as money laundering and fraud. By ensuring a transparent and accountable financial system, blockchain and DLT create a level playing field for individuals and businesses, particularly in regions where corruption and lack of transparency have hindered financial inclusion.

Blockchain-based platforms facilitate tokenization and fractional ownership of assets, allowing individuals to invest in assets that were traditionally inaccessible, such as real estate, art, or startups. These platforms enable fractional ownership, meaning individuals with limited funds can invest in a portion of an asset. This opens up investment opportunities to a broader range of individuals, promoting financial inclusion and wealth creation. And finally, Blockchain and DLT enable efficient and cost-effective micro-payments, making it feasible to transact small amounts of money. This capability is particularly valuable for individuals with low incomes or in the informal sector, who can access financial services such as microfinance or micro-insurance. By facilitating micro-transactions, blockchain and DLT empower individuals to engage in economic activities, accumulate savings, and mitigate financial risks.

Robo-Advisory Services

Robo-advisory services, which utilize algorithms and automation to provide investment advice and portfolio management, play a crucial role in promoting financial inclusion. Robo-advisory makes investment advice and portfolio management accessible to a wider range of individuals. Traditional financial advisory services often have high minimum investment requirements, making them inaccessible to individuals with limited financial resources. Robo-advisory platforms typically have lower minimum investment thresholds, allowing individuals to start investing in smaller amounts. This accessibility lowers the barriers to entry and enables individuals with modest savings to participate in investment opportunities. Robo-advisory services offer cost-effective investment solutions compared to traditional financial advisors. Traditional advisors typically charge high fees based on a percentage of assets under management, which can be prohibitive for individuals with smaller investment portfolios. Robo-advisory platforms often charge lower fees, as their automated nature reduces the need for human intervention. This cost-effectiveness makes professional investment advice affordable for individuals with limited financial resources, promoting financial inclusion.

Human financial advisors may exhibit biases or discrimination based on factors such as gender, race, or socioeconomic background. Robo-advisory services, being algorithm-based, are designed to be unbiased and objective. They provide investment advice based on quantitative data and algorithms, mitigating potential biases and ensuring fair and equal treatment for all users. This eliminates discriminatory practices and provides a level playing field for individuals seeking investment advice. Many robo-advisory platforms incorporate educational components to empower users with financial knowledge. These platforms often provide educational resources, articles, and tools to enhance users' understanding of investment concepts, risk management, and financial planning. By offering financial education, robo-advisory services empower individuals to make informed investment decisions and improve their financial literacy, promoting long-term financial inclusion.

Robo-advisory platforms offer customized investment portfolios based on individuals' financial goals, risk tolerance, and time horizon. By leveraging algorithms and automation, these platforms can provide personalized investment recommendations at scale. This customization allows individuals to align their investments with their specific needs and preferences, promoting inclusivity by catering to diverse investment requirements. Robo-advisory services streamline the investment process, making it simpler and more accessible. Users can set up investment accounts, monitor their portfolios, and make investment decisions through user-friendly online platforms or mobile applications. The simplified and intuitive user experience reduces barriers and makes investing more approachable for individuals who may be unfamiliar with traditional investment processes. And finally, robo-advisory services can scale their advice to accommodate a large number of users simultaneously. This scalability allows platforms to cater to a broader user base, including individuals who may have been traditionally underserved by human financial advisors due to capacity limitations. By leveraging technology, robo-advisory services can provide investment advice and portfolio management to a larger segment of the population, promoting financial inclusion on a broader scale.

Big Data Analytics and Credit Scoring

Big data analytics and credit scoring play a significant role in promoting financial inclusion by enabling a more accurate and inclusive assessment of creditworthiness. It allows financial institutions to analyze large volumes of diverse data from various sources, including transaction history, social media, and online behavior. This comprehensive analysis provides a more holistic view of an individual's financial behavior and creditworthiness, going beyond traditional credit scoring models that rely solely on limited financial data. By considering a broader range of data points, big data analytics enable a more inclusive assessment of creditworthiness, especially for individuals with limited credit history or unconventional financial profiles.

Big data analytics facilitate the development of alternative credit scoring models that incorporate non-traditional data sources. For individuals with limited access to formal financial services, alternative credit scoring models can consider factors, such as utility bill payments, rental history, or mobile phone usage patterns. By incorporating these alternative data sources, financial institutions can assess creditworthiness based on a more comprehensive and inclusive set of factors, providing opportunities for individuals who may have been excluded by traditional credit scoring models. Big data analytics enables real-time analysis of data, allowing financial institutions to make faster and more accurate lending decisions. This is particularly beneficial for individuals in urgent need of funds or facing time-sensitive financial situations. By leveraging big data analytics, financial institutions can quickly assess creditworthiness and provide timely access to credit, facilitating financial inclusion by addressing immediate financial needs.

Barriers to Digital Financial Inclusion

Digital financial inclusion refers to the availability, accessibility, and usage of digital financial services by individuals and businesses, particularly those who are underserved or financially excluded. It encompasses a range of services, including mobile banking, digital payments, online lending, insurance, and investment platforms. Digital financial inclusion aims to provide individuals with convenient, affordable, and secure access to financial products and services, enabling them to manage their finances, save, borrow, make payments, and build financial resilience; however, there are challenges and barriers which could potentially hinder the full realization of FinTech benefits for financial inclusion as discussed below.

Infrastructure Barriers

Limited access to reliable internet connectivity, particularly in rural and remote areas, hampers access to digital financial services. Slow internet speeds, connectivity gaps, and unreliable networks make it challenging for individuals to use online platforms and access digital financial tools. On the other hand, insufficient availability of digital devices, such as smartphones or computers, restricts individuals' ability to access and use digital financial services. Lack of technological infrastructure in areas with limited electricity or technological infrastructure exacerbates the digital divide. Incompatible systems and lack of interoperability among different financial service providers can limit the seamless transfer of funds and transactions between platforms. This fragmentation impedes the development of a cohesive digital financial ecosystem and restricts users' ability to access multiple services from different providers.

Financial Literacy

Limited financial literacy and digital skills among individuals hinder their ability to understand and effectively use digital financial services. Lack of knowledge about financial concepts, digital platforms, and cybersecurity risks undermines confidence in utilizing digital financial services. Many individuals, especially those in marginalized communities, lack the proper identification documents required for KYC procedures. This restricts their ability to open bank accounts, access credit, or engage in formal financial services, creating barriers to digital financial inclusion. The cost of digital devices, internet data, and transaction fees may be prohibitive for individuals with low incomes. High transaction fees or minimum balance requirements imposed by financial service providers can exclude economically vulnerable individuals from accessing and using digital financial services. The affordability of smartphones, data plans, and transaction costs needs to be addressed to ensure that digital financial services are accessible to all. Economic disparities and income inequality contribute to financial exclusion. Individuals with low incomes may struggle to meet the financial requirements set by financial institutions, such as minimum balance thresholds or creditworthiness criteria. This exclusion further exacerbates the digital divide and limits access to digital financial services.

Trust and Security Barriers

Many individuals, particularly those with limited experience with digital platforms, may lack trust in the security and reliability of digital financial services. Concerns about data privacy, cybersecurity threats, and fraudulent activities can deter individuals from adopting digital financial services. The collection and use of personal data in digital financial services raise concerns about privacy and data protection. Individuals may be reluctant to share their personal and financial information online, fearing misuse or unauthorized access. Ensuring robust data protection measures and building trust through transparency are essential for overcoming these barriers. The prevalence of fraud and cybercrime in the digital realm poses significant barriers to digital financial inclusion. Phishing attacks, identity theft, and fraudulent schemes erode confidence in digital financial services. Building strong cybersecurity frameworks, educating users about security measures, and implementing effective fraud prevention mechanisms are critical for mitigating these risks.

Regulatory and Policy Barriers

Fragmented regulatory frameworks and inconsistent standards across jurisdictions create barriers to the development of digital financial services. Diverse regulatory requirements and varying compliance burdens can impede innovation and limit the scalability of digital financial solutions. Insufficient regulatory support and outdated policies hinder the growth of digital financial services. Regulatory frameworks designed for traditional banking models may not adequately address the unique characteristics and risks associated with digital finance. Proactive regulatory approaches that foster innovation, promote competition, and ensure consumer protection are necessary for enabling digital financial inclusion. Inadequate consumer protection measures in the digital financial ecosystem can undermine trust and confidence. Individuals need assurance that their rights are protected, and effective mechanisms are in place to address grievances, disputes, and fraud-related issues. Strengthening consumer protection frameworks and establishing dispute resolution mechanisms can mitigate these barriers.

Regulatory Considerations for FinTech and Financial Inclusion

Regulatory considerations play a crucial role in facilitating the growth of FinTech, while ensuring financial inclusion and consumer protection. FinTech innovations often challenge traditional regulatory frameworks designed for traditional financial institutions. To promote financial inclusion through FinTech, regulators need to strike a balance between fostering innovation, maintaining systemic stability, and safeguarding consumer interests.

Regulators should adopt a proportionate approach to regulation, taking into account the nature, scale, and risks associated with FinTech activities. One-size-fits-all regulations may stifle innovation and hinder financial inclusion. Regulators should be flexible and adaptive, allowing for experimentation and innovation within well-defined boundaries.

Regulatory sandboxes provide a controlled environment for FinTech firms to test their products and services under regulatory supervision. Sandboxes allow regulators to assess potential risks and evaluate the impact of new technologies, while providing FinTech companies with the opportunity to navigate the regulatory landscape. This enables regulators to strike a balance between innovation and consumer protection.

Effective collaboration and coordination among regulators, policymakers, industry stakeholders, and FinTech firms are essential for addressing regulatory challenges and promoting financial inclusion. Open dialogue and information sharing can help regulators better understand FinTech's innovations and adapt regulations accordingly. Public-private partnerships can facilitate the development of inclusive FinTech solutions and promote shared goals.

FinTech firms must adhere to robust consumer protection measures to ensure the fair treatment of customers. Regulators should establish clear guidelines and standards for customer onboarding, disclosure of terms and conditions, data privacy, and complaint resolution mechanisms. Adequate safeguards should be in place to protect consumer funds and data, including cybersecurity measures and fraud prevention mechanisms.

KYC and AML regulations are critical for preventing financial crimes, such as money laundering and terrorist financing. However, stringent and burdensome KYC requirements can exclude vulnerable populations from accessing financial services. Regulators should explore innovative approaches to KYC and AML, such as digital identity verification and risk-based assessments, to strike a balance between compliance and inclusion.

Interoperability among FinTech firms and traditional financial institutions is essential to ensure seamless and inclusive financial services. Regulators should encourage data sharing and collaboration, enabling customers to access multiple services and platforms using a single interface. However, data sharing should be regulated to protect consumer privacy and ensure data security.

Regulators should prioritize financial education initiatives to enhance consumers' understanding of FinTech products and services. Promoting consumer awareness about risks, benefits, and the responsible use of FinTech can empower individuals to make informed financial decisions.

Regulators can collaborate with stakeholders to develop educational campaigns and resources.

As FinTech operates across borders, regulatory harmonization and international cooperation are crucial for promoting financial inclusion. Regulators should collaborate with international counterparts to develop consistent regulatory frameworks, share best practices, and address cross-border challenges. This can facilitate the expansion of FinTech services and enable the inclusion of underserved populations globally.

References

Abdulhakeem, S. A., & Hu, Q. (2021). Powered by blockchain technology, DeFi (Decentralized Finance) Strives to increase financial inclusion of the unbanked by reshaping the world financial system. *Modern Economy, 12*(01), 1–16. https://doi.org/10.4236/me.2021.121001

Agarwal, S., Alok, S., Ghosh, P., & Gupta, S. (2020a). *Financial inclusion and alternate credit scoring for the millennials: Role of big data and machine learning in FinTech* (pp. 1–38).

Agarwal, S., Qian, W., & Tan, R. (2020b). *Household finance: A functional approach* (pp. 1–352). Springer Singapore.

Al Mawali, N. R., Al Lawati, A. M., & Ananda, S. (2021). *Fourth industrial revolution and business dynamics: Issues and implications* (pp. 1–325). Springer Singapore.

Alrabei, A. M., Al-Othman, L. N., Al-Dalabih, F. A. N., Taber, T. A., Ali, B. J. A., & Amareen, S. M. (2022). The impact of mobile payment on the financial inclusion rates. *Information Sciences Letters, 11*(4), 1033–1044. https://doi.org/10.18576/isl/110404

Anderson, B., & Hardin, J. M. (2014). Credit scoring in the age of big data. *Encyclopedia of Business Analytics and Optimization, 15*(7), 549–557. https://doi.org/10.4018/978-1-4666-5202-6.ch049

Anisa, N. (2021). FinTech Peer to Peer lending as approach to encourage economic inclusion for rural communities in Indonesia. *SSRN Electronic Journal*, 1–19. https://doi.org/10.2139/ssrn.3846900

Beck, T., Senbet, L., & Simbanegavi, W. (2012, June). *Financial inclusion and innovation in Africa: An overview* (Policy Research Working Paper 6088 Abstract). https://doi.org/10.1093/jae/eju031

Berentsen, A., & Markheim, M. (2019). *Munich personal RePEc archive Peer-to-Peer lending, joint liability and financial inclusion with altruistic investors Peer-to-Peer lending, joint liability and financial inclusion with altruistic investors. 94963.*

Berentsen, A., & Markheim, M. (2021). Peer-to-peer lending and financial inclusion with altruistic investors. *International Review of Finance, 21*(4), 1407–1418. https://doi.org/10.1111/irfi.12333

Bianchi, M., & Briere, M. (2021). Robo-advising for small investors. *SSRN Electronic Journal*, 1–35. https://doi.org/10.2139/ssrn.3751620

Boitan, I. A. (2016). Crowdlending and financial inclusion—Evidence from EU countries. *Economic Alternatives, 4*, 418–432.

Buckland, J. (2012). *Hard choices: Financial exclusion, fringe banks, and poverty in Urban Canada*. University of Toronto Press. https://books.google.co.uk/books?id=rIzxrdsrjQAC

Butticè, V., & Vismara, S. (2022). Inclusive digital finance: The industry of equity crowdfunding. *Journal of Technology Transfer, 47*(4), 1224–1241. https://doi.org/10.1007/s10961-021-09875-0

Cámara, N., Research, B., & Tuesta, D. (2017, September). Measuring financial inclusion: A multidimensional index. *Bank of Morocco–CEMLA–IFC Satellite Seminar at the ISI World Statistics Congress on financial inclusion*.

Caplan, M. A., Birkenmaier, J., & Bae, J. (2021). Financial exclusion in OECD countries: A scoping review*. *International Journal of Social Welfare, 30*(1), 58–71. https://doi.org/10.1111/ijsw.12430

Capponi, A., & Lehalle, C.-A. (Eds.). (2023). Robo-advising: Less AI and more XAI? Augmenting algorithms with humans-in-the-loop. In *Machine learning and data sciences for financial markets: A guide to contemporary practices* (pp. 33–59). Cambridge University Press. https://www.cambridge.org/core/books/machine-learning-and-data-sciences-for-financial-markets/roboadvising-less-ai-and-more-xai-augmenting-algorithms-with-humansintheloop/71F1C1C2082552E4D70BA43561461B0B

Carbó, S., Gardener, E. P. M., & Molyneux, P. (2005). Financial exclusion in the UK. In *Financial exclusion* (pp. 14–44). Palgrave Macmillan UK. https://doi.org/10.1057/9780230508743_3

Chen, Y. J., & Chen, Y. M. (2022). Forecasting corporate credit ratings using big data from social media. *Expert Systems with Applications*, *207*(October 2021), 118042. https://doi.org/10.1016/j.eswa.2022.118042

Chinaka, M., Johnson, S., Kurtz, R. A., Verdi, R. S., & Cert, E. Y. A. (2014). *Blockchain technology-applications in improving financial inclusion in developing economies. Case study for small scale agriculture in Africa. by Signature redacted Signature redacted* (B.Sc. Mechanical Engineering).

Choudhury, S. R., & Bagchi, D. (2016). Financial exclusion—A paradox in developing countries. *IOSR Journal of Economics and Finance Ver. I, 7*(3), 2321–5933. https://doi.org/10.9790/5933-0703014045

Chung, S., Kim, K., Lee, C. H., & Oh, W. (2023). Interdependence between online peer-to-peer lending and cryptocurrency markets and its effects on financial inclusion. *Production and Operations Management, 32*(6), 1939–1957. https://doi.org/10.1111/poms.13950

Collard, S., Kempson, E., & Whyley, C. (2001). *Tackling financial exclusion: An area-based approach*. 52.

Demirgüç-Kunt, A., & Klapper, L. (2012). *Measuring financial inclusion: The global Findex database* (Policy Research Working Paper 6025).

Diniz, E., Birochi, R., & Pozzebon, M. (2012). Triggers and barriers to financial inclusion: The use of ICT-based branchless banking in an Amazon county. *Electronic Commerce Research and Applications, 11*(5), 484–494. https://doi.org/10.1016/j.elerap.2011.07.006

di Prisco, D., & Strangio, D. (2021). Technology and financial inclusion: A case study to evaluate potential and limitations of blockchain in emerging countries. *Technology Analysis and Strategic Management*, 1–14. https://doi.org/10.1080/09537325.2021.1944617

Division, P. (2004, September). Policy level response to financial exclusion in developed economies: Lessons for developing countries Elaine Kempson, Adele Atkinson and Odile Pilley The Personal Finance Research Centre University of Bristol September 2004 Report commissioned by Finance. *Personal Finance*, 1–49.

Donovan, K. (2011). *Mobile money for financial inclusion*. In *Information and communications for development 2012: Maximizing mobile*. The World Bank.

Eid, N., & Yang, J. (2018, August). Online financial inclusion and its implications for borrowers: Evidence from Peer-to-Peer lending. *SSRN Electronic Journal*. https://doi.org/10.2139/ssrn.3243499

Endress, T. (2023). *Business and management in Asia: Digital innovation and sustainability*. Springer Nature Singapore.

Etim, A. S. (2012). Ehrbeck et al. *Jack & Suri*, 1–13.

Fungáčová, Z., & Weill, L. (2015). Understanding financial inclusion in China. *China Economic Review, 34*, 196–206. https://doi.org/10.1016/j.chieco.2014.12.004

Guégan, D., & Hassani, B. (2018). Regulatory learning: How to supervise machine learning models? An application to credit scoring. *Journal of Finance and Data Science, 4*(3), 157–171. https://doi.org/10.1016/j.jfds.2018.04.001

Impact, S. (2012). *Measuring financial exclusion in Australia*. The Centre for Social Impact of National Australia Bank.

Jenik, I., Timothy, L., & Nava, A. (2017, March). *Crowdfunding and financial inclusion*. CGAP.

Jiang, J., Liao, L., Lu, X., Wang, Z., & Xiang, H. (2021). Deciphering big data in consumer credit evaluation. *Journal of Empirical Finance, 62*(August 2020), 28–45. https://doi.org/10.1016/j.jempfin.2021.01.009

Kata, R., Walenia, A., & Pyrkos, D. S. (2016). Financial exclusion of the rural population in Poland. *Journal of Agribusiness and Rural Development*, *9*(4). https://doi.org/10.17306/jard.2015.74

Kim, M., Zoo, H., Lee, H., & Kang, J. (2018). Mobile financial services, financial inclusion, and development: A systematic review of academic literature. *Electronic Journal of Information Systems in Developing Countries, 84*(5), 1–17. https://doi.org/10.1002/isd2.12044

Kirana, M. Y., & Havidz, S. A. H. (2020, August). Financial literacy and mobile payment usage as financial inclusion determinants. *Proceedings of 2020 International Conference on Information Management and Technology, ICIMTech 2020*, 905–910.

Konya, S., Küçüksucu, M., & Karaçor, Z. (2021). Panel Estimation of high-technology export determinants: Evidence from fast-growing countries. In M. H. Bilgin, H. Danis, E. Demir, & S. Vale (Eds.), *Eurasian Economic Perspectives: Proceedings of the 29th Eurasia Business and Economics Society Conference* (pp. 245–259). Springer International Publishing.

Lee, C. C., Chen, P. F., & Chu, P. J. (2023). Green recovery through financial inclusion of mobile payment: A study of low- and middle-income Asian countries. *Economic Analysis and Policy, 77*, 729–747. https://doi.org/10.1016/j.eap.2022.12.012

Lichtfous, M., Yadav, V., & Fratino, V. (2018). Can blockchain accelerate financial inclusion globally? *Deloitte Inside Magazine*, *19*.

Manta, A. (2019). Financial inclusion and gender barriers for rural women. *International Journal of Management*, *10*(5), 61–72. https://doi.org/10.34218/IJM.10.5.2019.006

Maskara, P. K., Kuvvet, E., & Chen, G. (2021). The role of P2P platforms in enhancing financial inclusion in the United States: An analysis of peer-to-peer lending across the rural–urban divide. *Financial Management, 50*(3), 747–774. https://doi.org/10.1111/fima.12341

Muhammad, T., Ngah, B. B., & Obad, A.-S. F. M. (2022). Financial exclusion in Northern Nigeria: A lesson from the developed countries. *AFEBI Islamic Finance and Economic Review*, *7*(01), 45. https://doi.org/10.47312/aifer.v7i01.565

Mukherjee, S., & Sood, K. (2020). Triggers and barriers of financial inclusion: A country-wise analysis. *Asian Economic and Financial Review*, *10*(9), 970–988. https://doi.org/10.18488/journal.aefr.2020.109.970.988

Mulia Rachman, K., & Sukmadilaga, C. (2022). Influence of Robo advisory in investment decision. *Journal of Digital Innovation Studies*, *1*(1), 1–20. https://doi.org/10.24198/digits.v1i1.37806

Ngendakumana, L., & Mashahanya, T. (2019). Causes of financial exclusion of micro, small to medium enterprises operating in Victoria falls, Zimbabwe. *Academic Research International*, *10*(4), 29–37.

Ohnesorge, J. (2018). *A primer on blockchain technology and its potential for financial inclusion* (Vol. 7, pp. 246–250).

Onay, C., & Öztürk, E. (2018). A review of credit scoring research in the age of Big Data. *Journal of Financial Regulation and Compliance, 26*(3), 382–405. https://doi.org/10.1108/JFRC-06-2017-0054

Óskarsdóttir, M., Bravo, C., Sarraute, C., Vanthienen, J., & Baesens, B. (2019). The value of big data for credit scoring: Enhancing financial inclusion using mobile phone data and social network analytics. *Applied Soft Computing Journal, 74*, 26–39. https://doi.org/10.1016/j.asoc.2018.10.004

Ozili, P. K. (2020). Financial inclusion in Nigeria: Determinants, challenges and achievements. *SSRN Electronic Journal, 99173*. https://doi.org/10.2139/ssrn.3557244

Philippon, T. (2019). *Nber working paper series on FinTech and financial inclusion*. National Bureau of Economic Research.

Ren, B., Li, L., Zhao, H., & Zhou, Y. (2018). The financial exclusion in the development of digital finance—A study based on survey data in the Jingjinji Rural Area. *Singapore Economic Review, 63*(1), 65–82. https://doi.org/10.1142/S0217590818500017

Savita, S. (2013). Financial inclusion in India: Do microfinance institutions address access barriers? *ACRN Journal of Entrepreneurship Perspectives, 2*(1), 60–74.

Schuetz, S., & Venkatesh, V. (2020). Blockchain, adoption, and financial inclusion in India: Research opportunities. *International Journal of Information Management*, *52*(February 2019). https://doi.org/10.1016/j.ijinfomgt.2019.04.009

Slimani, A., & Ziky, M. (2021). Crowdfunding and financial inclusion: A systematic literature review and a conceptual framework. *International Journal of Business and Economy, 3*(4), 25–37.

Tan, G. K. S. (2020). Robo-advisors and the financialization of lay investors. *Geoforum, 117*, 46–60. https://doi.org/10.1016/j.geoforum.2020.09.004

Tassabehji, R., & Isherwood, A. (2014). The case of crowdfunding in financial inclusion: A survey. *Strategic Change, 23*, 63–80. https://doi.org/10.1002/jsc

Ulwodi, D. W., & Muriu, P. W. (2017). Barriers of financial inclusion in Sub-Saharan Africa. *Journal of Economics and Sustainable Development, 8*(14), 66–81. www.Iiste.Org

Winn, J. K. (2015). *Mobile payments and financial inclusion: Kenya, Brazil, and India as case studies* (Legal Studies Research Paper No. 2015C29).

Wu, Y., & Pan, Y. (2021). Application analysis of credit scoring of financial institutions based on machine learning model. *Complexity, 2021*. https://doi.org/10.1155/2021/9222617

Xing, F., Cambria, E., & Welsch, R. (2019). *Intelligent asset management strategy* (p. 163).

Yasir, A., Ahmad, A., Abbas, S., Inairat, M., Al-Kassem, A. H., & Rasool, A. (2022). How artificial intelligence is promoting financial inclusion? A study on barriers of financial inclusion. *2022 International Conference on Business Analytics for Technology and Security, ICBATS 2022*, 1–6.

CHAPTER 9

Legal Framework for Digital Currencies

Introduction

Payment, clearing, and settlement services are undergoing revolutionary transformations by the advent of cryptocurrencies. Although these alternative modes of payment provide various advantages to users, however they entail anonymity and pseudonymity, since the transactions are performed by the exchange of tokens through a decentralized blockchain platform and involved parties are identified by a unique string of random numbers instead of personal information.

This chapter aspires to address the unique regulatory challenges brought about by the instant growth of this financial instrument due to the fact that it can facilitate tax evasion, illicit transactions, and the process of money laundering for criminals and terrorists who now have access to cash without the need to go through banks and conventional financial intermediaries. To this end, by expounding these risks and challenges, this chapter discusses legal framework reforms in the context of anti-money laundering and anti-terrorism financing regulations, particularly requirements on Know Your Client (KYC) rule for users on blockchain platforms and amendments to the laws requiring the disclosure of cryptocurrency users' identity.

B. Naysary and A. Tarazi, *The Digital Finance Era*,
https://doi.org/10.1007/978-981-97-3970-7_9

Regulation of Digital Currency Exchanges

The regulation of digital currency exchanges plays a critical role in ensuring the integrity of the digital currency market, protecting investors, and preventing illicit activities. Different jurisdictions have developed regulatory frameworks to govern the operation of digital currency exchanges. Many jurisdictions require digital currency exchanges to obtain licenses or register with the appropriate regulatory authorities. This process typically involves submitting detailed information about the exchange's ownership, management team, compliance procedures, and security measures. Licensing and registration requirements aim to ensure that exchanges meet certain standards of transparency, security, and compliance with applicable laws and regulations.

Digital currency exchanges are often subject to stringent AML and KYC regulations. These requirements oblige exchanges to implement robust measures to verify the identity of their customers, monitor transactions for suspicious activities, and report any suspicious transactions to the relevant authorities. AML and KYC regulations are crucial in preventing money laundering, terrorist financing, and other illicit activities. Digital currency exchanges are responsible for safeguarding the assets and information of their customers. Regulatory frameworks often include requirements for exchanges to implement robust security measures, including secure storage of digital assets, encryption protocols, and measures to protect against hacking and unauthorized access. Additionally, exchanges may be required to have adequate insurance coverage to protect against potential losses or breaches.

Regulators often implement measures to ensure fair and transparent trading on digital currency exchanges. These measures may include monitoring trading activities, implementing surveillance systems to detect market manipulation, and enforcing rules against insider trading and fraudulent practices. Regulators may collaborate with exchanges to establish monitoring mechanisms and conduct regular audits to maintain market integrity. Regulatory frameworks often require digital currency exchanges to provide regular reports on their operations, financial health, and customer protection measures. These reports may include information such as trading volumes, user statistics, compliance efforts, and financial statements. Transparent reporting helps regulators assess the overall health of the exchange, identify potential risks, and ensure compliance with regulatory requirements. Regulations for digital currency exchanges often include provisions aimed at protecting investors. These may include requirements for exchanges to disclose risks associated with digital currencies, provide clear information on fees and trading terms, and establish mechanisms for handling customer complaints and disputes. Some jurisdictions also require exchanges to maintain reserve funds to ensure the availability of customer assets in the event of insolvency or other financial difficulties.

Regulatory Approaches to Digital Currencies

United States

In the United States, regulatory approaches to digital currencies have evolved over time as regulators grapple with the unique characteristics and challenges presented by this emerging asset class. The regulatory landscape is complex, involving multiple regulatory agencies at the federal and state levels. At the federal level, the following bodies are responsible for making the required cryptocurrency regulation in the US—the Securities and Exchange Commission (SEC), the Commodity Futures Trading Commission (CFTC), the Federal Trade Commission (FTC), the Treasury Department, through the Internal Revenue Service (IRS), the Office of the Comptroller of the Currency (OCC), and the Financial Crimes Enforcement Network (FinCEN).

FinCEN, a bureau of the US Department of the Treasury, is responsible for enforcing AML and combating the financing of terrorism (CFT) regulations. FinCEN defines digital currencies as "convertible virtual currencies" and imposes certain reporting and record-keeping obligations on digital currency exchanges and administrators. Businesses engaged in money transmission involving digital currencies are classified as Money Services Businesses (MSBs) and are required to register with FinCEN.

The Securities and Exchange Commission (SEC) plays a crucial role in regulating digital currencies that qualify as securities. The Howey Test, derived from a landmark Supreme Court case, is used by the SEC to determine whether a digital currency offering constitutes a security. If a digital currency is classified as a security, it must comply with registration and disclosure requirements under the Securities Act of 1933 and the Securities Exchange Act of 1934. The SEC has also been active in pursuing enforcement actions against fraudulent or unregistered digital currency offerings.

The Commodity Futures Trading Commission (CFTC) regulates digital currencies that are considered commodities under the Commodity Exchange Act. Bitcoin, for example, is classified as a commodity by the CFTC. The agency oversees derivatives and futures contracts linked to digital currencies and has approved the operation of digital currency futures exchanges. The CFTC has jurisdiction over fraudulent activities and market manipulation in the digital currency derivatives markets.

The Office of the Comptroller of the Currency (OCC) is responsible for supervising and regulating national banks and federal savings associations. In July 2020, the OCC issued a letter clarifying that national banks have the authority to provide custody services for digital currencies. This move provided regulatory clarity and opened the door for traditional banks to enter the digital currency custody business.

Internal Revenue Service (IRS) treats digital currencies as property for federal tax purposes. In 2014, the agency issued guidance stating that digital currency transactions are subject to capital gains and losses taxation. Taxpayers are required to report their digital currency transactions and pay taxes accordingly. In recent years, the IRS has also been focused on ensuring compliance with digital currency tax obligations and has initiated efforts to educate taxpayers about their tax responsibilities.

In addition to federal regulations, digital currency businesses may be subject to state-level regulations, particularly those related to money transmission. Each state has its own money transmitter licensing requirements and regulations. Some states have enacted specific laws or regulatory frameworks for digital currencies, such as the BitLicense in New York. State regulators often collaborate with federal agencies to ensure compliance and address potential risks associated with digital currencies.

European Union

In the European Union (EU), regulatory approaches to digital currencies have been developed to address the challenges and opportunities presented by this emerging technology. The EU has taken a comprehensive and coordinated approach to regulate digital currencies across its member states.

European Securities and Markets Authority (ESMA) is responsible for promoting investor protection and ensuring the orderly functioning of financial markets in the EU. It has issued guidelines and opinions on the regulatory treatment of digital currencies, particularly initial coin offerings (ICOs). ESMA has emphasized that ICOs may fall under existing EU securities regulations and highlighted the need for issuers and intermediaries to comply with prospectus requirements and conduct adequate risk disclosures.

The European Banking Authority (EBA) is responsible for establishing a harmonized regulatory framework for banking activities within the EU. It has issued warnings and guidelines on the risks associated with digital currencies, including AML and consumer protection concerns. The EBA has stressed the need for financial institutions to conduct thorough due diligence on their digital currency-related activities and implement robust AML measures.

The European Central Bank (ECB), as the central bank for the eurozone, has been closely monitoring digital currencies. While not directly regulating digital currencies, the ECB has issued warnings about the potential risks they pose to financial stability and has advocated for a consistent approach to regulation within the EU. The ECB is also exploring the possibility of developing a central bank digital currency (CBDC) for the eurozone.

The EU has proposed the Markets in Crypto-Assets Regulation (MiCA) framework to regulate digital currencies and related activities uniformly across the member states. MiCA aims to establish a comprehensive regulatory regime for issuers of crypto-assets, digital asset service providers, and trading platforms. It introduces licensing requirements, capital requirements, and the conduct of business rules for digital asset service providers. MiCA also includes provisions for investor protection, custody of digital assets, and cross-border operation of service providers.

The EU's AML directives, particularly the Fifth Money Laundering Directive (5AMLD), impose AML and counter-terrorism financing obligations on digital currency businesses. The directive requires virtual asset service providers to register with competent authorities, conduct customer due diligence, and report suspicious transactions. It also extends AML requirements to digital wallet providers and custodian wallet providers.

The General Data Protection Regulation (GDPR), which came into effect in 2018, applies to digital currency businesses that process personal data of EU residents. It sets out strict requirements for data protection and privacy, including obtaining consent for data processing, implementing appropriate security measures, and ensuring transparency in data processing practices.

While the EU provides a harmonized framework, member states have some flexibility in implementing and enforcing regulations related to digital currencies. Some countries have adopted additional regulations or guidelines specific to digital currencies. For example, France has implemented a legal framework for initial coin offerings, and Germany has recognized digital currencies as financial instruments.

United Kingdom

In the United Kingdom, regulatory approaches to digital currencies have been developed to address the opportunities and risks associated with this emerging technology. The regulatory landscape in the UK focuses on striking a balance between fostering innovation and ensuring consumer protection.

The Financial Conduct Authority is the primary regulatory authority responsible for overseeing digital currencies in the UK. The FCA has implemented a registration regime for digital currency businesses under the Money Laundering, Terrorist Financing, and Transfer of Funds (Information on the Payer) Regulations 2017 (MLRs). Digital currency businesses that fall within the scope of the MLRs must register with the FCA and comply with anti-money laundering (AML) and Know Your Customer (KYC) requirements. The UK government and the FCA are committed to protecting consumers in the digital currency space. The FCA requires digital currency businesses to provide clear and fair information to consumers, ensure adequate security measures to protect customer assets, and have robust complaint handling procedures in place. Consumer education initiatives are also promoted to raise awareness of the risks associated with digital currencies. The FCA operates a regulatory sandbox, which provides a controlled environment for digital currency businesses to test innovative products and services in collaboration with the regulator. This allows businesses to explore new technologies and business models while ensuring compliance with regulatory requirements.

The Financial Services Compensation Scheme (FSCS) provides protection to customers of authorized financial services firms in the event of their failure. However, it's important to note that not all digital currency activities fall within the scope of the FSCS, and customers should carefully assess the protection offered by specific digital currency services.

The UK tax authority, Her Majesty's Revenue and Customs (HMRC), has provided guidance on the taxation of digital currencies. It classifies digital currencies as assets for tax purposes, and transactions involving digital currencies are subject to capital gains tax. Businesses accepting digital currencies as payment are also subject to applicable tax laws.

Regulatory Challenges and Considerations

Regulating digital currencies presents several challenges and considerations for regulatory authorities. The unique nature of digital currencies, their global reach, and the evolving technological landscape require careful assessment and adaptation of regulatory frameworks.

Technological Complexity

Digital currencies, such as cryptocurrencies, are built on complex underlying technologies like blockchain. Regulators need to have a thorough understanding of these technologies to effectively regulate and supervise digital currencies. Keeping up with the rapid pace of technological advancements in the digital currency space poses a challenge, as regulators must continuously update their knowledge and adapt their regulatory approaches accordingly.

Cross-Border Transactions

Digital currencies operate across borders, making cross-border transactions seamless and efficient. However, this poses challenges for regulators as they need to coordinate with international counterparts to address issues such as money laundering, terrorist financing, and tax evasion. Harmonizing regulatory approaches and establishing effective mechanisms for cross-border cooperation are essential for addressing these challenges.

Market Volatility and Investor Protection

Digital currency markets are known for their high volatility and potential for speculative trading. Regulators face the challenge of protecting investors from market manipulation, fraudulent schemes, and excessive risk-taking. Developing measures to ensure transparency, enforce fair trading practices, and educate investors about the risks associated with digital currencies is crucial for investor protection.

Consumer Education and Awareness

Digital currencies are relatively new and complex financial instruments. Many consumers lack a comprehensive understanding of how digital currencies work, the associated risks, and the potential for fraud. Regulators play a vital role in educating the public about digital currencies, providing guidelines on safe practices, and raising awareness about potential scams and fraudulent schemes.

Money Laundering and Illicit Activities

Digital currencies can be used for illicit purposes due to their pseudonymous nature and ease of cross-border transactions. Regulators face the challenge of implementing effective AML measures to prevent money laundering, terrorist financing, and other illicit activities. Balancing the need for privacy and financial transparency is a critical consideration for regulators to address this challenge.

Regulatory Coordination and Harmonization

As digital currencies transcend national borders, regulatory coordination and harmonization become crucial. Achieving consistent regulatory approaches across jurisdictions helps to prevent regulatory arbitrage, fosters investor confidence, and promotes global financial stability. Collaborative efforts between regulators, international organizations, and standard-setting bodies are necessary to establish common frameworks and standards for regulating digital currencies.

Innovation and Market Development

Regulators must strike a balance between promoting innovation and ensuring market integrity. Overly restrictive regulations can stifle innovation and hinder the development of new technologies and business models. Regulators need to foster an environment that encourages responsible innovation while protecting against potential risks and maintaining market confidence.

Scalability and Systemic Risks

The scalability of digital currencies and the potential for widespread adoption raise concerns about their impact on financial stability and systemic risks. Regulators must carefully assess the risks associated with the growth of digital currencies and develop appropriate safeguards to mitigate potential threats to the broader financial system.

Legal Framework and Jurisdictional Challenges

Digital currencies often challenge existing legal frameworks and jurisdictional boundaries. Regulators must navigate complex legal landscapes to ensure that digital currencies are subject to appropriate regulations. Determining the legal status of digital currencies, clarifying their treatment under existing laws, and adapting regulatory frameworks to accommodate technological innovations present significant challenges for regulators.

Anti-Money Laundering (AML) and Know Your Customer (KYC) Requirements

AML and KYC requirements play a crucial role in mitigating the risks of money laundering, terrorist financing, and other illicit activities in the digital currency space. These requirements are designed to ensure that digital currency service providers have appropriate measures in place to verify the identity of their customers, monitor transactions, and report suspicious activities to the relevant authorities.

AML Regulations for Digital Currency Businesses

AML regulations are designed to prevent money laundering, terrorist financing, and other illicit activities. Digital currency service providers are required to implement robust AML measures to detect, prevent, and report suspicious transactions. Digital currency service providers must implement systems to monitor and analyze customer transactions. This involves identifying patterns of suspicious activities, such as large transactions, frequent transfers, or unusual transaction flows. If a service provider detects any suspicious transactions or activities, they are legally obligated to report them to the appropriate authorities. Suspicious Activity Reports (SARs) detail the nature of the suspicious activity and any relevant customer information. AML requirements follow a risk-based approach, meaning that service providers must assess the risks associated with their customers and transactions. Enhanced due diligence measures are applied to high-risk customers, ensuring that the level of scrutiny aligns with the perceived risk. Service providers are required to establish comprehensive AML compliance programs. These programs outline policies and procedures for identifying and mitigating money laundering risks, training staff, conducting internal audits, and maintaining records of AML activities. Digital currency service providers may be required to submit regular reports to regulatory authorities, providing information on their AML policies, procedures, and effectiveness. These reports help regulators assess the overall compliance of service providers and identify potential areas for improvement.

KYC Obligations and Customer Due Diligence

KYC procedures involve verifying the identity of customers and assessing their risk profiles. Digital currency service providers, including exchanges, wallet providers, and other platforms, are typically required to collect and verify certain information from their customers. Customers are required to provide identification documents such as passports, driver's licenses, or national identification cards. The service provider verifies the authenticity of these documents to establish the customer's identity. Customers are often required to provide proof of their residential address, such as utility bills, bank statements, or government-issued documents. This helps ensure that the customer's address is legitimate and matches the information provided during the registration process. Customer Due Diligence (CDD) involves assessing the risk profile of customers based on factors such as their occupation, source of funds, transaction patterns, and geographic location. Higher-risk customers, such as politically exposed persons (PEPs) or those from high-risk jurisdictions, may require enhanced due diligence measures. KYC requirements also include ongoing monitoring of customer transactions and activities. Service providers must conduct periodic reviews of customer information, verify the legitimacy of transactions, and identify any unusual or suspicious activities.

Consumer Protection and Investor Safeguards

Consumer protection and investor safeguards play a vital role in promoting trust, confidence, and responsible participation in the digital currency ecosystem. Given the unique characteristics of digital currencies, regulatory frameworks and industry best practices are necessary to ensure the protection of consumers and investors. Digital currency service providers, including exchanges, wallets, and investment platforms, should provide clear and transparent information to consumers and investors. This includes disclosing the risks associated with digital currencies, potential fees and charges, terms and conditions, and any limitations or restrictions that may apply to their services. Comprehensive disclosure helps consumers make informed decisions and understand the nature of their involvement in the digital currency market.

Protecting the security of consumers' digital currency holdings is essential. Service providers should implement robust security measures to safeguard customers' funds and personal information. This includes using secure encryption protocols, multi-factor authentication, cold storage for cryptocurrencies, and regular security audits. Adequate security measures reduce the risk of hacking, theft, and unauthorized access to consumers' digital assets. Digital currency service providers should respect consumers' privacy rights and handle their personal information in accordance with applicable data protection regulations. Consumers should be informed about how their data will be used, stored, and shared. Clear privacy policies and practices help build trust and ensure that consumers' personal information is protected.

Establishing mechanisms for handling consumer complaints and disputes is crucial. Digital currency service providers should have effective processes in place to address and resolve consumer complaints in a timely manner. This includes providing channels for communication, maintaining records of complaints, and escalating issues when necessary. By promptly addressing consumer concerns, service providers can enhance trust and maintain good customer relationships.

Educating investors about the risks and complexities of digital currencies is essential. Service providers, regulators, and industry associations should collaborate to provide educational resources, guidelines, and best practices for investors. These resources can cover topics such as risk management, responsible investment strategies, identifying scams and fraudulent schemes, and understanding the volatile nature of digital currency markets. Investor education helps individuals make informed investment decisions and protects them from potential pitfalls.

Regulatory authorities play a crucial role in establishing and enforcing consumer protection and investor safeguards in the digital currency industry. Regulators should develop and enforce clear rules and regulations to ensure fair and transparent practices. This includes licensing requirements for service providers, regular audits and inspections, and the establishment of dispute resolution mechanisms. Effective regulation and oversight provide consumers and investors with confidence in the market and protect them from fraudulent activities.

Some jurisdictions require investors to meet certain eligibility criteria or accreditation standards to participate in certain types of digital currency investments. These requirements aim to ensure that investors have the necessary knowledge, experience, and financial capacity to understand and bear the risks associated with specific investment opportunities. Accreditation and suitability criteria help protect less sophisticated or vulnerable investors from investing in high-risk or complex digital currency products. Digital currency service providers and regulators should collaborate to implement measures to detect and prevent fraud in the digital currency ecosystem. This includes conducting thorough due diligence on digital currency offerings, monitoring for fraudulent activities and market manipulation, and taking swift action against fraudulent operators. Anti-fraud measures help maintain market integrity and protect investors from financial harm.

Taxation of Digital Currencies

Income tax considerations for digital currencies vary by jurisdiction, and it's important for individuals and businesses involved in digital currency transactions to understand their tax obligations.

Tax liabilities typically arise when certain events occur involving digital currencies. These events can include the sale or exchange of digital currencies for fiat currency or other assets, receiving digital currency as payment for goods or services, mining or staking digital currencies, and receiving airdrops or forks. Each jurisdiction may have its own specific rules for determining taxable events.

In some jurisdictions, digital currencies are treated as property or assets, similar to stocks or real estate, while in others, they may be treated as currencies or commodities. The classification can impact the applicable tax rates, deductions, and reporting requirements.

When digital currencies are sold or exchanged for fiat currency or other assets, capital gains tax may apply. The tax liability is calculated based on the difference between the acquisition cost and the proceeds from the sale or exchange. Short-term capital gains, for assets held for a year or less, may be subject to higher tax rates compared to long-term capital gains.

In some cases, the receipt of digital currencies as payment for goods or services may be considered ordinary income. The value of the digital currency received at the time of the transaction is included in the individual's taxable income. The tax liability is calculated based on the fair market value of the digital currency at the time of receipt.

Mining digital currencies to earn rewards or transaction fees may result in taxable income. The value of the rewards or fees received is typically included in the individual's taxable income at the fair market value at the time of receipt. Mining expenses, such as equipment costs or electricity bills, may be eligible for deductions or credits.

Taxpayers involved in digital currency transactions are generally required to report their income and gains on their tax returns. Depending on the jurisdiction, specific reporting forms or schedules may be required. It's essential to keep accurate records of digital currency transactions, including dates, values, and any associated expenses, to comply with reporting requirements.

For individuals or businesses engaged in cross-border digital currency transactions, additional tax considerations come into play. Tax treaties, foreign exchange rules, and reporting requirements can impact the taxation of digital currency transactions involving multiple jurisdictions. It's crucial to understand the tax obligations in both the home jurisdiction and the jurisdiction where transactions occur.

In some cases, taxpayers may be able to deduct certain expenses related to digital currency transactions, such as mining equipment costs, transaction fees, or losses from the sale or exchange of digital currencies. Deductions and losses can help offset taxable income or capital gains, reducing the overall tax liability. However, specific rules and limitations apply, and it's important to consult with a tax professional for guidance.

International taxation presents various challenges when it comes to digital currencies due to their borderless and decentralized nature. Digital currencies operate across national borders, making it challenging to determine the jurisdiction where tax obligations arise. Different countries may have varying tax rules and interpretations, leading to potential conflicts or gaps in taxation. Determining the appropriate tax jurisdiction for digital currency transactions can be complex, especially in the absence of clear international tax standards.

Taxation of digital currency activities may depend on the concept of a "permanent establishment" (PE) in international tax law. A PE generally refers to a fixed place of business through which a company conducts its business activities. However, in the case of digital currencies, where operations can be decentralized and conducted remotely, establishing a physical presence may be challenging. The absence of a PE can create difficulties in determining the tax obligations in different jurisdictions.

Transfer pricing issues may arise in international digital currency transactions involving related entities. Transfer pricing refers to the pricing of goods, services, or intellectual property transferred between related entities within a multinational enterprise. It aims to ensure that transactions between related entities are conducted on an arm's length basis. Determining the fair value of digital currency transactions for transfer pricing purposes can be complex, especially when market prices are volatile or difficult to ascertain.

Double taxation is a significant concern in the international taxation of digital currencies. Double taxation occurs when the same income or transaction is subject to tax in more than one jurisdiction. With digital currencies, it is possible for a single transaction to involve multiple jurisdictions, each with its own tax rules. This can lead to potential double taxation unless mechanisms such as tax treaties or bilateral agreements are in place to mitigate this issue.

International tax reporting and compliance can be complex for individuals and businesses involved in digital currency transactions. Taxpayers need to navigate the requirements of multiple jurisdictions, including reporting their income, gains, and transactions accurately. The lack of standardized reporting frameworks and the complexity of digital currency transactions make it challenging for taxpayers to meet their reporting obligations in different jurisdictions.

Digital currencies are highly volatile, and their values can fluctuate significantly in short periods. When transactions involve converting digital currencies into fiat currency or vice versa, exchange rate fluctuations can impact the taxable amount. Determining the appropriate exchange rate for tax purposes can be challenging, especially when transactions occur across different time zones or involve multiple conversions.

Given the cross-border nature of digital currencies, international cooperation is crucial to address taxation challenges. Cooperation among tax authorities, regulatory bodies, and international organizations is necessary to develop consistent tax rules and standards for digital currencies. Initiatives such as the OECD's Base Erosion and Profit Shifting (BEPS) project and discussions on international tax reforms aim to address these challenges and ensure fair and efficient taxation in the digital economy.

Regulatory Sandboxes and Innovation

A regulatory sandbox is a framework established by regulatory agencies to facilitate the testing and experimentation of new financial technologies, products, or services. It allows innovators, including digital currency businesses, to operate in a limited and controlled environment, typically with relaxed regulatory requirements. The primary purpose is to strike a balance between promoting innovation and protecting consumers and maintaining financial stability.

Regulatory sandboxes are designed to encourage experimentation and innovation in digital currency-related technologies and business models. By providing a controlled environment, businesses can explore and refine their products and services without facing the full regulatory burden that applies to the wider financial industry. This flexibility allows for the testing of new ideas, business models, and technological advancements.

One of the significant advantages of regulatory sandboxes is the close collaboration between innovators and regulatory authorities. Businesses participating in the sandbox engage in regular dialogue and consultations with regulators, enabling them to better understand and navigate the regulatory landscape. This interaction fosters a mutual learning process, where regulators gain insights into emerging technologies, while businesses gain guidance on compliance requirements.

Regulatory sandboxes often provide certain exemptions or relaxations from specific regulatory requirements. These can include exemptions from certain licensing obligations, reduced capital requirements, temporary relief from compliance obligations, or streamlined regulatory processes. The goal is to strike a balance between consumer protection and the promotion of innovation.

While regulatory sandboxes aim to promote innovation, consumer protection remains a key consideration. Regulatory authorities establish guidelines to ensure that participating businesses adhere to certain consumer protection standards. This may include requirements related to data privacy, security measures, disclosure of risks, and transparent communication with customers. The sandbox environment provides an opportunity to assess the impact on consumers and address any potential risks or vulnerabilities.

Regulatory sandboxes are typically time-limited, allowing businesses to test their innovations within a specified period. At the end of the sandbox period, businesses are expected to transition to full compliance with applicable regulations. The sandbox experience enables businesses to refine their models and operations, gather evidence of their viability, and prepare for compliance with regulatory requirements once they exit the sandbox.

Regulatory sandboxes involve ongoing monitoring and evaluation by regulatory authorities. The authorities closely observe the performance of participants, assess risks, and identify potential policy implications. Insights gained from sandbox experiments can help regulators adapt existing regulations, develop new regulatory frameworks, and foster an ecosystem that supports innovation while mitigating risks.

References

Aggarwal, M. (2023). *Cryptocurrency regulation in the US in 2023*. LegaMart.

Akins, B. W., Chapman, J. L., & Gordon, J. M. (2015). A whole new world: Income tax considerations of the bitcoin economy. *Pittsburgh Tax Review, 12*(1), 24–56. https://doi.org/10.5195/taxreview.2014.32

Alam, N., Gupta, L., & Zameni, A. (2019). *FinTech and Islamic finance: Digitalization, development and disruption*, (pp. 1–178).

Arsi, S., Ben Khelifa, S., Ghabri, Y., & Mzoughi, H. (2021). Cryptocurrencies: Key risks and challenges. In *Cryptofinance* (pp. 121–145). WORLD SCIENTIFIC. https://doi.org/10.1142/9789811239670_0007

Bal, A. (2015). *Chapter 14—How to Tax Bitcoin?* (D. B. T.-H. of D. C. Lee Kuo Chuen, Ed.; pp. 267–282). Academic Press. https://www.sciencedirect.com/science/article/pii/B978012802117000014X

Bamodu, O. O. (2003). The regulation of electronic money institutions in the United Kingdom. *Journal of Information Law &Technology, 2003*(December).

Browne, R. (2023). EU lawmakers approve world's first comprehensive framework for crypto regulation. *CNBC*.

Carvalho, C. E., Pires, D. A., Artioli, M., & de Oliveira, G. C. (2021). Cryptocurrencies: Technology, initiatives of banks and central banks, and regulatory challenges. *Economia e Sociedade, 30*(2), 467–496. https://doi.org/10.1590/1982-3533.2021v30n2art08

Dewey, J. (2019). *Blockchain & cryptocurrency regulation* (pp. 488–499). https://www.acc.com/sites/default/files/resources/vl/membersonly/Article/1489775_1.pdf

Dziura, M., Jaki, A., & Rojek, T. (2020). *Restructuring management. models—changes—development*.

Fanusie, Y. J., & Robinson, T. (2018). Bitcoin laundering: An analysis of illicit flows into digital currency services. *Center on sanctions and illicit finance ...*, 15.

Fauzi, M. A., Paiman, N., & Othman, Z. (2020). Bitcoin and cryptocurrency: Challenges, opportunities and future works. *Journal of Asian Finance, Economics and Business*, *7*(8), 695–704. https://doi.org/10.13106/JAFEB.2020.VOL7.NO8.695

Feinstein, B. D., & Werbach, K. (2021). The impact of cryptocurrency regulation on trading markets. *Journal of Financial Regulation, 7*(1), 48–99. https://doi.org/10.1093/jfr/fjab003

Frick, T. A. (2019). Virtual and cryptocurrencies—regulatory and anti-money laundering approaches in the European Union and in Switzerland. *ERA Forum, 20*(1), 99–112. https://doi.org/10.1007/s12027-019-00561-1

Gross, A., Hemker, J., Hoelscher, J., & Reed, B. (2017). The role of secondary sources on the taxation of digital currency (Bitcoin) before IRS guidance was issued. *Journal of Accounting Education, 39*, 48–54. https://doi.org/10.1016/j.jaccedu.2017.02.001

Harris, J., Vargas-padilla, N. A., Leckar, S. C., Mullin, K., Sorokin-altmann, J., Aw, C. R. L., & Taff, B. R. S. (2008). American University Washington College of Law. *Articles in Law Reviews & Other Academic Journals*, *III*(1).

Hossain, M. B. (2023). Acquiring an awareness of the latest regulatory developments concerning digital assets and anti-money laundering. *Journal of Money Laundering Control*, *ahead-of-print*(ahead-of-print). https://doi.org/10.1108/JMLC-10-2022-0147

Jani, S. (2018). *The growth of cryptocurrency in India: Its challenges & potential impacts on legislation* (Issue April). https://doi.org/10.13140/RG.2.2.14220.36486

Lee, J., Long, A., McRae, M., Steiner, J., & Gosnell Handler, S. (2015). Bitcoin basics: A primer on virtual currencies. *Business Law International, 16*(1), 21–46.

Lipton, A., Sardon, A., & Schär, F. (2020). *Currency, and the future of money*.

Mahari, R., Hardjono, T., & Pentland, A. (2022). AML by design: Designing a central bank digital currency to stifle money laundering. *MIT Science Policy Review, 3*, 57–65. https://doi.org/10.38105/spr.j0hildxtyi

Mehrotra, V., & Bhatia, M. (2022). *Blockchain and financial market innovation* (pp. 128–150).

Mullan, P. (2014). *The digital currency challenge shaping online payment systems through US financial regulations.*

Mullan, P. C. (2016). *A history of digital currency in the United States.*

Naheem, M. A. (2019). Exploring the links between AML, digital currencies and blockchain technology. *Journal of Money Laundering Control, 22*(3), 515–526. https://doi.org/10.1108/JMLC-11-2015-0050

Pocher, N., & Veneris, A. (2022). Privacy and transparency in CBDCs: A Regulation-by-Design AML/CFT Scheme. *IEEE Transactions on Network and Service Management, 19*(2), 1776–1788. https://doi.org/10.1109/TNSM.2021.3136984

Rupeika-Apoga, R., Dārziņš, E., Filipovs, D., & Wendt, S. (2023). *Competitors and partners at the same time: On the role of Fintech companies in the Latvian financial market* (pp. 115–138).

Sater, S. (2020). Do We Need KYC/AML: The bank secrecy act and virtual currency exchanges. *Arkansas Law Review, 73*(2), 397.

Silva, E. C., Silva, M. M., & da. (2022). Research contributions and challenges in DLT-based cryptocurrency regulation: A systematic mapping study. *Journal of Banking and Financial Technology, 6*(1), 63–82. https://doi.org/10.1007/s42786-021-00037-2

Taeihagh, A., Ramesh, M., & Howlett, M. (2021). Assessing the regulatory challenges of emerging disruptive technologies. *Regulation and Governance, 15*(4), 1009–1019. https://doi.org/10.1111/rego.12392

TAN, Y. (2022). Legal governance of digital currencies and regulatory sandboxes in the blockchain era. *Proceedings of the 2022 7th International Conference on Financial Innovation and Economic Development (ICFIED 2022), 648*, 995–1000. https://doi.org/10.2991/aebmr.k.220307.164

Terranova, G. (2022). Are stablecoins good money? Finding a balance between innovation and consumer protection: The European and the United State perspective. In *Rivista di Diritoo Bancario.*

Vondrrrkovv, A. (2018). Regulation of virtual currency in the European Union. *SSRN Electronic Journal.* https://doi.org/10.2139/ssrn.2896911

Wechsler, M., Perlman, L., & Gurung, N. (2018). The state of regulatory sandboxes in developing countries. *SSRN Electronic Journal.* https://doi.org/10.2139/ssrn.3285938

Yanchao, Y. (2021). On the legal attributes of digital currency. *Social Sciences in China, 42*(2), 123–141. https://doi.org/10.1080/02529203.2021.1924463

Zhang, Z., Chen, Y., Chow, S. S. M., & Hanaoka, G. (2007). *Provable Security* (Vol. 3, pp. 435–454).

CHAPTER 10

New Generation of Participants in Financial Industry

Introduction

As a sizable portion of global wealth and capital will be handed over to millennials in the next coming decades, studying the generational aspect of technology acceptance in financial market and the use of alternative modes of payment, investment and financing is gaining more significance. In light of the theory of generation which postulates the idea that understanding the mindset in each generation provides insight into upcoming issues confronting the economy, this chapter attempts to highlight the characteristics of new generation of participants in the financial market who are well-known for their tech-savviness and tendency to embrace digital transformations.

Additionally, this chapter discusses some of the root causes of this favorable view of millennials toward FinTech and cryptocurrency such as lack of trust in conventional banking industry (according to the millennial disruption survey report 73% of respondents preferred financial services from online platform like Google, Amazon, Apple, and PayPal rather than their own banks), higher returns compared to conventional investment options, cryptocurrencies as a suitable retirement portfolio item, convenient and constant access.

B. Naysary and A. Tarazi, *The Digital Finance Era*,
https://doi.org/10.1007/978-981-97-3970-7_10

Generational Differences and Technology Adoption

Generational differences play a significant role in shaping technology adoption patterns, including within the realm of FinTech. Each generation possesses unique characteristics, experiences, and attitudes that influence their acceptance and utilization of new technologies. Understanding these generational differences is crucial for FinTech companies and financial institutions to tailor their products and services effectively. This section explores some key aspects related to generational differences and technology adoption.

Understanding Generational Cohorts

Generational cohorts are groups of people who were born and raised during a specific period and share common experiences, events, and cultural influences. These cohorts are often used to analyze societal and behavioral trends, including technology adoption. Here are the main generational cohorts and their defining characteristics:

Silent Generation

Born between 1928 and 1945, the Silent Generation experienced significant historical events such as World War II and the Great Depression. They were raised during a time of economic hardship and tend to value stability, loyalty, and traditional values. Members of this generation may have limited technology adoption compared to later generations, but some have embraced technology later in life.

Baby Boomers

Born between 1946 and 1964, the Baby Boomers witnessed a period of post-war economic prosperity and societal change. They were heavily influenced by events like the Civil Rights Movement and the Vietnam War. Baby Boomers have seen the rise of various technologies throughout their lives, from television to personal computers and the internet. While they may have been slower to adopt certain technologies, many have embraced digital tools and platforms in recent years.

Generation X

Born between 1965 and 1980, Generation X experienced social and cultural shifts, including the rise of dual-income households, divorce rates, and the advent of personal computers and video games. They are often referred to as the "latchkey generation" as many grew up with working parents. Generation X was exposed to the early stages of digital technology and witnessed the growth of the internet and mobile phones. They are generally adaptable to technology but may have a more balanced approach to its usage.

Millennials (Generation Y)

Born between 1981 and 1996, Millennials were the first generation to grow up with widespread access to the internet and personal technology devices. They experienced the rapid advancements in technology, such as social media, smartphones, and streaming services. Millennials are known for their comfort with technology and are often early adopters of new digital platforms and innovations.

Generation Z

Born between 1997 and 2012, Generation Z is the first fully digital-native generation. They have grown up with smartphones, social media, and on-demand services. Generation Z is characterized by its fluency in technology, a desire for instant gratification, and a preference for digital communication. They have unique expectations regarding convenience, personalization, and social impact.

Generation Alpha

Born between 2013 and 2025, they are expected to be the most formally educated and technologically immersed generation to date. Growing up in a world highly influenced by climate change, evolving gender norms, and ongoing global tensions, they very likely interact with technology that is currently in developmental stages, such as advanced AI and augmented reality.

Baby Boomers and FinTech Adoption

Baby Boomers often prioritize financial security and stability. They value the concept of a "good job" and have a strong work ethic. Many Baby Boomers aim for long-term employment with companies that offer retirement benefits and pension plans. They tend to prioritize saving for retirement and building a nest egg to ensure a comfortable and secure future. Baby Boomers typically have a higher level of trust in traditional financial institutions, such as banks, credit unions, and brokerage firms. They are more likely to use these institutions for their financial needs, including savings accounts, checking accounts, and investment products. Baby Boomers often prefer face-to-face interactions with financial advisors or bank representatives when seeking financial guidance or making important financial decisions. Baby Boomers have a high rate of homeownership compared to younger generations. They view homeownership as a sign of financial stability and an essential component of wealth accumulation. Many Baby Boomers have invested in real estate as a means of building equity and securing their financial future. Baby Boomers generally exhibit a more conservative approach to investing. They tend to favor low-risk investment options, such as bonds, certificates of deposit (CDs), and mutual funds. Baby Boomers prioritize capital preservation and are often cautious about market volatility and potential financial losses. They may seek investment strategies that provide steady income and protect their accumulated wealth. Baby Boomers are at or nearing retirement age, and thus retirement planning is a significant focus for many. They are concerned with ensuring they have enough savings to maintain their desired lifestyle during retirement. Baby Boomers may actively seek professional financial advice to create retirement income strategies, manage their pensions and Social Security benefits, and navigate healthcare costs. While Baby Boomers were not born into the digital era, many have adapted to technology in recent years. They have increasingly embraced online banking, mobile payment apps, and digital financial tools. However, their adoption of technology may be slower compared to younger generations, and they may still prefer some traditional methods of financial management. Baby Boomers often prioritize leaving a financial legacy for their children and grandchildren. They may engage in estate planning, including writing wills, establishing trusts, and considering gifting strategies. Baby Boomers may also view passing on financial knowledge and values as an important part of their legacy.

Generation X and FinTech Adoption

Generation X is often characterized by a strong desire for financial independence and self-reliance. They witnessed economic shifts and experienced financial challenges, such as the recession in the early 1990s and the global financial crisis of 2008. As a result, Generation X tends to prioritize financial stability, building wealth, and being prepared for unexpected financial setbacks. Generation X tends to be more pragmatic and practical when it comes to financial decisions. They value financial security and are more likely to focus on long-term financial goals such as homeownership, retirement planning, and saving for their children's education. Generation X often seeks a balance between enjoying their current lifestyle and planning for future financial needs.

Generation X generally exhibits a greater inclination toward investment compared to younger generations. They are more likely to invest in stocks, mutual funds, and other investment vehicles to grow their wealth. They understand the importance of building assets and making strategic investment choices to secure their financial future. Generation X often carries higher levels of debt, including mortgages, student loans, and credit card debt. They may have accumulated debt during their younger years for education or homeownership. However, they also tend to be diligent in managing their debt and prioritizing debt repayment. They may seek strategies to reduce their debt burden and maintain a good credit score.

Generation X is known for their entrepreneurial spirit and willingness to diversify their income sources. They may engage in side businesses, freelance work, or investment ventures to supplement their primary income. This entrepreneurial mindset allows them to create additional financial security and flexibility. Generation X, having experienced economic uncertainty and financial crises, may exhibit a level of skepticism toward financial institutions and traditional financial advice. They tend to be cautious and research-driven in their financial decisions, seeking multiple opinions and conducting their due diligence before making significant financial commitments.

Generation X has adapted to technological advancements, although not as early as younger generations. They have embraced online banking, digital payment methods, and mobile applications for financial management. Generation X utilizes technology to enhance their financial management and streamline processes, but they may still appreciate the option of in-person interactions and value customer service. Many of the Generation X individuals find themselves in the "sandwich generation" situation, where they are simultaneously responsible for caring for their aging parents and supporting their own children. This financial burden can impact their financial attitudes and behaviors, as they may need to juggle multiple financial obligations and prioritize caregiving responsibilities.

Millennials and FinTech Adoption

Millennials are often characterized by a strong sense of financial consciousness. They prioritize financial stability, budgeting, and saving. Many Millennials grew up during economic recessions, such as the 2008 financial crisis, which influenced their cautious approach to money management. They tend to be more conscious of their spending habits and are more likely to save for emergencies and future goals. Millennials, known as digital natives, are highly adept at utilizing technology for various aspects of their financial lives. They are early adopters of FinTech innovations and readily embrace digital tools for budgeting, investing, and managing their finances. Millennials are comfortable using mobile apps, online banking, and digital wallets for their financial transactions. Many Millennials carry significant amounts of student loan debt, which can impact their financial attitudes and behaviors. They tend to be proactive in managing their debt and exploring strategies for repayment, such as income-driven repayment plans or refinancing options. Millennials may be more cautious about taking on additional debt and prioritize debt reduction strategies.

Millennials recognize the importance of saving for the future, including retirement planning. However, they often face challenges such as student loan debt and rising living costs, which can hinder their ability to save. Despite these challenges, Millennials strive to contribute to retirement accounts. They may also seek alternative investment options that align with their values, such as socially responsible investing.

Millennials value financial education and seek resources to improve their financial literacy. They are proactive in researching personal finance topics and may turn to online platforms, podcasts, and blogs for guidance. Millennials are eager to understand concepts like investing, budgeting, and building credit to make informed financial decisions. They value flexibility and autonomy in their careers, and these alternative work arrangements provide them with additional financial opportunities. Millennials may invest in their own businesses or explore platforms that offer gig work.

Millennials often prioritize investments that align with their values and have a positive social or environmental impact. They are more likely to engage in impact investing, which involves investing in companies or funds that address social or environmental issues. Millennials place importance on corporate social responsibility and may choose to support businesses with ethical practices. Millennials value transparency and authenticity from financial institutions. They seek trusted and transparent financial services providers who prioritize ethical practices and are committed to meeting their needs. Millennials may be more willing to switch financial institutions or explore FinTech alternatives if they find the traditional banking system lacking in transparency or offering subpar customer experiences. Millennials tend to seek input and collaborate with peers and family members when making financial decisions. They value recommendations and insights from trusted sources and may seek advice from friends, family, or online communities. Millennials are open to learning from others' experiences and sharing their own to navigate the complexities of personal finance.

Generation Z and FinTech Adoption

Generation Z tends to be pragmatic and cautious when it comes to financial matters. Growing up during the Great Recession and witnessing the financial struggles of previous generations, they prioritize financial stability and are more risk-averse in their decision-making. They are likely to prioritize saving and seek financial independence at an early age.

Generation Z is the first generation to grow up fully immersed in digital technology. They are highly comfortable with technology and rely heavily on digital platforms for their financial activities. Generation Z embraces FinTech solutions, mobile banking apps, and digital payment methods. They value convenience, speed, and accessibility in their financial interactions.

Generation Z is characterized by a strong entrepreneurial spirit. They are eager to pursue self-employment, start their own businesses, or engage in side hustles. Generation Z recognizes the potential of new economic models and alternative income streams. They are more open to exploring freelancing and the sharing economy to achieve financial goals.

Generation Z seeks financial education and resources to develop their financial literacy. They understand the importance of financial knowledge and are proactive in learning about budgeting, investing, and personal finance management. Generation Z leverages online platforms, social media, and educational apps to access financial information and enhance their financial skills. Generation Z places a strong emphasis on social and environmental issues. They prioritize investments that align with their values and support companies with sustainable and ethical practices. Generation Z seeks investment opportunities that contribute to positive social impact, such as environmental sustainability, diversity, and social justice. Generation Z is more aware of the potential pitfalls of debt. They have witnessed the financial struggles of previous generations burdened with student loans and credit card debt. Generation Z tends to be cautious about taking on debt and seeks alternative options such as scholarships, grants, or community college to reduce student loan burdens. They prioritize financial planning to minimize future debt obligations.

Generation Z is known for its activism on various social and political issues. They extend their activism to financial matters, demanding transparency, fairness, and accountability from financial institutions. Generation Z expects financial institutions to align with their values and address social and environmental concerns. They may choose to support banks and FinTech companies that demonstrate a commitment to ethical practices.

Generation Z exhibits a strong inclination toward saving and investing. They are focused on building financial security and are more likely to prioritize saving for emergencies, education, and homeownership. Generation Z recognizes the power of long-term investing and may start investing at an early age, leveraging apps and platforms that offer fractional investing or robo-advisory services. Generation Z is highly influenced by digital media, influencers, and peer recommendations. They seek validation and recommendations from online communities, social media platforms, and trusted influencers before making financial decisions. Generation Z values authenticity and may be more receptive to financial advice from relatable sources.

Impact on the Financial Market

The financial behavior of various generations has a significant impact on the financial system as a whole. The financial system, which encompasses banks, financial institutions, markets, and regulatory bodies, is shaped by the behaviors, preferences, and needs of different generations.

Different generations have distinct preferences and expectations when it comes to financial products and services. For example, younger generations, such as Millennials and Generation Z, have grown up in a digital age and expect seamless, convenient, and tech-enabled financial experiences. This has led to the rise of digital banking, mobile payments, and FinTech innovations. Financial institutions need to adapt to these preferences and provide the technology-driven solutions that meet the expectations of younger generations.

Each generation has its own investment preferences and risk tolerance levels, which influence the dynamics of financial markets. For instance, Baby Boomers have traditionally preferred more conservative investment options, such as fixed-income securities and real estate, while younger generations are often more interested in technology stocks, impact investing, and cryptocurrencies. These shifts in investment pattern can impact asset prices, market volatility, and the overall functioning of financial markets.

The financial behavior of different generations shapes the demand for financial services. For instance, Baby Boomers nearing retirement may require retirement planning services, estate planning, and products that provide stable income streams. Millennials and Generation Z, on the other hand, may seek out services that cater to their specific needs, such as student loan refinancing, robo-advisory platforms, and access to affordable credit. Financial institutions need to adapt their product offerings to meet the evolving demands of different generations.

The financial behavior of one generation can impact the wealth accumulation and transfer to the next generation. As older generations transfer their wealth to younger generations, it can have implications for wealth distribution, investment strategies, and economic dynamics. Understanding the financial behavior of different generations is crucial for financial institutions and wealth management firms to effectively address intergenerational wealth transfer needs.

References

Aseng, A. C., Ekonomi, P., & Keguruan, F. (2020). Factors influencing generation Z intention in using Fintech digital payment services. *Cogito Smart Journal, 6*(2), 155–166.

Bencsik, A. (2016). Y and Z Generations at workplaces. *Journal of Competitiveness, September.* https://doi.org/10.7441/joc.2016.03.06

Carlin, B., Olafsson, A., Pagel, M., & Anderson, B. C. (2017). FinTech adoption across generations: Financial fitness in the information age. In *NBER working papers* (Vol. 23798).

Dadwal, S. S. (2019). *Handbook of research on innovations in technology and marketing for the connected consumer*. IGI Global. https://books.google.co.uk/books?id=yDG1DwAAQBAJ

Daqar, M. A. M. A., Arqawi, S., & Karsh, S. A. (2021). FinTech in the eyes of Millennials and generation Z (the financial behavior and FinTech perception). *Banks and Bank Systems, 15*(3), 20–28. https://doi.org/10.21511/bbs.15(3).2020.03

Daragmeh, A., Lentner, C., & Sági, J. (2021). FinTech payments in the era of COVID-1: Factors influencing behavioral intentions of 'Generation X' in Hungary to use mobile payment. *Journal of Behavioral and Experimental Finance, 32*, 100574. https://doi.org/10.1016/j.jbef.2021.100574

Das, A., & Das, D. (2020). Perception, adoption, and pattern of usage of fintech services by bank customers: Evidences from Hojai District of Assam. *Emerging Economy Studies, 6*(1), 7–22. https://doi.org/10.1177/2394901520907728

Dospinescu, O., & Dospinescu, N. (2021). FinTech services and factors determining the expected benefits of users: Evidence in Romania for millennials and generation Z. *E&M Economics and Management, 24*(2), 101–118.

Hernaus, T., & Polos, N. (2014). Work design for different generational cohorts. *Journal of Organizational Change Management, 27*(4), 615–641. https://doi.org/10.1108/JOCM-05-2014-0104

Holyoke, L. (2009). Engaging the adult learner generational mix Laura Holyoke Erick Larson. *Journal of Adult Education, 38*(1), 12–21.

Kapoor, C., & Solomon, N. (2015). Understanding and managing generational differences in the workplace. *Worldwide Hospitality and Tourism Themes, 3*(4), 308–318. https://doi.org/10.1108/17554211111162435

Lee, Y.-K. (2023). Higher innovativeness, lower technostress? Comparative study of determinants on FinTech usage behavior between Korean and Chinese Gen Z consumers. *Asia Pacific Journal of Marketing and Logistics, 35*(7), 1663–1681. https://doi.org/10.1108/APJML-05-2022-0402

Memon, I. A., & Jakhiya, M. (2021). How ready the GEN-Z is to adopt FinTech? *International Conference on Computational Intelligence and Knowledge Economy (ICCIKE)*, 565–570.

Miskan, N. H., Hussin, N. L., Muhamad, N., Esa, M. M., & Aziz, N. E. M. (2021). The financial technology (M-Banking) adoption among baby-boomers in twenty-first century. *International Journal of Academic Research in Business and Social Sciences, 11*(8), 1579–1583. https://doi.org/10.6007/IJARBSS/v11-i8/10703

Multidisiplin, P., Rizqa, D., & Prayogi, I. A. (2023). Financial technology acceptance in baby boomers generation. *Jurnal Indragiri, 3*(1), 10–15.

Petroulas, E., Brown, D., & Sundin, H. (2010). Generational characteristics and their impact on preference for management control systems. *Australian Accounting Review, 20*(54), 221–240. https://doi.org/10.1111/j.1835-2561.2010.00099.x

Rahim, N., & F., Bakri, M. H., Fianto, B. A., Zainal, N., & Hussein Al Shami, S. A. (2023). Measurement and structural modelling on factors of Islamic FinTech adoption among millennials in Malaysia. *Journal of Islamic Marketing, 14*(6), 1463–1487. https://doi.org/10.1108/JIMA-09-2020-0279

Singh, A. K., & Sharma, P. (2023). A study of Indian Gen X and Millennials consumers' intention to use FinTech payment services during COVID-19 pandemic. *Journal of Modelling in Management, 18*(4), 1177–1203. https://doi.org/10.1108/JM2-02-2022-0059

Solarz, M., & Swacha-lech, M. (2021). Determinants of the adoption of innovative FinTech services by millennials. *E&M Economics and Management, 24*(3), 149–166.

Stevanin, S., Palese, A., Bressan, V., Vehvil, K., & Kvist, T. (2018). Workplace-related generational characteristics of nurses: A mixed-method systematic review. *Journal of Advanced Nursing, January*, 1245–1263. https://doi.org/10.1111/jan.13538

Subagyo, A., Abraham, J., Mursitama, T. N., Rahim, R., & Multazam, M. T. (2019). *WoMELA-GG 2019: The 1st Workshop on Multimedia Education, Learning, Assessment and its Implementation in Game and Gamification in conjunction with COMDEV 2018, Medan Indonesia, 26th January 2019, WOMELA-GG*. European Alliance for Innovation (EAI). https://books.google.co.uk/books?id=zMhdEAAAQBAJ

Thi, N., Phuong, H., Thuy, N. D., Giang, T. L., Thi, B., Han, N., Hieu, T. H., & Long, N. T. (2022). Determinants of intention to use FinTech payment services: Evidence from Vietnam' generation z. *International Journal of Business, Economics and Law, 26*(1), 354–366.

Vaicondam, Y., Jayabalan, N., Qureshi, M. I., & Khan, N. (2021). FinTech adoption among millennials in Selangor. *Academy of Entrepreneurship Journal, 27*(5).

CHAPTER 11

The Road Ahead

Introduction

The concept of money has undergone a fascinating journey, evolving with human civilization from simple barter systems to sophisticated digital currencies like Bitcoin. Throughout history, the function of money—as a medium of exchange, a unit of account, and a store of value—has remained constant, but its form and the institutions surrounding it have dramatically evolved. While it is difficult to predict the future of money, its fascinating history suggests that further transformations are yet to come, potentially revolutionizing how we think about value, exchange, and finance. This chapter presents the concluding remarks, including an overview of the evolution of money, revamping the advancement of digital currencies and their implications and finally the emerging trends in the future.

Overview of the Evolution of Money

In ancient times, trade primarily existed in the form of barter—direct exchange of goods and services without any intermediary. While straightforward, bartering was inefficient for multiple reasons: the double coincidence of wants, indivisibility of certain goods, and the absence of a standard measure of value. The limitations of the barter system led to the adoption of commodity money, which is any item valued by society

B. Naysary and A. Tarazi, *The Digital Finance Era*,
https://doi.org/10.1007/978-981-97-3970-7_11

and has intrinsic value. Commodity monies like livestock, salt, grain, and eventually precious metals like gold and silver acted as a medium of exchange. These commodities were durable, divisible, and had intrinsic value, making them suitable for use as money. Although commodity money provided a more stable medium of exchange than bartering, it still had limitations, like inconvenience, in transporting large quantities of metal. This led to the use of representative money, where items like paper notes or coins would represent a certain amount of a commodity stored elsewhere. In the twentieth century, the need for a more flexible and manageable monetary system led to the decoupling of currency from physical commodities. Governments began to issue money that was not backed by a physical commodity but rather by the strength and stability of the issuing government. This is known as fiat money. In the latter part of the twentieth century, as technology advanced, electronic forms of payment like credit and debit cards began to emerge. These digital forms of money made transactions even more efficient, removing the need for physical presence and enabling global commerce. The twenty-first century saw an even more radical shift with the invention of cryptocurrencies like Bitcoin. These digital or virtual currencies use cryptography for security and are decentralized, operating on technology called blockchain. Unlike traditional currencies, they are not controlled by a single entity, like a government or financial institution.

The Future of Money: A Glimpse into a Digital Horizon

Money, as we know it, has been evolving since its inception. From the barter system to coins made of precious metals, from paper bills to plastic cards, and now to digital bytes, the concept of money has been a subject of continuous innovation. As we look into the future, we see an amalgamation of technology, governance, and social change shaping the next frontier of money. The most notable development in recent years has been the emergence of cryptocurrencies like Bitcoin and Ethereum. While Bitcoin and Ethereum have gained mainstream attention, there are thousands of other cryptocurrencies, each with its unique features and use-cases. For instance, Ripple aims to make cross-border transactions more efficient, and Monero focuses on providing enhanced privacy. As the technology matures, we can expect more specialized cryptocurrencies catering to specific niches. Non-Fungible Tokens (NFTs) have added a new dimension to the crypto landscape. These unique digital assets offer a way to monetize and authenticate everything from art to real estate. The idea of "ownership" is being redefined in the digital world, thanks to NFTs. These decentralized systems promise more significant financial freedom, reduced transaction fees, and increased privacy. However, they also bring challenges, such as scalability and regulatory acceptance. Recognizing the advantages of digital currencies, various nations are experimenting with or have already launched their own Central Bank Digital Currencies. CBDCs aim to provide the stability of conventional money and the efficiency of blockchain technology. Countries like China and Sweden are in the advanced stages of implementing CBDCs, which could eventually replace physical cash. CBDCs could be revolutionary, but they also pose significant challenges. On the one hand, they promise efficient transactions and financial inclusivity. On the other hand, they could give central banks an unprecedented level of control over monetary policy, potentially leading to concerns about privacy and financial surveillance. The introduction of CBDCs could also shake up the geopolitical landscape. If a country's CBDC gains international acceptance, it could challenge the global dominance of currencies like the US Dollar. This has implications for trade, diplomacy, and global power dynamics. Stablecoins, which are cryptocurrencies pegged to stable assets like the US dollar, offer another avenue for digital growth. They offer the best of both worlds: the stability of traditional money and the efficiency of digital transactions. One of the most promising aspects of digital currencies is their potential to provide financial services to the unbanked populations. Decentralized Finance (DeFi) platforms, operating on blockchain technology, offer services like lending, borrowing, and trading without the need for traditional financial institutions.

In a digital economy, data takes on a form similar to money. Platforms like Facebook and Google already "pay" users for their data by offering free services. In the future, data marketplaces could become more structured, allowing individuals to sell their data for monetary benefits directly. As data becomes more valuable, the need for robust security measures increases. Blockchain technology offers potential solutions, but the transition to a data-driven economy also necessitates stronger cybersecurity protocols.

Emerging Trends and Future Scenarios

Decentralized Autonomous Organizations (DAOs)

As the future of money unfolds, we are witnessing the rise of Decentralized Autonomous Organizations (DAOs), which are essentially organizations run through rules encoded as computer programs on the blockchain. DAOs could become the financial institutions of the future, offering an array of financial products and services without the need for centralized control. The implications are profound, not just for how we manage and distribute resources, but also for how we conceptualize organizational structures. In the realm of DAOs, governance tokens could serve as a form of digital money that also bestows voting rights. This creates a more democratic and decentralized method for decision-making, impacting everything from monetary policy to community projects.

The Role of Artificial Intelligence (AI) and Machine Learning (ML)

Financial transactions will increasingly involve automated systems, driven by AI and ML algorithms. These technologies can predict market trends, automate trading, manage risk, and even offer financial advice. The integration of AI into financial systems will revolutionize how decisions are made and transactions are executed. As with any technology, AI and ML come with their own sets of challenges, including ethical concerns about data privacy and algorithmic bias. Oversight and regulation will be crucial in ensuring that these technologies are implemented responsibly.

Social and Cultural Implications

The way we perceive and use money is deeply rooted in social and cultural norms. As digital currencies and financial technologies become more prevalent, they will inevitably impact our social structures. NFTs have revolutionized how we perceive the value of digital art, collectibles, and even tweets. The ability to tokenize virtually anything (from real estate to time) has shifted our understanding of ownership and value. The ethos of decentralized finance challenges traditional trust systems, which are usually centralized, like banks or governments. Younger generations, who are more comfortable with digital technologies, may find it easier to adapt to new forms of money. This could lead to a generational divide in financial practices and preferences.

Conclusion: The Uncharted Territory Ahead

The future of money is like an unfolding novel, with each chapter revealing new complexities, characters, and plot twists. The interplay of technology, society, and individual behavior will write this story, influenced by factors we can predict and many that we cannot. The only certainty is that change is inevitable, and the future of money will be a reflection of broader shifts in technology, culture, and global events. Adapting to these changes will require flexibility, innovation, and a willingness to venture into the unknown. As we stand on the cusp of this financial frontier, one thing is clear: the future of money offers a world of possibilities limited only by our imagination and our willingness to adapt, innovate, and navigate the challenges and opportunities that come our way.

References

El Faqir, Y., Arroyo, J., & Hassan, S. (2020). An overview of decentralized autonomous organizations on the blockchain. *Proceedings of the 16th International Symposium on Open Collaboration*. https://doi.org/10.1145/3412569.3412579

Guihong, Z. (2006). The rise of decentralized autonomous organizations: opportunities and challenges. *South Asian Survey, 85*(5), 4–23.

Hassan, S., & De Filippi, P. (2021). Decentralized autonomous organization. *Internet Policy Review, 10*(2), 1–10. https://doi.org/10.14763/2021.2.1556

Hsieh, Y. Y., Vergne, J. P., Anderson, P., Lakhani, K., & Reitzig, M. (2018). Bitcoin and the rise of decentralized autonomous organizations. *Journal of Organization Design, 7*(1), 1–16. https://doi.org/10.1186/s41469-018-0038-1

Kumar, R., Grover, N., Singh, R., Kathuria, S., Kumar, A., & Bansal, A. (2023). Imperative role of artificial intelligence and big data in finance and banking sector. *2nd International Conference on Sustainable Computing and Data Communication Systems, ICSCDS 2023—Proceedings*, 523–527. https://doi.org/10.1109/ICSCDS56580.2023.10105062

Makalesi, A., Article, R., Esra, T. F. S. U., & ALP COŞKUN, Y. Kararlarında Yapay Zekanın Rolü ve, Doğu Teknik Üniversitesi, O., & Bölümü, İ. (2022). The role of artificial intelligence in investment decisions and applications in the Turkish finance industry. *Gaziantep Üniversitesi Sosyal Bilimler Dergisi, 21*(4), 2208–2222.

Santana, C., & Albareda, L. (2022). Blockchain and the emergence of Decentralized Autonomous Organizations (DAOs): An integrative model and research agenda. *Technological Forecasting and Social Change, 182*(July), 121806. https://doi.org/10.1016/j.techfore.2022.121806

Wang, S., Ding, W., Li, J., Yuan, Y., Ouyang, L., & Wang, F. Y. (2019). Decentralized autonomous organizations: concept, model, and applications. *IEEE Transactions on Computational Social Systems, 6*(5), 870–878. https://doi.org/10.1109/TCSS.2019.2938190

Index

B. Naysary and A. Tarazi, *The Digital Finance Era*,
https://doi.org/10.1007/978-981-97-3970-7

The manufacturer's authorised representative in the EU is Springer
Nature Customer Service Centre GmbH, Europaplatz 3, 69115 Heidelberg,
Germany. If you have any concerns regarding our products, please
contact ProductSafety@springernature.com

Printed and bound by CPI Group (UK) Ltd, Croydon, CR0 4YY
30/09/2026
02225254-0005